BLACK ENTREPRENEURSHIP IN AMERICA

D0060860

BLACK ENTREPRENEURSHIP
IN AMERICA

Shelley Green and Paul Pryde

Transaction Publishers
New Brunswick (U.S.A.) and London (U.K.)

Second paperback printing 1997

Copyright © 1990 by Transaction Publishers, New Brunswick, New Jersey 08903.

This book is printed on acid-free paper that meets the American National Standard for Permanence of Paper for Printed Library Materials.

Library of Congress Catalog Number: 88-35599
ISBN: 0-88738-290-8 (cloth); 1-56000-885-7 (paper)
Printed in the United States of America

Library of Congress Cataloging-in-Publication Data

Green, Shelley.
    Black entrepreneurship in America/Shelley Green and Paul Pryde.
    p. cm.
    Includes index.
    ISBN: 0-88738-290-8
1. Afro-Americans—Economic conditions. 2. Afro-American business enterprises. 3. Entrepreneurship—United States. I. Pryde, Paul. II. Title.
E185.8.G776   1989
338'.04'08996073—dc19   88-35599
                                                                      CIP

Contents

Preface

Most published works on the economic conditions of black America propose to redress black poverty and high unemployment by redistributing existing resources. From this perspective, either opportunities, via civil rights and affirmative action statutes, or income, through social welfare spending, should be redistributed to people unfit for competition in the American marketplace. Our book proposes an alternative view. We proceed from the assumption that black economic progress does not depend on a renewed struggle for unattained civil rights. Nor does it depend on the restoration of funding for an acronymic jungle of social welfare programs. Rather it demands that black Americans respond creatively to both economic opportunities and problems as the American and larger world economy undergo a major transformation. In the long run, we argue, black economic development must rely on successful risk-taking and innovation; that is, on the entrepreneurial ability of the black American community.

For the past two decades, black Americans have depended on affirmative action and public spending to protect their rights and improve their fortunes. Middle-class blacks have met with relative success in applying these politically based strategies toward upward mobility. Federal laws enacted during the prosperous 1960s required the recruitment, hiring, and promotion of qualified blacks. In addition, they went far to eliminate racial discrimination in housing and public accommodations, and provided new opportunities for black-owned businesses.

During the same period, Americans launched a panoply of public-sector programs to combat poverty. Beyond providing a reliable, if meager, source of income for chronically poor blacks, increased antipoverty spending generated thousands of new jobs for black social service professionals and administrators. For the first time, blacks were free to compete for the jobs created by simultaneously expanding public and private sectors. Not surprisingly, comparative income studies show that the gap between black and white middle-class professionals has narrowed perceptibly since the 1960s.

vii

Nonetheless, affirmative action programs remain but a partial solution to problems made worse by poorly designed antipoverty programs. The plight of America's poor, white as well as black, cannot be realistically addressed without taking into account a broad range of social and economic policies. Relying, we grant, on 20/20 hindsight, it is now obvious that:

1. The new laws required employers to treat qualified whites and blacks identically, and expanded jobs in the helping professions where black college graduates were heavily concentrated. Thus blacks for whom racial prejudice had been a principal obstacle to economic advancement—that is, those who were well educated to begin with—benefited most.
2. For people of few skills and little education, the new civil rights laws conferred the empty right to compete for jobs they had neither training nor skills to fill. Income transfer programs, which provided money in inverse proportion to effort, made poverty easier to tolerate but harder to escape.
3. The economic expansion and social optimism of the 1960's, brought about by the rapid growth of the economy, moved Americans away from self-protection in the marketplace. Inclined toward sharing their good fortune, they widely endorsed legal reforms and public spending to eradicate racial discrimination and poverty.

Together, an expanding economy and accelerated social welfare spending promoted the growth of a sizable, if not entirely secure, black middle class. At the bottom, one third of American blacks are at risk of becoming a permanent underclass. Clearly, all blacks have not benefited in equal measure over the past twenty years. What has gone wrong? To a large degree, worsening black poverty represents a failure of policymakers, however well-intentioned, to understand the income gap between blacks and whites as a development problem. Nor have most middle-class blacks and their political leaders demonstrated a proclivity for pursuing economic goals by way of economic development. As Schumpeter points out, the "development" of a community does not occur through changes forced upon its economic life from without, but by economic changes arising from its own self-directed initiatives.

If blacks have not yet realized their economic potential, they have become increasingly aware that somewhere along the line, an essential ingredient for their economic progress has been omitted. We believe the missing ingredient is entrepreneurship. We also believe that having located the problem, we must begin with a new and more accurate assessment of black economic behavior. Like the two-faced god, Janus, who guarded the portals of Rome by looking backward to the city's past and forward to its future, black Americans must turn both inward and outward for solutions. We hope our book, by stimulating that first and critical step of honest self-examination, provides a useful roadmap for new, more entrepreneurial development perspectives among black Americans.

We wish to thank the Institute for the Study of Economic Culture at Boston University, under the direction of Dr. Peter L. Berger, for providing the research and funding support that made this study possible.

Acknowledgments

While they may ardently disagree with our final product, we would like to thank the following individuals and organizations for their generous advice and support in the preparation of this book:

Gavin Chen, Frank Fratoe, and Richard Stevens from the Minority Business Development Agency; Maria McFadden and Julie Lane Gay from the Institute for the Study of Economic Culture; Timothy Bates; Barry Levine; Robert Woodson; Pat Jacobs; Juliet Walker; Malcolm Griffith; T. M. Alexander; John Raye and the Majestic Eagles; Grace Goodell; Mark Dreyer.

In particular, we want to acknowledge our research associates, Anne Marie Jensen, Cassandra Walton, Jessica Scheer/Derek Dorman, Carlton Henry/Andy Goldfarb for their research contributions to chapters 2, 3, 4, and 5, respectively.

Finally, our heartfelt thanks to Irving Horowitz, Esther Luckett, Scott Bramson, and Mary Curtis, our publisher and editors from Transaction.

1

The Case for Black Entrepreneurship

Aged forty-two in 1819, Frank McWorter operated a commercial farm, manufactured saltpeter, and speculated in land on the Kentucky frontier. In 1830 he moved his family west to Illinois, where he homesteaded and steadily expanded his business ventures. In 1835 he bought an eighty-acre tract and built his own town. Christened New Philadelphia, the community represented a distinct aberration in American frontier history; its founding father and proprietor, chief developer, and promoter was a black American.

Until the courts changed his name in 1837, Frank McWorter went by the common and legal title of "Free Frank." Born on a South Carolina plantation, the son of a black slave woman and her Scotch-Irish master, he lived as a slave for forty-two years. Nevertheless, beginning in slavery and continuing in freedom, he accumulated enough wealth to buy his own freedom and that of every member of his family, sixteen people in all. As attested to by his biographer and descendant, Juliet Walker, through a remarkable mix of skill, perseverance, and ingenuity, Frank McWorter overcame tremendous odds to become the sine qua non of creative capitalism: a successful entrepreneur.[1]

A unique set of circumstances drove Frank McWorter to use his entrepreneurial talent. He needed surplus capital to buy freedom for himself and his family. The frontier environment provided him with some extraordinary opportunities. Even so, the most unusual—and noteworthy—aspect of Frank McWorters story is the method he chose to pursue his goals. While the majority of people stand in awe before seemingly insurmountable obstacles, the Frank McWorters of the world are calculating how to surmount or subvert them. In the same way, promoters of black economic development should stop endlessly rehashing the awesome nature of black economic problems. Like the creative capitalist, they must begin to view obstacles as challenging opportunities for a broad range of economic and social achievements.

In his classic theory of modern economic development, Schumpeter considers the creative capitalist, or entrepreneur, directly responsible for economic development in industrialized societies. Entrepreneurs initiate the development process by putting together new combinations of resources, or enterprises.[2] Subsequent studies have elaborated on Schumpeter's view.

Sociologist Albert Shapero sketches both broad and narrow definitions of entrepreneurial development. Widely, he characterizes developing communities as "self-renewing," as having the capacity to absorb change, undertake new initiatives, create opportunities, and promote diversity. Narrowly, he views entrepreneurship in relation to commerce, as seminal to the formation and development of "profit-oriented business."[3]

By contrast, psychologists have concentrated on the nature of individual entrepreneurs, and how particular cultures and societies influence individual entrepreneurial behavior. McClelland has linked societies and cultures stressing achievement with higher levels of entrepreneurship and more rapid economic development. Because of their high achievement drive, entrepreneurial types seek out the risk and responsibility of innovative, profit-oriented activities.[4]

Frank McWorter fits the entrepreneurial patterns outlined by Schumpeter, Shapero, and McClelland. Yet his story is a significant departure from mainstream black economic history. Entrepreneurship, measured in the narrow sense of business development, has not been widely practiced among black Americans. Using 1980 census data, Bates calculated the relative levels of entrepreneurship among different racial and ethnic groups in the American work force. Only 1.75 percent of blacks—as compared with 5.02 percent of whites, 3.76 percent of Asians, and 3.16 percent of Hispanics—fell into the self-employed category.[5]

Why have so few black Americans become entrepreneurs? Is the reason, as many would have it, that blacks have faced too many racial barriers to succeed in business? Or, as still others assert, do blacks themselves lack a cultural predilection for entrepreneurship? Whatever their starting point—racism, cultural determinism, or some combination of these and other factors—concerned observers agree on the desirability of increasing entrepreneurial activity among black Americans.

Amid current debates about black well-being, including the slate for black economic progress, entrepreneurship has received short shrift. "Economic life," says Jacobs, "develops by grace of innovating."[6] Adds Gilder, "Capitalist creativity is guided not by an invisible hand, but by the quite visible and aggressive hand of management of entrepreneurship."[7] We agree. As in any self-renewing, viable community, entrepreneurship can and must become the engine of black economic development.

At the same time, we emphatically disagree with those who consider black entrepreneurship more of a far-off hope than an imminent possibility. Across the economic spectrum, blacks have both rising aptitudes for and opportunities to engage in entrepreneurial pursuits. We concede that aptitude and opportunity alone will not produce more black entrepreneurs. Significant barriers remain in place. Today's obstacles, however, are not the same as those faced by civil rights leaders twenty years ago. Entrenched in long-standing behavior patterns among black Americans as well as in the structure of the American marketplace, they have not been addressed and may even have been exacerbated by the success of equal opportunity and affirmative action programs.

Understanding the barriers to black entrepreneurship, and thereby to black economic development, requires looking at the problem from an entrepreneurial viewpoint. Any potential entrepreneur responds to a double calculation of risk and reward: real and perceptual. If the real risk of engaging in entrepreneurial activities has declined for blacks over the past twenty years, the perceptual risk has remained high. Concomitantly, if the real rewards for black entrepreneurs have increased, the perceptual rewards have not risen high enough. As with aptitude and opportunity to wax entrepreneurial, these phenomena seem to hold true across the black economic spectrum.

Over the past two years, the so-called bifurcation of black America into a rising middle class and a rapidly deteriorating underclass has been the subject of widespread debate. As yet no one has attempted to understand its significance in entrepreneurial terms. To do so requires tracing the history of both groups from their southern roots, through their outward migration, to the evolution of their respective positions in American society over the past two-and-a-half decades.

Since Douglas Glasgow, former head of the Department of Social Work at Howard University, coined the term "black underclass," the causes of and cures for black poverty in America have once again become the object of national attention.[8] The self-destructive behavior and low productivity associated with the underclass have been attributed to a value system undermined by the absence of strong middle-class role models. With many adherents of this view, we believe government can and should do little to inculcate the "missing" values. Instead we would rely on family, neighborhood schools, churches, and other community-based institutions to transmit desirable codes of morality and behavior.

As frustration mounts over seemingly intractable problems of poverty and an array of social programs that have cost American taxpayers over $20 billion during the past decade, we also face the danger of absolving government from any responsibility toward the poor. In fact, we believe the state must play a pivotal role in encouraging, even requiring, the poor to become productive. How people pursue their economic interests, or refuse to, as the case may be, is shaped as much by the institutions that govern economic activities as by attitudes about work, welfare, and wealth. Attitude, behavior, and structure interact with each other in a spiral of causation.

In a controversial article for the *Atlantic Monthly,* Nicolas Lemann links the Chicago underclass to the fact that middle-class blacks have moved to the suburbs over the past twenty years. In the process they have left behind a population whose origins in the tenant farms of the rural South ill-prepared them for modern urban life. Without more urbanized, upwardly mobile blacks to serve as role models, the black poor have failed to develop the discipline and mental habits essential to economic and social development.[9]

Prior to World War I, 80 percent of black Americans lived in rural areas of the deep South, the vast majority in the cotton belt states of Mississippi, Alabama, Louisiana, Georgia, and South Carolina.[10] For most, tenant farming and sharecropping were the only ways to earn a living. Born of a need for cheap labor and reinforced by racism, the structure of southern agriculture was particularly pernicious. In addition to depriving black families of their freedom, it severed the connection between effort and reward.

After the Civil War, white southern farm owners parceled out their land among black and white tenants known as sharecroppers. Although more whites than blacks sharecropped, the conditions under which the two races farmed were significantly different. Whites tended to work the smaller holdings of less arable hilly areas and to produce a greater diversity of crops. Most blacks worked on large cotton-growing estates under the supervision of white planters and their overseers.[11]

Southern agriculture consisted of a four-tiered labor structure. Cash tenants, who rented their land but controlled growing and marketing decisions, occupied the top income-producing berth, while wage laborers, paid daily as they were needed, subsisted at the bottom. In between lay share tenants and croppers. Share tenants owned some of their equipment, paid rent for the use of their land, and were able to retain between two thirds and three fourths of the cash value of their crops. Their position contrasted markedly with that of sharecroppers, who, because they owned no equipment and had no means for renting the land they farmed, paid landowners half of the crops produced. Cash tenants were the least common type of black agricultural worker. During the 1920s and 1930s, as the cotton belt economy declined and agricultural mechanization increased, thousands of displaced black share tenants and croppers shifted into the lowest and least secure position of wage laborer.

The sharecropping system was designed to keep workers in a perpetual state of dependency and indebtedness. Because workers had no resources of their own, landlords advanced them food, clothing, and supplies on credit at selected stores, most of which charged exorbitant prices at exorbitant interest rates. Croppers unable to repay their debts were legally forbidden to leave their landlords, who generally contrived to keep their workers in debt. Independent decision-making and self-reliance, from crop planting to marketing to growing a family vegetable garden, were discouraged, as was provision of education to tenant children. Families were crowded into primitive wooden shacks, lacking, in many cases, even the basic amenity of an outdoor toilet. Diets high in calories but low in protein and vitamins left tenants in chronically poor health. Despite landlord attempts to control vagrancy, many sharecropper families moved frequently. For them, negative incentives prevailed. They got as much as they could out of a given plot or building before moving on to the next. The depleted soil and dilapidated housing they left behind passed unchanged to yet another set of tenants.

Landlords oversaw the messes created by the sharecropping system with an ingrained mixture of contempt and paternalism. If black houses were ramshackle, black crops meager, black families large and unhealthy, it was because blacks by nature were shiftless, lazy, and improvident. Black tenants, like children, needed constant supervision to maintain their modicum of existence.

It takes no great understanding of economic theory to grasp that entrepreneurial values and behavior did not flourish in a system that typically rewarded both sloth and diligence with the same economic consequence, debt. Moreover, indolence involved considerably less risk than aggression. Yet even with overwhelming odds against them, a fair number of black tenants and sharecroppers managed to escape the system. Despite the prevalence of landlords who applied negative incentives to encourage black industriousness, chiefly by taking away animals and equipment or throwing families off land, some positive incentives survived. Honest landlords in conjunction with large cotton crops and high prices permitted more fortunate black cash and share tenants to accumulate land and personal property. Their success stories filled an important, if modest, niche at the top of the black, rural South's economic hierarchy. At its base, hundreds of thousands of blacks subsisted in an atmosphere of extreme poverty and growing disillusionment.[12]

By 1960, less than one fourth of American blacks lived and worked in the cotton belt states. The decline of cotton and the mechanization of agriculture, together with fluctuations in the overall growth and prosperity of the U.S. economy, generated waves of black emigration out of the rural South. Initially, many moved to small southern towns, but thousands of later migrants left directly for the urban North. Three time periods—1910 through the early 1930s, the early 1930s through the late 1940s, and the mid-1950s through the 1960s—profile their exodus and the conditions that induced it.

The first wave, 1910 through the early 1930s, occurred as the result of combined "push–pull" economic factors. On the one hand, a series of natural disasters, increased world competition, and falling prices significantly reduced demand for labor in the cotton industry. On the other, World War I and restrictive immigration laws greatly increased the demand for labor in northern cities. In two decades, nearly one-and-a-half million rural southern blacks moved North, most to urban industrial centers.

The second wave responded, again, to both push and pull factors. Large-scale mechanization of the cotton industry began in the 1930s, replacing mules with tractors for plowing the soil, but leaving to black workers the labor-intensive tasks of hand weeding and picking. During the 1930s, government programs encouraged mechnization and discouraged high cotton yields, and black laborers found themselves working fewer and fewer days per year. By the late 1940s, hand weeding gave way to herbicides, relegating a sole function, picking, to blacks. Throughout this process, black agricultural workers lost security and income as they moved downward from the position of share tenant or cropper to that of wage laborer. Oppressive as it was, the paternalistic "welfare" system that had undergirded plantation-style agriculture disappeared forever from the scene. Landowners no longer had to provide a back-up system of material resources for tenants and croppers on whose labor they depended. In the end, black plantation workers faced two choices: they could either move away or resign themselves to increasingly dire poverty and starvation.

During the 1930s, the Great Depression curtailed black movement north, but northward migration resumed in force as a result of the economic boom spawned by World War II. In all, over two million blacks made their way to northern cities between 1930 and 1950.

The final and greatest wave of black migration from South to North took place between 1950 and 1970. By the mid-1950s, hand picked cotton, along with the remaining rural black labor force, had become obsolete in southern states. Push greatly outweighed pull factors, as nearly three million blacks moved en masse into inner cities of the North and West. Most skipped the transitional process of living in small southern towns, and lacked the motivational structure and coping skills characteristic of the earlier migrants. Bates and Fusfeld have chronicled the reasons why, as they put it, "The migrants were moving to the big city at the wrong point in history."[13] To begin with, they were among the least skilled and educated of Americans. Manufacturing no longer relied on a large pool of unskilled and semiskilled labor, and demand for the labor they were able to provide had shrunk. In addition, they were competing with large numbers of better-educated, more highly skilled white migrants from rural areas. National economic growth, following the boom years of World War II, had slowed down. Finally, jobs were moving to the suburbs, areas beyond the geographic reach of most recent black immigrants.

Trends visible in the 1950s have since become constant and determinant elements of black urban life in America. While better-educated and skilled blacks prospered, the economic well-being of the less educated declined.

From 1953 onward, high black unemployment has been a permanent fixture of the American economy. During the 1960s, a combination of general prosperity and eliminated racial barriers made more jobs than ever before available to blacks. Unlike historic demands for black labor, however, the new jobs required education and skills.

Nearly seven million blacks left the rural South between 1910 and 1970. The magnitude and urgency of black migration had a cataclysmic effect on American social, economic, and political institutions. Even so, institutional processes were slow to react to the enormous personal hardship experienced by hundreds of thousands of individual blacks. The entire panoply of social service and welfare programs Americans, black and white, now take for granted is in fact a very recent phenomenon.

Most federal aid programs for the poor originated from New Deal legislation in the 1930s. Responding to burgeoning unemployment and political unrest, the newly elected Roosevelt administration enacted the Federal Emergency Relief Act in the spring of 1933. For the first time in American history, the federal government distributed cash benefits to the destitute. During the winter of 1933–1934 alone, over one fifth of all Americans received some form of federal assistance. Effective as a temporary stabilizing measure, cash supports quickly shifted into the more publicly acceptable form of work relief. The rural poor, who suffered the greatest and most irreversible losses during the Great Depression, benefited least from New Deal legislation. Thwarted by local political structures and lack of Congressional support, the Farm Security Administration awarded fewer than 2,000 tenant purchase loans to more than one million black tenant farmers.[14]

Among New Deal initiatives, the Social Security Act of 1935 heralded a significant structural change in the position of the federal government toward poverty. Yet it, too, was tied specifically to earned, work-related benefits. Until 1950, Aid to Families with Dependent Children (AFDC), established under the auspices of the Social Security Act, provided assistance solely to children left parentless because of death, desertion, or disablement. Direct public assistance to the poor remained primarily a function of individual states and localities throughout the Great Depression and into the 1950s. Thus, while the New Deal left an enduring legacy of federal antipoverty programs, it did so chiefly by getting the American public used to the idea of direct federal intervention against poverty.[15]

The War on Poverty was launched in 1964 as part of Lyndon Johnson's agenda for a Great Society. It marked the beginning of a new era of federal antipoverty programs. In striking contrast to the New Deal, which had emerged from an atmosphere of economic crisis, the Great Society was ushered in during an era of unparalled domestic prosperity. Nonetheless, like its New Deal counterpart, the quietly but hugely expanded Social Security system became the most far-reaching element of the Great Society agenda. In addition, as had the New Deal, the Great Society depended on a narrow, tenuous political base. As black demands for economic equality—and the structural reforms to undergird them—increased, coalitions among black civil rights leaders and white liberals deteriorated. Lacking a broad base of political support, the Great Society and subsequent antipoverty programs have since foundered on the shoals of politically unpopular welfare spending and a hesitation among political leaders to institute genuine antipoverty reforms.[16]

The unpopularity of federal antipoverty programs, which the majority of Americans lump together under the term "welfare," does not stem from either hard-hearted indifference or obtuseness. To paraphrase welfare and poverty analyst Hugh Heclo, when it comes to antipoverty policy, what Americans want from their policymaking they do not have, and what they have they do not want.[17]

In fact, American attitudes toward poverty, and what government should do about it, have changed very little over the past forty years. Public opinion polls taken in 1948, 1961, 1981, and 1984 indicate that a majority of Americans believe government should play a role in helping poor people. Yet Americans draw sharp distinctions between the "deserving" and "undeserving" poor. As a result, public response to government antipoverty spending varies depending on the words used to describe specific programs. If, for example, nearly 70 percent of Americans polled in 1984 thought the government was spending too little "caring for the poor," over 75 percent believed government "welfare" programs gave away "too much" (41 percent) or "about enough" (34.4 percent).[18]

"Caring for the poor" translates into assisting people hard hit by adverse circumstances, such as widows, orphans, or the physically disabled. These people, through no fault of their own, must rely on public support. Americans also approve of funds for education, training, and counseling to give the less fortunate new or better job opportunities. In fact Americans appear eager to support poor people they view as willing to help themselves. Paradoxically, many Americans who staunchly defend free enterprise and minimal government interference in the economy also demand that the government provide jobs for all Americans willing to work. A helping hand from government or any other source should get people back on their feet and moving in the direction of self-reliance.

"Welfare" programs, as perceived by most Americans, do not provide deserving poor people with resources for becoming more independent. They simply transfer wealth directly from the able-bodied working to the equally able-bodied but nonworking. In addition, Americans believe administrative incompetence and government corruption prevent most welfare benefits from reaching the intended recipients.

The largest and fastest-growing group of aid recipients in urban ghettos is single black mothers and their dependent children. Rightly or wrongly, the average American does not consider them "deserving poor." According to opinion surveys, while the American public strongly approves of child care support for a widow and her children (81 percent), only 52 percent would provide similar assistance to families with absentee fathers. A mere 15 percent would offer public support to families headed by nonmarried, nonworking mothers.[19]

According to a recent analysis of blacks and welfare policy, in 1983 16 percent of all black American families received cash benefits from state and federal welfare agencies. By 1985, almost half of black families were headed by women and over half of black children lived in female-headed households. Currently two thirds of black female-headed families fall below the poverty line.[20] Contrary to their negative stereotype, many black single mothers on welfare work. However, most cannot earn enough on minimum wage salaries, even working full time, to get off welfare. The vast majority of single black mothers who emerge from poverty do so by marrying or remarrying.[21]

Deciding whether welfare payments have encouraged chronic welfare dependency and contributed to the general deterioration of poor, inner-city neighborhoods depends in part on where one turns for analysis. A number of studies have found no evidence linking welfare payments to either rising birth rates among single mothers or nuclear family breakdowns.[22] Nevertheless, common sense dictates that as a cure for the destitution of chronically poor blacks, many of whom descend from generations of desperately poor, socially atomized rural migrants, welfare has become a kind of economic methadone, replacing one form of dependency with another.

Bates and Fusfeld point out that when transfer payments dip too low, as they did between 1964 and 1968, the ghettos break out in riots. When they rise too high, the incentive to work erodes and an important source of low-wage labor for the American economy dries up. Under the present system, American policymakers face the continual choice of applying either the carrot of higher transfer payments or the stick of greater law enforcement to maintain a precarious equilibrium between the ghetto economy and the economy at large. According to this view, welfare payments operate chiefly to maintain economic stability in and outside the ghetto; they are not designed to help poor people out of chronic poverty.[23]

Despite the gaping faults of the current welfare system, blacks have been better off as wards of the state than as serfs of southern agriculture. A quarter century ago, more than half of all American blacks lived in poverty. Less than a third do today. Infant mortality rates among black children have dropped, and life expectancy has risen for blacks at all economic levels.[24]

Even so, more income does not necessarily translate into economic progress. No one would assert that a family receiving $10,000 a year in government welfare grants is as well off as the family of a struggling young medical resident earning not much more. *How* one makes money is as important as how much one makes. If promoting jobs and decreasing welfare dependency in black communities is to be initiated by a new policy agenda for black economic development, specific objectives and the means for obtaining them must be made clear.

The Split in Black America

Of the 28.6 million American blacks who make up 12 percent of the total U.S. population, between two and four million fall into the chronically poor "underclass."[25] According to the Chicago blacks interviewed by Lemann, the split between middle- and lower-class blacks has deep roots in black American culture. In the agrarian and small town atmosphere of the South, clear divisions stood out between two-parent black families who worked hard and saved to get ahead and unmarried or separated black families who drifted around the countryside and hustled on the wrong side of town. From the former rose most of the black middle class and from the latter, the underclass.[26]

When civil rights and affirmative action opened doors for aspiring middle-class blacks, they rapidly moved up and out of poor, inner-city neighborhoods. As a rule, they did not gain their new economic advantages through entrepreneurship. If, over the past twenty-five years, the underclass has relied on the marginal benefits of increased social welfare spending, the black middle class has also staked its economic fortunes on an expanding public sector. Although blacks have made impressive strides forward as skilled craftsmen and professionals, by far the largest single employer of the newly designated black middle class has been government. Between 1970 and 1980 alone, the percentage of blacks in the public sector rose from 21 to 27 percent. At the same time, total numbers of black self-employed and receipts from black businesses fell.[27] Clearly, most middle-class blacks have chosen the safe and sure route up the economic ladder. Given the convergence of a deprived socioeconomic history with publicly provided opportunities, theirs was a purely rational economic decision. It was not an entrepreneurial one.

Economic development is not the same as economic growth. Economic growth has to do with changes in the aggregate measure of output, employment, and income—in other words, *how much* is produced. Economic development, by contrast, has to do with changes in the technology, institutions, and economic arrangements by which growth is achieved. Growth and development are mutually reinforcing processes. As growth occurs it introduces and necessitates change in the production of goods, the operation of institutions, and the structure of economic arrangements. Economic development responds to growth as a continuous process of adaptation to changing economic circumstances. The entrepreneur provides the engine for development by organizing new arrangements to take advantage of the opportunities or solve the problems arising from an economic environment in flux.[28]

In addition to new ideas and technologies, entrepreneurial firms create most of the new jobs in our economy.[29] It follows that if we want to create jobs in black communities and enable them to adapt more readily to economic change—in other words, to become the subjects rather than the objects of economic events—we must overcome the remaining barriers to black entrepreneurship. Here, we should make clear that our definition of entrepreneurship extends beyond the narrow definition of commercial risk-taking to education, health care, and the delivery of other public and private goods and services.

Business formation in black communities, defined as a broad range of entrepreneurial activity, depends largely on the capital and labor markets of the American economy. Risk capital, the single most important determinant of the business formation rate in any community, has generally not been available to companies formed by blacks or located in areas where blacks are heavily represented in the population. Current tax codes do not encourage investments in a wide variety of risky, sometimes questionable enterprises, or in productive activities organized by or providing employment to poor people. This lack of incentives is no cosmic accident. Organizing financial markets to encourage investments in poor people has simply not been a national priority. Yet restructured capital markets would provide only a partial solution to black poverty. Labor markets must also operate differently. Black interests will not be served until increasing numbers of blacks, middle-class as well as poor, are able to get the jobs generated by increased business formation in black communities. More blacks must seek and obtain appropriate educations and experience, from learning basic skills to organizing complex entrepreneurial ventures. More would-be employers must be appropriately compensated for assuming the risk of hiring unskilled, low-income people.

Black America must begin to address its chronic problems of unemployment, welfare, and low capital accumulation by adopting entrepreneurial approaches with which it is neither familiar nor comfortable. Government expansion has reached the point of diminishing returns. Throughout the industrialized and so-called Third World, governments are handing over entire functions and industries to the private sector. Fueled in large part by a universal dissatisfaction with the inability of government to manage or adapt to rapidly changing economic circumstances, the trend encompasses a broad range of activities, from the privatization of local economic development and entire national economic sectors, to the creation of tax-advantaged enterprise zones in over half of U.S. states, to the offering of public stock in government-owned industrial corporations in Britain and France.

Because over 50 percent of all college-educated U.S. blacks are employed in the public sector, and 26 percent of all black families depend to some degree on public services and transfer payments, a shrinking government represents a trend black Americans can neither change nor afford to ignore.[30] Like any major economic shift, it presents both problems and opportunities. On the one hand, as private firms and individuals assume more of the responsibility for producing "public goods," the decreasing size and responsibility of government may result in reduced upward mobility, job security, and status for blacks in public service. On the other, it will create new opportunities for those who are nimble and creative—in a word, entrepreneurial enough to exploit the possibilities that always accompany change.

The black community's ability to generate and sustain entrepreneurial activities, from state-of-the-art computer firms to day care centers, will depend largely upon the availability of substantial amounts of risk capital for investment into new, unproven, but promising endeavors. Prevailing orthodoxy has held that since the black community lacks the money to finance the large numbers of risky ventures needed to make a dent in black unemployment, entrepreneurial strategies at best provide a Band-Aid solution to black economic problems. We believe the prevailing wisdom is wrong. Black America has enough money to make a substantial start toward financing its own development. It also has within reach the tools for attracting substantial investment from white America. Tax reforms passed in 1985 should reduce black America's tax burden by nearly $2 billion a year.[31] A significant part of the reduction will go toward the purchase of basic necessities by those in the lowest income brackets. The remainder, however, will flow to blacks whose economic circumstances would permit them to save and invest it. In other words, tax reform will have given black America approximately $1 billion to invest in its own development between 1985 and 1990. Yet we know that the added capacity will not translate easily into increased entrepreneurial activity among black Americans. The reasons have to do with both black economic culture and the encompassing structures of the American marketplace.

Black Culture and Entrepreneurship

Until recently, observations of entrepreneurial behavior focused largely on the psychology of individuals. If, the line of reasoning seemed to go, one could discover what made entrepreneurial individuals tick, they might be produced in larger and more effective quantities. Although this method has augmented our appreciation of entrepreneurs and our awareness of their indispensable contributions to modern economic life, it has done little to increase our understanding of the underlying social processes that brought them into existence.

The model of entrepreneurial decision-making we will use considers external factors, referred to as "opportunity structures," in relation to the inherent capacity of individuals to perceive and act on given opportunities.[32] Opportunity structures encompass the social, economic, technological, and political conditions exogenous to the choices and decisions of individual entrepreneurs. Every society has individuals who are better positioned to take advantage of entrepreneurial opportunities, because of their relative access to opportunity structures, their greater native ability, or both. Entrepreneurs who successfully act on available opportunities move economies and societies to new stages of development.[33]

We have noted the long-recognized contribution of entrepreneurship to economic development. As the awareness of the entrepreneurial role in development has increased, so has the need to understand the cultural contexts in which specific types of economic change occur. From Weber's Protestant ethic to McClelland's individual achievement motivation, to Hagen's overcompensating "out" groups, a variety of analyses have attempted to construct a cultural basis for entrepreneurial behavior.[34]

In the mid-nineteenth century, Tocqueville observed that community-level institutions, by serving as a bridge between individual decision-makers and large social institutions, performed an important function in American society.[35]

Anthropologist Goodell has termed these so-called "mediating" or "middle-range" structures "routine fields of interaction." As the central arenas of most human activity, "routine fields" form a locus for entrepreneurial behavior. Essentially, they operate as incubators for initiative and risk-taking, saving and investment, habits of work and laziness, and decisions to join others in common endeavors. Cultures evolve from the repetition and intensity of routine interactions. Over time, daily routines evolve into legally defined social institutions.[36]

What qualities distinguish a dynamic entrepreneurial culture? Shapero outlines four:

- *resilience*—the capacity to respond effectively to change.
- *creativity and innovation*—the ability and willingness to experiment.
- *initiative*—the desire and power to begin and carry through useful projects.
- *diversity*—enough variety to protect against unforeseen circumstances and provide for a creative environment.[37]

Shapero maintains that localized economic development programs provide the best means for stimulating entrepreneurial growth among low-performance groups. Instead of importing a few large-scale industries from the outside, they encourage a diversity of new companies from within the community. Specifically, he ties the potential for entrepreneurial dynamism to the "cultural fit" between local entrepreneurs and their communities.

> The entrepreneur, even when drawn from a minority or immigrant group, is part of the fabric of the culture in which he is found. The entrepreneur lives close to and is part of the culture of the country and locale. He is attuned to place and custom, and has an intimate awareness of what can and cannot be done with local resources. Unlike the manager of an immigrant industrial plant, the local entrepreneur does not have to be "oriented," taught how to understand the local natives, given language lessons, taught about local customs.[38]

As does the overall American culture of which it forms a part, the subculture of black Americans represents a distinctive set of shared values expressed in a distinctive "way of life." In this particular study, we are interested in the economic characteristics of black culture. How did they come into existence? How have they changed? How have black Americans, individually and as a group, fared economically as a result of their distinctive cultural experiences?

In the following chapters we will attempt to locate both the barriers to and facilitators of black entrepreneurship in the United States. Having surveyed the relationship of black entrepreneurs to the opportunity structures in which they operate, we will descriptively apply Shapero's yardsticks of entrepreneurial culture to black families, schools, and voluntary associations. Our premise is that these institutions, in which most of the daily activities of most black Americans take place, serve as the principal mediators between individual black economic decisions and the opportunity structures in American society that positively or negatively reinforce them. We will look especially at how individual black entrepreneurs have acted as Schumpeter's "creative destroyers."[39] Unlike Schumpeter, who confined his definition to those who feed the capitalist engine by replacing old goods with new, we will broaden our scope. In addition to businesses, black "creative destroyers," or entrepreneurs, have ultimately formed and transformed black families, churches, and schools. They have performed an integral role in shaping and reshaping American social, political, and economic institutions at all levels.

We want to make our intentions clear. This study does not attempt to provide theoretical proof that black entrepreneurship offers the best and only means for sustained economic progress among black Americans. Nor does it claim to offer a systematic explanation for the cultural basis of black entrepreneurship. At best, we have embarked on a new way of viewing black economic development through the prisms of entrepreneurship and culture. Always, we assume that understanding entrepreneurship from inside black

America requires looking at it as a social phenomenon played out under uniquely American circumstances.

From the fictional creations of Horatio Alger to real-life John D. Rockefellers, Andrew Carnegies, and Stephen Jobs, Americans have spun indelible myths about their larger-than-life entrepreneurial heroes. As those who achieve far beyond conventional measures of wealth, fame, and power, entrepreneurial giants epitomize the quintessentially American fantasy of rugged, untrammeled individualism. Yet real-life entrepreneurs are as much product as producer of the societies in which they live and operate. One has only to compare the fabulous entrepreneurial successes of a Hong Kong with their conspicuous absence elsewhere to realize that not all social environments elicit equal levels of entrepreneurial success. Given our awareness that economic development in the black community will depend largely on its entrepreneurial talent, we are behooved to understand the unique economic culture that has evolved from the relationship between black Americans and the larger American society.

Notes

1. Walker, Juliet, *Free Frank: A Black Pioneer on the Antebellum Frontier* (Lexington: The University Press of Kentucky, 1983).
2. Schumpeter, Joseph, *The Theory of Economic Development* (Cambridge: Harvard University Press, 1955).
3. Shapero, Albert, *Entrepreneurship: Key to Self-Renewing Economies* (College of Administration, Ohio State University, August 1981, p. 20).
4. McClelland, David, *The Achieving Society* (Princeton: Van Nostrand, 1961).
5. Bates, Timothy, "An Analysis of Minority Entrepreneurship: Utilizing the Census of Population Public Use Samples" (Fourth progress report on MBDA contract, August 1985).
6. Jacobs, Jane, *Cities and the Wealth of Nations* (New York: Random House, 1984, p. 39).
7. Gilder, George, *Wealth and Poverty* (New York: Basic Books, 1981, p. 37).
8. For a recent update see Glasgow, Douglas, "The Black Underclass in Perspective" in *The State of Black America 1987* (New York: National Urban League, January 1987).
9. Lemann, Nicholas, "The Origins of the Underclass" *(Atlantic Monthly,* June and July 1986).
10. Bates, Timothy and Fusfeld, Daniel R., *The Political Economy of the Urban Ghetto* (Carbondale, Illinois: Southern Illinois University Press, 1984).
11. Ibid.
12. Ibid.
13. Ibid., p. 116.
14. Heclo, Hugh, "The Political Foundations of Antipoverty Policy" in Danziger and Weinberg (eds.), *Fighting Poverty: What Works and What Doesn't* (Cambridge: Harvard University Press, 1986).
15. Ibid.
16. Ibid.

17. Ibid., p. 326.
18. Ibid., pp. 326–332.
19. Ibid. pp. 329–330.
20. Joint Center for Political Studies, "Tax and Welfare Policy Options: Implications for Minorities and the Poor" (Washington, D.C.: 1986, p. 16).
21. Ibid.
22. Ibid. See also Wilson, William J., *The Truly Disadvantaged* (Chicago: University of Chicago Press, 1987, pp. 77–81, and for opposing viewpoint Murray, Charles, *Losing Ground: American Social Policy, 1950–1980* (New York: Basic Books, 1984).
23. Bates and Fusfeld, op. cit., pp. 207–212.
24. Joint Center for Political Studies, op. cit., p. 18.
25. *The Washington Post,* "Blacks in America 1986: While Most Gain, Millions Suffer" (Monday, January 20, 1986).
26. Lemann, op. cit.
27. Hill, Robert B., "The Black Middle Class: Past, Present and Future" in *The State of Black America 1986* (New York: National Urban League, 1986, p. 50). See also Kotkin, Joel, "The Reluctant Entrepreneurs," (*Inc.* September, 1987, p. 81).
28. Gilder, op. cit.
29. Armington and Odle, "Sources of Employment Growth, 1978–1980" (Waltham, Massachusetts: Bentley College, second annual small business research conference, March 11–12, 1982, pp. 5–6). Also Birch, David L., *The Job Generation Process* (Cambridge: MIT Program on Neighborhood and Regional Change, 1979). As well as Teitz, Michael B., *Small Business and Employment Growth in California* (Berkeley: University of California Press, March 1981).
30. Swinton, David, "Summary of Simulation Results for the Tax Reform Act of 1985" *Final Report: Summary of Simulation Results for the Tax Reform Act of 1985* (Atlanta: Southern Center for Studies in Public Policy, January 1986, p. 1).
31. Greenfield, Sidney M. and Strickon, Arnold, in Aubey, Strickon, and Greenfield (eds.), *Entrepreneurs in Cultural Context* (Albuquerque: University of New Mexico Press, 1979, p. 17).
32. Ibid., p. 343.
33. Shapero, Albert and Sokol, Lisa, "The Social Dimensions of Entrepreneurship" in Kent, Sexton, and Vesper (eds.), *Encyclopedia of Entrepreneurship* (Englewood Cliffs, New Jersey: Prentice-Hall, 1982, pp.74–75).
34. Tocqueville, Alexis de, *Democracy in America* (Garden City, New York: Anchor Books, Doubleday, 1969, based on the 13th edition, 1850).
35. Goodell, Grace, "The Importance of Political Participation for Sustained Capitalist Development" (*European Journal of Sociology* 26: 93-127).
36. Shapero, Albert, "The Role of Entrepreneurship in Development at the Less-Than-National Level" in Friedman and Schweke (eds.), *Expanding the Opportunity to Produce* (Washington, D.C.: Corporation for Enterprise Development, 1981, p. 31).
37. Ibid., p. 26.
38. Schumpeter, Joseph A., *Capitalism, Socialism and Democracy* (New York: Harper and Row, 1950, p. 83).

2

Blacks in the Marketplace

Introduction

Black business development has been the subject of extensive research and policy analysis over the past two decades. Spurred by black gains in civil rights and a desire to promote similar progress in black economic conditions, the research has focused on four principle areas: economics, business management, psychology, and sociology.[1]

The economic approach primarily looks at the financial characteristics of minority firms and the economic environments in which they operate. It places a strong emphasis on the financial resources available to minority entrepreneurs, and generally assumes that low business formation and growth result from a lack of equity or debt capital. Much of the economic research has been hampered by a paucity of sound empirical data on the economic characteristics of black businesses.

Business management concentrates on the nonfinancial characteristics of firms—management, planning procedures, technical capabilities in producing goods and services, and market strategies. A number of government programs attempt to provide these organizational resources to minority businesses.

Psychological methods stress the individual human resources that an entrepreneur brings to the operation of a business. In policy terms, entrepreneurial psychologists have advocated increasing the formal entrepreneurial training and business experience of minorities.

By contrast, the sociological approach contends that minority business ownership is a group-level phenomenon that depends largely on the resources of social groups for its development. The Minority Business Development Agency (MBDA) at the Department of Commerce considers the sociological perspective one of the most potentially lucrative avenues of research on black businesses.

As the principle investigator for the MBDA in the area, sociologist Frank Fratoe has defined a series of internal and external social factors that influence the development of minority businesses.[2] From an internal perspective, says Fratoe, "group self-help support networks" play a critical role in the formation and success of ethnic minority businesses. As the resources and institutions closest to the individual—family, friends, voluntary associations—they provide a range of support that enables the individual entrepreneur to start and maintain a successful business.[3] In addition to internal factors, Fratoe collects under the term "larger social environment" external conditions influencing minority entrepreneurship.[4] These have less to do with sociology and more to do with macroeconomics, business development, and government policy.

The objective of this chapter will be to analyze the social, economic, and political framework in which black entrepreneurship has taken place. While all four analytical approaches—economic, business management, psychological, and sociological—will be used as points of departure to highlight various issues, we intend to emphasize the sociological perspective. Among other topical areas we will include a chronological history of black participation in business, the demographic characteristics of black businesses and business owners, black capital and labor markets, and government assistance to minority businesses. Underlying our discussion is the question of how conditions in the marketplace impinge on the development of entrepreneurial institutions within the black American community.

A Chronology of Black Business

In 1968, Eugene Foley published a brief but cogent framework for creating more jobs in predominately black urban ghettos. He believed an important part of the solution lay in putting existing resources to more effective use. A major step in that direction consisted of stimulating the growth of the critically underdeveloped black business sector of low-income neighborhoods. Foley offered a concise sketch of black American businesses at that point in time.

> The picture, then, of the Negro in business is that of a small businessman—a very small businessman—generally not a very good businessman and, frankly to date, not a very significant factor in the Negro community.[5]

In 1984, nearly two decades after Foley submitted his proposal to public policymakers, Bates described a distressingly similar business climate in inner-city areas. Ghettos, as he referred to them, encompassed an economic system in which racially and culturally unassimilated minorities remained trapped in a vicious circle of poverty.[6] The best and the brightest moved up and out "taking with them the great bulk of entrepreneurial talent."[7] Along with human resources, capital and income also flowed away from rather than into poor neighborhoods. The combined result was to make self-sustained economic growth in the ghetto increasingly elusive.

Over time, suggested Bates, business development could staunch and even reverse such resource drains. New businesses would offer viable economic opportunities to highly skilled and talented ghetto residents, keeping them inside the community. The large numbers of ghetto unemployed would have access to stable employment opportunities. Locally owned businesses serving markets outside the ghetto would multiply indigenous capital and income in two ways: by increasing spending within the community and by bringing in new sources of income and capital.

As both Foley and Bates acknowledged, historical precedents indicated that increasing entrepreneurship to break the poverty cycle among the urban poor presented some formidable challenges.

The Turn of the Century

At the turn of the century, W.E.B. Du Bois made the first systematic effort to observe and analyze the development of black American businesses. The preface to *The Negro in Business,* first published in 1899, sets forth the rationale for his investigation:

> For a Negro then to go into business means a great deal. It is, indeed, a step in social progress worth measuring. It means hard labor, thrift in saving, a comprehension of social movements and ability to learn a new vocation—all this taking place, not by concerted guided action, but spontaneously here and there, in hamlet and city, North and South.[8]

His methods, also outlined in the preface, indicate a strong bias toward the economic and business management types of analysis:

> We need to know accurately the different kinds of business ventures that appear, the order of their appearance, their measure of success and the capital invested in them. We need to know what sort of men go into business, how long they have been engaged and how they managed to get a start. Finally, we should know where this economic advance is being most strongly felt, and what the present tendencies are.[9]

Du Bois separated black business along class or caste lines, which he believed had resulted from the very different position of blacks under slavery and as freedmen. Thus blacks who as slaves were house servants, field hands, and plantation mechanics became respectively barbers, gardeners, and builders after emancipation. General merchants, bankers, and manufacturers tended to come from that small group of black elite who had obtained their freedom prior to the official end of slavery. If Du Bois' "evolutionary" business categories fail to hold up under close scrutiny, his analysis does provide valuable information about the numbers and types of black businesses in existence at the turn of the century. According to a state by state, territory by territory breakdown, Du Bois and his researchers estimated 5,000 American blacks were then engaged in private enterprise. Most were crowded into the personal services and retail trades and primarily successful because they provided resources blacks would otherwise have to do without. "Peculiar instances," observed Du Bois, "of the advantage of the disadvantage."[10] As the anecdotal speeches and profiles in the second half of *The Negro in Business* suggest, Du Bois and other black leaders realized the enormity of the gulf between the need for blacks to succeed in business and the progress they had made thus far. Exorted Professor John Hope of the Atlanta Baptist College:

> Business seems to be not simply the raw material of the Anglo Saxon civilization, but almost the civilization itself. It is at least its mainspring to action. Living among such a people is it not obvious that we cannot escape its most powerful motive and survive? To the finite vision, to say the least, the policy of avoiding entrance in the world's business would be suicide to the Negro. Yet as a matter of great account, we ought to note that as good a showing as we have made, that showing is but as pebbles on the shore of business enterprise.[11]

In 1907, Booker T. Washington published the only other early work on black enterprise, titled identically, *The Negro in Business*. Washington did not attempt a scientific analysis of blacks businesses; instead, he promoted business as a way of life for the young, educated black male. He filled his book with inspirational profiles of black men who had made it in the world of business and expounded at length on the virtues of education and Christian morality. The two combined, he stressed, "Make a man valuable as a citizen, make him more industrious, make him earn more, make him upright."[12] Preached this early minister of black economic salvation, "Our pathway must be up through the soil, up through swamps, up through forests, up through streams and rocks, up through commerce, education and religion!"[13]

The American Dilemma and the Myth of Negro Business

In his Nobel Prize–winning exegesis on black America, Gunnar Myrdal observed the ideological—and practical—dilemma facing middle-class black professionals and businessmen. Even as they fought against blocked social and economic opportunities, they had to protect the limited resources offered by a segregated environment.[14]

Originally a two-volume effort of nearly 2,000 pages, *The American Dilemma* devoted less than ten pages to black businesses in the United States. The fact that black businessmen received but a passing nod amid a cursory examination of the black middle class reflects a prevailing notion about black economic progress at mid-century. However pressing the social and economic problems of black Americans, entrepreneurship was not perceived by either policymakers or the black community as providing a significant part of proposed solutions.

What Myrdal had to say about black business circa 1944 was not encouraging. The bulk of black businesses still consisted of small retail establishments that, due to their size and limited stocks, were at a severe competitive disadvantage relative to white retail shops. Although the majority of black stores relied on an exclusively black clientele, they garnered only 5 to 10 percent of all black consumer dollars. Reasoning their businesses had a better chance of succeeding at a distance from stores that sold similar goods, black retailers increased the odds against them by choosing poor locations. Myrdal calls such choices manifestations of an "attitude" about the special requirements of black businesses. In this case, blacks chose not to locate their businesses according to the economically sound principle that competition increases business volume. Instead, they succumbed to an economically irrational "attitude" that succeeded only in isolating them from the larger flow of retail business in their communities. The inability of many black retailers to perceive and take advantage of business opportunities clearly impeded the growth and diversity of black businesses.

Added to the limitations of size, type, and location, all black businesses had difficulty getting credit, partly due to racial prejudice but also because of their marginal ability to make a profit. Combined deficiencies in the business environment meant that black businesses suffered from a chronic inability to reproduce themselves. Even if a talented supply of replacements had been available, most black enterprises at the time were too small, inefficient, and unattractive to draw or train potential young entrepreneurs.

The almost complete monopoly by some black businesses within their communities—hotels, funeral parlors, beauty and barber shops—contributed greatly to their success. Yet blacks also failed in businesses where they initially held an advantage. For example, in catering, laundry work, and the building trades, blacks had a long history of skills and experience. Observed Myrdal, "Not only has the Negro caterer lost out because he has not had capital, but also because he has often failed to modernize his business and be efficient generally."[15] Blacks did not choose to go into the laundry business. The building trades were taken over by technology and labor policies that discriminated against blacks. A dearth of black manufacturers, said Myrdal, was even more easily explained. Given little capital, an inferior education, and no opportunity to gain experience, the average black faced nearly insurmountable obstacles in becoming a successful producer of manufactured goods.

Besides small retail establishments, Myrdal reported the minor success of a few black banks and building and loan associations, along with the relatively greater success of black insurance companies. Black banks were compromised by their small size and restricted investment opportunities. By contrast, black insurance companies performed better than any other capitalist enterprise in the black community. In 1939, sixty-seven black insurance companies underwrote $13 million in policies and employed 8,000 workers. They stood at the apex of black businesses in America. Because white insurance companies charged black customers higher premium rates, discrimination contributed substantially to their success. Practically all American families—black, white, rich or poor—subscribed to some form of insurance. For the black and poor, life insurance companies guaranteed little more than burial payments. In fact, black insurance companies worked hand-in-hand with black undertakers—the only black business group in America whose proportions in the black population rivaled those of their white counterparts in the white population.

As opposed to the broad social policies dealt with in *The American Dilemma,* E. Franklin Frazier's contemporaneous *Negro in the United States* looked at institutional development within the black American community. Frazier attempted to understand the degree to which blacks had assimilated the larger culture and as a result whether they had successfully integrated into American society.

In Frazier's view, the general character of black business had not changed since the beginning of the century:

> The vast majority of black business enterprises have continued to be small establishments catering to the wants of a segragated world not served by the business enterprises of the larger white community.[16]

Why, by 1949, had black Americans failed to develop a larger and more prosperous business sector? The core reason, concluded Frazier, was that blacks "lacked experience in buying and selling, which are at the heart of the spirit of business."[17] He concurred with Myrdal that the future of black business success lay in an integrated business and financial community that would allow blacks to obtain gradually the skills they needed to prosper as businessmen.

Frazier's explanation was a significant departure from earlier analyses of black business patterns. Instead of racial prejudice and economic exclusion, it focused on the internal shortcomings of black business culture. To support his "missing business experience" hypothesis, Frazier scanned black American business from an historical perspective, beginning with a description of entrepreneurial ventures prior to the Civil War. The majority were small personal services operated by freedmen in northern and southern cities. Northern blacks, who had a larger variety of available opportunities, engaged in a limited degree of merchandising and manufacturing. Following the Civil War, a small group of black businessmen formed the Freedman's Savings and Trust Company. The purpose of the organization was to foster thrift and prosperity among the newly freed black masses. Proclaimed Frederick Douglass, one of its founders:

> The mission of the Freedman's Bank is to show our people the road to a share of the wealth and well being of the world. It has already done much to lift the race into respectability, and with their continued confidence and patient cooperation, it will continue to reflect credit upon the race and promote their welfare.[18]

Although the original mission failed, a small group of businessmen organized under its auspices became the founding fathers of black banking and insurance industries.

Frazier did not completely omit racism from his analysis. He considered poverty and an inability to obtain credit as important factors in the retardation of black enterprise. In particular, he stressed the invidious effect of black exclusion from the larger marketplace. Nevertheless, he attributed the primary cause of failure to a missing social and cultural factor—a tradition of buying and selling within the context of everyday life in the black community.

Black Capitalism

Developed in the late 1960s and early 1970s, "Black Capitalism" constituted a movement by blacks to gain control over the business development of their own communities. At the same time they reached out into the encompassing marketplace for new entrepreneurial resources.[19] Directing business growth in the black community was considered the first step toward achieving a powerful black economic presence in the larger American economy. Essentially, Black Capitalism called for a new kind of social and economic contract among racial groups in America—one based on mutual self-interest rather than integration.

In 1974, Cross attempted to lay out the philosophical foundations of Black Capitalism as well as ways in which it could be put into practice. He described the "wealth forbidding conditions" of America's inner cities, areas he maintained "were structured to prevent the accumulation of wealth."[20] Black Capitalism had the potential to usher in a new era of black economic progress, one based on entrepreneurial development inside ghetto communities. As opposed to donating jobs, giving blacks the opportunity to obtain entrepreneurial skills was the way to make black communities more productive. To overcome entrepreneurial deficiencies, talented black entrepreneurs had to be recruited from and into economically segregated ghettos.

However small and restricted, said Cross, blacks had a long tradition of entrepreneurship. Stripped of the protective mantle of enforced segregation, that tradition was rapidly eroding. Meanwhile, despite legal advances, black Americans as a group were not becoming more entrepreneurial. Believing the key to economic progress in the ghetto was to make investments in slum areas profitable, Cross proposed tax deductions that would entice mainstream American business into ghettos. In place of the Community Development Corporations (CDCs) then under consideration, he suggested the creation of entrepreneurial development centers:

> These centers (established in ghetto storefronts) would evaluate business proposals, assist in preparing loan applications, help establish bookkeeping systems, and explore sources of financing for ghetto businesses. They would evaluate and make recommendations on locations and types of business needed in the community, and help develop and implement business programs which would improve economic conditions in the community by working with local groups, city, state, and federal agencies.[21]

Cross was adamant that the building of wealth in American ghettos must be the prerogative of business, not government. He predicted the failure of CDCs, which he believed rested on the false premise that "creative entrepreneurship and black affluence can develop in a quasi-socialistic enclave where the production and marketing are community controlled."[22] Above all, restrictions and centralized control, familiar signatures of large-scale economic development plans coordinated and managed by government, were to be avoided.

Economic Development in the Urban Ghetto

In 1984, sixteen years after Foley and his research staff noted the complete absence of studies on the economic structure of urban ghettos, Bates and Fusfeld published *The Political Economy of the Urban Ghetto*. Tracing the formation of modern urban ghettos through vast waves of black migration from South to North during the first half of the century, they examined the relationship between ghettos and the mainstream American economy. According to their analysis, two interlinked processes operated to maintain an ongoing cycle of urban poverty. First, ghettoized low-wage workers provided a cheap source of labor to the larger American economy, and second, blacks and other minorities were crowded into the low-wage labor force. While the mainstream economy received the benefits of a cheap and plentiful labor supply, low-income workers found themselves trapped in an environment that offered them little opportunity to learn new skills. Static and debilitating social processes served to perpetuate the system internally.[23]

According to Bates and Fusfeld, the history of black entrepreneurship "has been shaped by limited access to credit, limitations in educational and training opportunities and prevailing attitudes about the roles that minorities should assume in society."[24] Over the past two decades blacks have begun to reverse their historical limitations. The business community has diversified. As older traditional businesses decline, new "emerging" lines of business are replacing them. Emerging businesses are larger, more profitable, and integrated into the broader marketplace. By providing jobs and attracting capital to low-income black neighborhoods, they may take the lead in developing the entrepreneurial potential of the ghetto.

Participation of Blacks in Business

According to a business evolution model developed by MBDA, the total number of minority business enterprises results from three processes: business formation, growth, and failure.[25] It follows that a combination of low business formation and high business failure produces a low business participation rate. Despite the advances of "emerging" black enterprises, overall black business development continues to fit this pattern.

In a September 1986 article for *Inc.*, Kotkin held the poor business performance of black Americans directly responsible for their position at the bottom of the economic ladder.[26] Blacks are more underrepresented in business than in any other occupational category. Their participation rates are low compared not only with whites but to other minority groups, notably Asian-Americans and Hispanics. Using 1980 census data, Bates calculated the following percentages of self-employment for different racial and ethnic groups:

Nonminorities	5.02%
Asians	3.76%
Hispanics	3.16%
Blacks	1.75%[27]

His figures correspond roughly with those produced by Bearse from the 1976 census.[28] Using a slightly different numerical analysis, in 1982 the MBDA calculated about 63 nonminority (white) businesses for each 1,000 persons in that population group. Comparable statistics for all minorities reveal a participation rate of 14 per 1,000 persons. For blacks the rate is 9 per 1,000—the lowest of all minority groups.[29]

While a business participation rate does not capture the full range of black business issues, it illustrates a general condition. It is especially significant when combined with the fact that black businesses also have the highest failure rates. In 1984, Stevens quantified minority business formation and failure rates among Asians, Hispanics, and blacks. Asians had the highest level of business participation, and blacks the lowest, while Hispanics fell in between; Stevens therefore expected Asian businesses to have higher formation and lower failure rates than the other two groups. To his surprise, although formation rates were predictably high for Asians (20.7 percent), medium for Hispanics (17.2 percent), and low for blacks (14.9 percent), corresponding failure rates among the three groups were almost identical. Steven concluded from his findings that of the two major problems facing black entrepreneurs— low business formation and high business failure—the more critical element was business formation.[30]

Social Group Phenomena

Using the 1980 census, Fratoe compared business participation rates across racial and ethnic groups. His data provided important new information on the low business participation rates of blacks.

The 1980 census was the first to ask for the identification of ancestry, permitting collection of ethnic data from Americans regardless of how many generations they were removed from their country of origin. The analysis focused on fifty groups which, taken together, comprised nearly the entire universe (97 percent) of all persons reporting a single ancestry. Ancestry groups were cross-tabulated by self-employment to ascertain the business participation rate for each group. The rate was defined as the number of self-employed per 1,000 population of a group. People of single ancestry who reported self-employed status were also cross-tabulated by income.

Fratoe found 4.9 percent of all persons reporting a single ancestry group were self-employed in 1980. Their mean income was $18,630, of which $13,960 was from nonfarm self-employment. Business participation rates ranged from a high of 117.4 for Russians to a low of 10.6 for Puerto Ricans. Besides Puerto Ricans, other groups who were more than 50 percent below the U.S. average were Subsaharan Africans, Dominicans, Haitians, Vietnamese, Mexicans, Hawaiians, Jamaicans, Filipinos, and Ecuadorians. For the predominantly black ancestry groups, business participation rates were:

1. Subsaharan African   13.6%
2. Dominican   14.6%

3.	Haitian	15.5%
4.	Jamaican	21.5%

Among all ancestry groups, 48.9 out of every 1,000 persons reported self-employment, while among every 1,000 Subsaharan Africans, fewer than 14 were self-employed.

Corresponding mean incomes among predominantly black groups were:

1.	Subsaharan African	$11,260.00
2.	Dominican	$13,870.00
3.	Haitian	$19,100.00
4.	Jamaican	$15,320.00

The largest black West Indian groups, Jamaicans and Haitians, have business participation rates (21.5 and 15.5 percent) above those of Subsaharan Africans. Jamaicans, Haitians, and Dominicans also have higher mean incomes than Subsaharan Africans. In fact, the mean Haitian income was above the national average of $18,630.

Ancestry groups reporting self-employed persons with high and low business participation rates generally corresponded with the groups having high and low mean incomes. Of the ten groups with the highest business participation rates, five were also among the groups with the highest mean incomes— Russian, Rumanian, Austrian, Lebanese, and Syrian. The relationship was even more pronounced among groups with low business participation rates. Of ten groups in the low participation category, eight were also among the bottom ten in income—Subsaharan African, Puerto Rican, Vietnamese, Ecuadorian, Mexican, Dominican, Hawaiian, and Jamaican.[31]

Characteristics of Black Self-Employed

Conducted as a special project in 1969 and incorporated into the economic census in 1972, the Commerce Department initiated the Survey of Minority-Owned Business Enterprises (SMOBE) to provide comprehensive survey data on minority businesses. Until that time, comprehensive data on black business owners was virtually nonexistent. Following the pioneer attempt of Du Bois at the beginning of the century, only a few scattered studies—one by Pierce in 1944, another by the Drexel Institute in Philadelphia in 1964, and a third by the Indiana Business School in 1968—had tried to systematically record the number, type, and location of black enterprises in the United States.

The SMOBE provides separately published economic data on businesses owned by blacks, Hispanics, Asians, and American Indians. Each survey reviews entire firms rather than separate establishments or subsidiaries. The data cover number of firms, gross receipts, number of paid employees, and annual payrolls. These figures are presented by geographic area, industry, size of firm, and legal form of organization. In 1982, the most recently published economic censuses covered manufacturing, mining, construction industries, retail and wholesale trade, service industries, and selected transporation activities among minority firms.

As a result of a new census report, the Characteristics of Business Owners (CBO), demographic characteristics of business owners have also been determined. First published in 1987, the CBO provides data about the characteristics of minority-owned businesses (including those owned by women) as well as those of the nonminority (white male) universe. Initial data were collected through a statistically selected mail survey and then combined with administrative records from the 1982 economic census. This information may prove a valuable resource for empirically testing various theories about business ownership. Systematically collected demographic information about different ethnic businesses was previously unobtainable. The following sections present the statistical descriptions of black business owners from the CBO report. In some cases the results validate many hypotheses about black business owners; in others they present evidence contrary to established notions.

Age and Business Experience

The majority of black business owners are between 35 and 44 years of age. Across all racial and ethnic groups, this age group produces the most business owners. Yet only 17.3 percent of black owners fall into the 25 to 34-year-old category, the lowest for this age range among all groups. Blacks also have the lowest percentage of business owners under age 25, 1.8 percent, compared with 3.3 percent for nonminority male owners, 4.0 percent for white females, and 3.6 percent for Hispanics and other minority groups. Among black business owners, more than 49 percent are between the ages of 35 and 54, a higher percentage than for either female or white male business owners.

Work Experience

Black business owners had the lowest percentage response, 10.9 percent, to the question of whether the owners had previously owned a business. Nonminority males had the highest at 22.1 percent, followed by other minorities and Hispanics at 17.7 and 15 percent, respectively.

Over half of black business owners who worked as full- or part-time employees had at least ten years of work experience. At 54.8 percent, among all business owners they placed second only to white males, 61.1 percent of whom had ten or more years of work experience. More than half of black business proprietors had greater than ten years of work experience, with nearly 27 percent reporting more than twenty years. Across all groups, sole proprietorships made up over 90 percent of business ownerships, but at 95 percent was highest for blacks. Numbers of years of work experience was higher among black partnerships and corporations—57.4 and 57.7 percent, respectively—than for black individual proprietorships.

Slightly over half, 52.6 percent, of black business owners had no managerial experience. Only women, at 54.6 percent, ranked lower in this category. In addition, fewer than 12 percent of black owners had worked in a managerial capacity for more than ten years. They fell considerably behind the 21.2 percent of white male owners with ten or more years of experience as managers.

Education

Business owners who had completed high school formed the largest educational category across all groups. Among black business owners, 25.4 percent had a high school education and 30 percent had some college. In this respect, they compared favorably with business owners from other ethnic groups. However, blacks also had a much higher percentage of owners with less than a high school education, 25.3 percent. At 30.4 percent, only Hispanics had a higher proportion of owners with less than a high school education. In all other groups the percentage was less than 15 percent.

A relatively large number of black business owners, 15.3 percent, had some postgraduate education. Nevertheless, out of a range of one to five years of college, they also had the second lowest percentage of owners with at least one year of college education. Hispanics rated the lowest at 38.4 percent, blacks were 45.3 percent, women and white males 52 percent, and other minority owners 60 percent.

Veterans' Status

Almost half of white male business owners, 43.2 percent, were veterans of the armed services. Black owners came in second with nearly one third (30 percent) listed as veterans. At 22.6 and 16.2 percent, Hispanics and other minorities lagged significantly behind black and white males in terms of participation in the armed services.

The social and economic significance of military service for black males cannot be underestimated. Research indicates that although white, high-school-educated veterans do about as well in civilian life as white non veterans, the military has a substantial positive impact on men who have not finished high school or are black. Because the military does not teach blacks specific skills that prepare them for the civilian job market, it is thought that the positive effect must in large part be cultural. According to researchers, the military serves as a "bridging environment" by teaching black youth "how to cooperate and how to cope with the bureaucratic complexity of large-scale organizations."[32] Moreover, says Moskos, who reported this research in an article for *The Atlantic Monthly,* the Army emphasizes the connection between effort and reward as opposed to race and reward. In the words of a black veteran:

> The Army showed me that life can be hard no matter what your color. No race has it easy.[33]

Exposure to Other Self-Employed Individuals

Sociological studies have shown that entrepreneurial role models positively affect entry into business ownership. Studies have consistently reported that a majority of entrepreneurs had parents who were self-employed either as business owners or professionals. The evidence for entrepreneurs is congruent with a repeatedly verified observation concerning occupational inheritance; occupationally, children tend to follow in their parents' footsteps. It is also consistent with the fact that many new business ventures emerge from small family firms, in environments where individuals can gain the direct knowledge and experience required to conduct a business.

In response to the question of whether owners had close relatives who were self-employed or owned a business, blacks registered the lowest number of positive responses. Women owners had the highest percentage, 40.4 percent, followed by white males at 38.5 percent. Asked whether the owner had worked for a close relative who owned a business or was self-employed, blacks again had the lowest positive responses, 7.3 percent. This contrasted sharply to nonminority males, who at 18.7 percent gave over double that percentage of "yes" responses, and women, 13.8 percent of whom had worked for a close relative.

Legal Form of Organization

In 1982, sole proprietorships represented 95.2 percent of all black-owned businesses and contributed 52.9 percent of business sales and receipts. Partnerships accounted for less than 2 percent of black business ownerships. Individual proprietorships brought in most of the profits in agricultural services, construction, transportation, retail trade, and the service industries.

Although some analysts have emphasized the small number of black corporations as a serious handicap,[34] our own bias is that more emphasis should be concentrated on the low percentage of black partnerships. The evolution to corporate status results from the expansion of existing small firms. A key ingredient to this expansion is the risk sharing and expertise pooling made possible through the joint founding of companies. We would also contend that the low level of black business partnerships is connected with the dearth of informal savings networks in the black community. As we will discuss at length in Chapter 5, traditional rotating credit associations have provided a substantial portion of the investment capital for new businesses.

Summary of the Characteristics of Black Business Owners

Among black males, Bearse and Johnson have found that the variables most highly correlated with business ownership are licensable occupation—indicative of education, skills, and experience—and part-time work status. Other influential factors on the choice to become an entrepreneur include geographic location, age, ownership of assets, industry background, and opportunity costs.[35] To understand how each of these operates, we go back to Bates.

Capable Entrepreneurs

Although still considerably behind their white counterparts, black entrepreneurs have made impressive strides in narrowing gaps in education and self-employment income. Bates notes that blacks have made the greatest gains in lower-paying areas such as personal services and the least in high-paying areas such as finance, insurance, and real estate. Among all ethnic minorities in the United States, only black American Indian males have gained so little in overall earnings from self-employment.

Bates observes the most rapid increases in black entrepreneurship are in the so-called "emerging" lines of business: finance, insurance, and real estate; professional services; business services; wholesale trade; and manufacturing. Blacks in these fields are on average younger, better educated, and earn higher returns than those who are self-employed in more traditional lines of black enterprise or salaried. Bates encapsulates the profiles of most and least likely to succeed black entrepreneurs as follows:

Least Likely to Succeed	**Most Likely to Succeed**
weak educational backgrounds	strong educational backgrounds
undercapitalized firms	higher income
small firms	larger firms

retail and service fields	emerging lines of business
slow or negative growth rates in	rapid growth rates of all firms in
all firms in geographic location	geographic area[36]

The profile of the "emerging" black entrepreneur reflects one of the most significant trends in black business today. As the lower-paid, less-educated traditional entrepreneurial pool declines, a relatively smaller but more aggressive emerging sector is beginning to take up the slack. Even so, blacks are still the least likely of highly educated minorities to pursue self-employment, primarily because of opportunity costs. For the majority, professional, corporate and government employment remain more attractive options.

Industry Divisions

From 1977 to 1982, black-owned businesses increased significantly in the services and retail trade sectors. Service businesses comprised 43.4 percent of black businesses, well above the services proportion for whites and other minorities. By contrast, black businesses are disproportionately underrepresented in the wholesale trade, manufacturing, and finance industries.

For black firms with employees, only the mining and services sector showed growth between 1977 and 1982; during the same period, black manufacturing and construction significantly declined. With the exception of agriculture, which had a decrease in firms but an increase in employment, both the number of firms and levels of employment moved downward in all other categories of black business.

Sales and Receipts

The black retail trade and services sectors, with the largest share of black-owned businesses, also had the highest number of sales and receipts in both 1977 and 1982. Sales and receipts in the services industry increased at an annual rate of 11.4 percent between 1977 and 1982. The industry also had the largest absolute gain in sales receipts—more than $1 billion. Black firms in retail trade increased sales by 4.2 percent per year.[37]

Subindustries with the largest annual increases in sales and receipts between 1977 and 1982 were miscellaneous retail trades, including drug and liquor stores; nondurable goods such as paper products, groceries, and raw materials; trucking and warehousing; and personal and health services.

Metropolitan Statistical Area Distribution

Between 1977 and 1982, Dallas–Fort Worth and Houston registered the largest increases in the number of black-owned businesses—an over 80 percent jump. Black businesses increased more than 50 percent in most metropolitan statistical areas (MSAs) with previously existing high numbers of black businesses. Half of these same MSAs reported decreases in employment. In addition, seven of the ten MSAs with the largest number of black firms showed decreases in the number of firms with employees.

In older, heavily urbanized states, black businesses have concentrated in metropolitan commercial areas. For example, 84 percent of black businesses in Illinois in both 1977 and 1982 were in Chicago, and over 80 percent of Pennsylvania's black firms were in Philadelphia.

Growth in Black-Owned Businesses by Region and State

Over the past decade the overall number of black-owned businesses has increased significantly, from 231,203 in 1977 to 339,239 in 1982. More than two thirds of this growth occurred in the service and retail trades. Several industries with few black ownerships—finance, mining, and wholesale trade—also recorded large percentage increases. Predominately rural states— Utah, Maine, Idaho, Alaska, and North Dakota—had the largest proportional growth in black-owned business.

Nevertheless, employment growth in black-owned business decreased 3.3 percent between 1977 and 1982, an indication that most of the growth in the number of black businesses represented self-employed entrepreneurs with few or no employees. On the other hand, states such as Hawaii, Utah, Montana, and Wyoming showed significant increases in employment among black firms. In general, black businesses have flourished in the "Sunbelt" region of the United States—a geographic area encompassing states in the South and Southwest.

Black Business Performance

Swinton and Handy found that the state of the business cycle and the overall level of black consumer purchasing power had the most significant effect on black business receipts. By contrast, the condition of the local economy and the expansion of the black consumer market appear more important determinants of black firm growth. In addition to market factors, resource availability in the form of both finance capital and highly skilled professional and managerial labor correlated strongly with the profitability and growth of black firms. A related boost came from the general expansion of professional and managerial workers in nonminority, mainstream businesses. One of the most interesting findings reported by Handy and Swinton was that the physical segregation of black communities had no measurable impact on black business growth. Given the presence of adequate markets, capital, and labor, their data suggest, "Black businesses can grow effectively irrespective of the level or trends in segregation."[38]

Access to Markets

Bates has outlined two areas he considers of related importance in expanding the market opportunities of black businesses.

The first has to do with making major structural changes in urban markets. For example, the growth of government and corporate administrative services in inner cities has created a demand for complementary services. Between 1972 and 1977, the number of ancillary black businesses in urban centers doubled.

Second, opportunities created by government policy reforms could induce better-educated, younger black entrepreneurs to create and expand firms in finance, insurance and real estate, contracting, wholesaling, manufacturing, and business services.[39] As we shall explain subsequently, government programs and policies designed to accomplish this task have thus far fallen short of the mark.

Handy and Swinton have raised the additional point that black businesses rely heavily on a local black clientele. The higher the level of black family income, the higher the growth of black business sales and receipts.[40]

Capital Availability

> The Negro businessman, furthermore, encounters greater difficulties in securing credit. This is partly due to the marginal position of Negro business. It is also partly due to prejudiced opinions among whites concerning the business ability and personal reliability of Negroes. In either case, a vicious circle is in operation keeping Negro business down.[41]

Historically, blacks have faced obstructions to many lines of capital access because of discrimination. As the above quote illustrates, its legacy has helped shape the business climate surrounding black enterprises. Although it is true that restricted access to commercial credit has inhibited the growth of black business, the perceived influence of racial discrimination on black business development has become a distorted and damaging myth in the black community. Small businesses can develop despite restrictions in commercial capital markets. The business "success stories" of Chinese, Japanese, Koreans, and West Indians provide ample proof that alternative sources of capital can be and have been found.

Small Business Financing

Small businesses depend on financing from both internal and external sources for their successful operation and expansion. In addition, the financing needs of small businesses vary for different industries and at different stages of business formation.[42] The principal concern in external financing is having open access to capital at competitive rates. Internal sources of capital range from personal savings and equity financing to family funds. In other cases, ethnic community resources go toward community business investments. Finances for start-up "mom and pop" firms come primarily from personal savings and loans from close relatives or friends. Slightly larger "small businesses"—particularly those of entrepreneurs developing new products, services, means of production, or distribution channels—depend for capital on financial institutions and organized venture capital firms as well as loans from friends, relatives, and other informal investors.

Black Wealth

Personal equity investment is especially important for new and growing firms. It is an immediate source of capital that can be leveraged to maximum benefit. Hence, the amount of wealth that a community has is an important determinant for successful business development.

Although blacks make up 12 percent of the nation's households, they hold only 4 percent of all personal wealth.[43] As of 1979, blacks had approximately $211 billion in personal wealth, compared to $4.875 trillion held by whites. Furthermore, the average black household had about one third the wealth of the average white household—$24,608 for blacks compared with $68,891 for whites.[44]

The black–white difference in per capita wealth is greater than the difference in family or household wealth because blacks have larger families. In March 1979, the average white household consisted of 2.74 persons, while the average black household was made up of 3.10 persons. The per capita wealth of blacks was $7,938; that of whites, $25,142. The average household wealth of whites was therefore 2.8 times that of blacks, and white per capita wealth 3.2 times greater.

Blacks have far less wealth than whites for two reasons. First, in every asset category examined, a smaller proportion of blacks than whites own assets. Asset holdings are a major source of capital that can be used to leverage business and personal loans. For example, 62.4 percent of white families had equity in a home, compared with 47.9 percent of black families. Second, in most asset categories, the average value of black holdings was far less than the average value of white holdings. Among families who had equity in their homes, the average white family had accumulated $35,599 while the average black family had accumulated only $25,589.

Composition of Wealth

Only 7 percent of black wealth is invested in financial assets, compared with 28 percent of white wealth. Moreover, while 95.3 percent of white households have financial assets of some type, only 78 percent of black households do. All told, blacks hold a mere 1.1 percent of personally held financial assets in the United States.

Furthermore, nearly a quarter of black households have no significant financial assets. Among those that do, the value of holdings for the average white household was ten times the value of the average black household: $20,413 for whites and $2,180 for blacks.

Black Banks

> The Negro-managed bank and insurance company will not get away from the fact that the Negroes are poor and the segregated Negro community cannot offer any range of investment opportunities such that investment risk can be minimized. Indeed, it is difficult to see a real future for a segregated Negro financial system. Basically, it is nothing but a poor substitute for what the Negroes really need: employment of Negroes in white-dominated financial institutions and more consideration for them as insurance or credit seekers.[45]

In 1971, there were 29 black banks with $460 million in assets and $419 million in deposits.[46] These figures represented less than 1 percent of the institutions, assets, and deposits of the entire U.S. commercial banking sector. By 1982, the asset and deposit base of black banks had tripled. Compared with a 6 percent increase in the total number of banks in the system, their numbers increased by 50 percent. In the same period, the equity position of black banks moved from 5 to 8 percent of assets.[47]

Numerous studies have compared the profitability and portfolio composition of black banks to those of various classes of nonblack banks. They have led to a general concensus that black banks are less profitable that their nonblack counterparts as well as significantly different in asset and liability composition.

Brimmer has concluded that black banks face too many obstacles—the overwhelming one being their small size—to have a significant impact on the economic development of the black community. According to Brimmer, black banks operate at a substantial disadvantage in terms of both operating costs and efficiency. They suffer from substantially greater loan losses and a severe shortage of management talent.

Because of their small size, black banks have played a minor role in business financing. Against the background of their 1969 operating results, Brimmer cautioned, "The multiplication of (black banks) should not be encouraged in the belief that they can make a major contribution to the financing of economic development in the black community [since] most of the black banks might be viewed primarily as ornaments."[48] Instead, he recommended that large nonminority banks be give the authority, along with any necessary government tax credits and loan default insurance, to provide equity financing for urban economic development.

Bates and others have subsequently challenged Brimmer's summary dismissal of black banks as a viable means for financing black economic development. In 1973, FDIC economist John Boorman provided evidence that although black banks suffered from relative inefficiency and poor management in their early years of operation, their performance improved substantially over time.[49] Six years later, in 1979, Bates and Bradford concluded that, in conjunction with government-guaranteed loan protection and development banks specifically created for long-term loans, black banks could serve as an essential part of the financial apparatus needed to stimulate black business expansion.[50] Even more recently, in 1984, Bates and Fusfeld have pointed out that black banks may look bad precisely because they are doing what they were intended to do, channeling numerous small savings deposits from individual householders and businesses back into their communities in the form of loans:

> Smaller account size necessarily means more paperwork and extra teller labor time per deposit dollar, and this raises personnel expenses relative to deposits. While this represents "inefficiency" in a sense, it reflects, more accurately, the fact that the financial performance of black banks and S & Ls is affected by the economic characteristics of the markets they serve. If black financial institutions reported mean deposit sizes and personnel costs that were identical to the national averages, we would suspect that they were not serving the lower-income saver that typifies the inner-city population.[51]

Sources of Capital for Black Businesses

Access to capital has long been considered a major inhibiting factor in the formation of new black businesses. However, based on the 1982 CBO data, nearly a third of all business owners reported they had no starting capital requirements. Blacks (30.7 percent) and women (35.5 percent) constituted the highest number of owners in this category. In addition, only 10 percent of black business owners indicated commercial banks as sources of equity-based capital for business starts.

The fact that many black businesses have either not needed or used banks and other financial institutions to borrow capital for their businesses does not mean that a lack of formal sources of capital has been a minor problem for black businesses. In the first place, the majority of black businesses created without start-up capital are sole proprietorships earning less than $10,000 annually; were formal financing available, more blacks might be in business for themselves. In the second place, a lack of access to formal sources of capital can seriously hinder the expansion and development of businesses already in existence. Finally, the types of black business most likely to bring large-scale benefits to the community, what Bates and others refer to as "emerging" lines of business, require significant amounts of capital from the outset.[52]

Rotating Credit Associations

Sociologists and historians of ethnic enterprise have identified rotating credit associations as an important resource for financing ethnic enterprises in American.[53] Rotating credit associations, informal clubs of friends, and other trusted co-ethnics who make regular contributions to a fund, the whole of which is given to each contributor in rotations, have been a main source of business investment for groups like the Chinese, Japanese, Koreans, and West Indians. As we will elaborate in Chapter 5, there is no evidence native-born American blacks ever developed rotating credit associations or other informal ethnic group networks to support their business efforts.

Summary of Capital Availability

In addition to perceiving high opportunity costs in starting a business, blacks are among the least likely of ethnic groups to have large personal wealth holdings. Historical and contemporary research makes it abundantly clear that the largest source of start-up capital for new businesses comes from personal savings or loans from family and friends. Blacks are less than twice as likely as Asians or Hispanics to rely on their families for such loans. Group-based savings networks for business investment purposes have not traditionally been used by the black American community.[54] These realities have profoundly affected the course of black entrepreneurship. Fewer blacks form businesses. Many who do rely heavily on long-term debt for financing. Newer and younger firms, which have the most potential for succeeding in emerging lines of business, are also the most highly leveraged. For example, the construction business, which is among the more lucrative sectors of black enterprise, is particularly vulnerable to failure because of a heavy reliance on debt.[55] Taken together, the limits imposed by a lack of personal sources of business "seed" capital have severely handicapped black business formation and viability.

Government Assistance

Government focus on black business development came in the aftermath of civil disorders in the 1960s.[56] Over the past two decades, government involvement has grown to the extent that in fiscal year 1984, minority businesses received an estimated $9.5 billion in contracts, grants, and loans from federal agencies.

The Office of Minority Business Enterprise (OMBE) was established in 1969 by President Nixon as part of his promised efforts to spearhead "Black Capitalism." By executive order, Nixon created the OMBE to provide management and technical assistance, information, and advocacy in the private sector for minority business development. Today, the renamed Minority Business Development Agency (MBDA) functions within the Commerce Department. With Washington, D.C. headquarters serving as research and information hub, MBDA's six regional offices disperse technical advice and information to a network of over one hundred local business development centers around the country.[57]

The Small Business Administration (SBA) has been the government agency responsible for directing financial assistance to black and other minority enterprises. SBA has initiated two major type of programs: loan assistance and preferential procurement of federal contracts.

Loan Programs

The primary activity of the SBA has been to encourage long-term loans to small businesses. In terms of number of businesses assisted, the largest loan program was the now-defunct Economic Opportunity Loan (EOL) program. It was designed to help low-income entrepreneurs, both minority and non-minority, who operated very small businesses. Initially, the EOL program provided loan maturities of fifteen years with a loan ceiling of $25,000, and restricted eligibility to applicants below the family poverty line. Eligibility requirements were then broadened, and the ceiling of EOL loans raised to four times the original level; in 1980 it reached $100,000.

In dollar volume, the largest loan program has been the 7(A) program, which consists largely of bank loans guaranteed against default by the SBA. The 7(A) program has specifically targeted minority businesses, particularly larger and more promising firms. Over 80 percent of all SBA loan approvals in the 7(A) program have been guaranteed bank loans, as have a substantial number of SBA-approved EOLs. Although SBA claims its loan approvals have exceeded 30,000 annually, the actual number of firms assisted has been considerably lower due to the nondisbursal of approved loans and the use of new loans to refinance some already made.

Another SBA-connected loan program is the Minority Enterprise Small Business Investment Company project (MESBIC), which was started in conjunction with the Office of Minority Business Enterprise. As privately owned, privately managed venture capital corporations, MESBICs are supposed to furnish the following services to minority-owned firms:

1. Venture capital by purchasing an equity interest in the business.
2. Long-term capital by lending funds—normally subordinated to other creditors—to the business, often with warrants permitting MESBIC to purchase an equity position.
3. Guaranteed loans made by third parties.
4. General management and technical assistance.

Preferential Procurement Policies

The targeting of "set-asides" and procurement dollars to minority firms by corporations and government units has grown tremendously over the past decade. A major element of the procurement approach is the SBA's 8(A) program, which awarded $2.3 billion in contracts to minority firms in 1983. Increasingly, local governments and corporations are also using set-asides to support minority enterprise.

Minority business set-aside programs have their genesis in government policies designed to aid small businesses. Section 8 of the Small Business Act of 1953 was one of the initial set-aside measures. Section 8 authorized the SBA to enter into contracts with government agencies having procurement powers and to fulfill the contracts by giving subcontracts to small businesses. During the 1960s, assistance was earmarked for minority entrepreneurs as part of the War on Poverty. Initially programs focused on entrepreneurs with very low incomes. As with EOL loans, eligibility for set-asides broadened during the 1970s to include minority businessmen in middle- and high-income brackets.

Following the 1967 amendment to the Economic Opportunity Act, SBA established a new program under section 8(A) that expressly directed federal contracts to minority-owned firms. Section 8(A) procurement contracts— amounting to a modest $8.9 million in 1969—grew to $208 million in 1973, $768 million in 1978, and $2.3 billion in 1983. Although SBA is not required to award 8(A) contracts exclusively to minorities, the program has largely operated as a minority set-aside operation. A 1978 SBA report indicated that 96 percent of 8(A) companies were owned by minorities.

Entry into the 8(A) program is contingent upon SBA approval of a business plan prepared by the prospective 8(A) firm. The plan identifies the types of assistance needed to create a profitable, self-sustaining business. The business plan projects the amount of 8(A) contract support needed for the firm to reach self-sufficiency; it also projects the firm's operating performance over three consecutive years. In theory, 8(A) firms use their contract support to attain self-sufficiency, at which point they "graduate" from the program. In reality, graduation is rare—a mere five firms graduated between 1975 and 1980.

Presidential executive orders and specific congressional legislation have mandated a second type of minority set-aside program at the individual agency level. Richard Nixon issued an executive order in 1970, calling for increased representation of small businesses—especially minority business concerns—among federal department and agency contractors. The Railroad Revitalization and Regulatory Reform Act of 1976 authorized creation of a Minority Resource Center within the Department of Transportation. One of the center's duties was to assist minority businesses in securing government contracts. As a result, within two years minority subcontracting with the federal government increased by $85 million.

In 1977, Congress passed the Local Public Works Employment Act (LPW), which provided $400 million worth of local public works for minority firms. The act featured a 10 percent set-aside provision favoring minorities.

In 1978, yet another subcontracting program was created through an amendment to section 8(D) of the Small Business Act. For federal contracts exceeding $500,000—$1 million for construction—the program required prime contractors to submit a subcontracting plan benefiting small firms in general and "socially and economically disadvantaged" individuals in particular.

Assessment of Government Assistance

By statistical measures, government loan and procurement programs show discouraging results. Nearly half of EOL participants fail to repay their loans. Eight to 9 percent of SBA loan approvals are never disbursed, while another 17 percent are used to cover the refinancing of earlier loans.

According to a 1981 report by the General Accounting Office, only 166 of 4,598 firms participating in the 8(A) program had graduated as competitive businesses. Even though a number of 8(A) firms have been given every form of available SBA assistance, they have not succeeded in becoming self-sufficient enterprises.

The MESBIC program has fared no better. MESBICs are undercapitalized and have cash-flow problems. Most are not able to cope successfully with the risks inherent in financing small minority businesses. Because of the extended periods before equity investments begin to yield dividends, MESBICs commonly generate negative cash flows. To cope with cash flow crises, they frequently avoid equity investments and, instead, grant only loans to minority firms. As a result, they have failed in the major purpose for which they were created—to provide the equity capital essential for minority business development.

In terms of job creation, the evidence shows that minority firms working on set-asides, as well as minority businesses in general, disproportionately employ minority employees. Construction and manufacturing firms are the most likely to create jobs filled overwhelmingly by minorities.

A serious problem with minority business set-aside programs is the so-called "salt-and-pepper" firms. Nominally, these firms are 50 percent owned by minorities, but the de facto owners and controllers do not belong to minority groups. Adhering to the letter if not the spirit of the law, many nonminority contractors establish 50 percent partnerships with minorities in order to obtain set-asides. Another drawback of set-asides is the higher procurement costs incurred by government as a result of using firms that may be less experienced and cost-effective than nonminority enterprises.

One of the most critical debates surrounding the viability of minority procurement and set-aside programs has resulted from the inconsistency in standards. Standards for firm eligibility vary from agency to agency within the federal government as well as among private corporations and local governments. In particular, the acceptance criteria used by SBA in its 8(A) program have been vague and inconsistent.

Minority business set-aside programs that demand efficient business performance are the most useful to the black community and to American society as a whole. Programs that provide minority enterprises with partial protection from competition in the awarding of procurement contracts are fundamentally different from 8(A) contracts. A federal agency that purchases goods or services from a minority vendor will—other things being constant—pick the low-cost supplier over the high-cost alternatives; similarly, the vendor that produces reliably will be favored over the alternative that produces haphazardly. Over time, therefore, procurement business will flow increasingly to the most efficient minority enterprises.

The Future

The growth of self-employment has resulted from several factors: economic conditions, the availability of opportunities for salaried employment, effects of the tax code on business formation, identification by entrepreneurs of unexploited opportunities, worker dissatisfaction, and the desire to supplement other income. No country or social or ethnic group has a constant potential stock of entrepreneurs. The environment in which the group operates, both internal and external, affects the numbers and types of new entrepreneurs.

In an earlier era, segregation and discrimination had a profoundly adverse effect on the formation and growth of black businesses. Black businesses were largely restricted to serving the black community, and blacks were denied access to capital and certain occupations. Black educational opportunities were limited. In addition to these external constraints, blacks have not possessed a strong "business culture" that might have countered, as it has among Asians and West Indians, the obstructions of a racially biased marketplace.

In a 1985 article for *Black Enterprise,* Brimmer evaluated the future of blacks in the public sector. "For many years," he pointed out, "most black civil rights leaders have been turning to Washington for both legislation and budget resources to provide economic underpinnings for black citizens."[58] In 1983, 23.9 percent of all employed black Americans held jobs in the public sector, compared with 14.7 percent of white employees. Until recently, the high number of blacks in government service has had a sound economic rationale. Jobs in the public sector have provided more money with less risk than those in the private sector. Although on average black men and women earn less than white men and women in government jobs, they have perceived the risks of working elsewhere as greater. Equally significant, according to Brimmer, is the fact that blacks "have historically encountered less discrimination in government than in the private sector."[59] But as Brimmer and many others warn, black dependence on the government must soon come to an end. The United States has entered an era of shrinking public and expanding private sectors. From now on, blacks will have to look to the private sector for economic opportunities.

Despite both advances and challenges, blacks have yet to translate economic progress into entrepreneurial take-off. In "The Reluctant Entrepreneurs," Kotkin collectively lambasts black Americans for their indifferent entrepreneurial performance.[60] He pointedly underscores the difference between the political and economic attainments of black Americans. Gaining city hall has not done much to improve the economic situation of inner-city constituents. Reflects James Johnson, former city manager turned real estate developer:

> When blacks took power, everyone thought the economy would change overnight. But government can only provide leads and open doors. Government cannot create entrepreneurs. It can't turn a ghetto into a nice neighborhood.[61]

More black Americans than ever before have the combination of skills, opportunity, and motivation to go into business for themselves. By 1975, more black than white male college students were studying business and opting for business careers.[62] A highly trained cadre of black professionals sits bottlenecked at midlevel administrative and management positions in white-owned companies.[63] The pull factor of perceived opportunities together with the push factor of a shrinking public sector will undoubtedly propel more and more Americans, black and white, into entrepreneurial pursuits.

Urban America holds many of the most promising opportunities for black entrepreneurs. Blacks are poised to take advantage of the post–World War II transformation of older industrial areas in the Northeast and the "Sunbelt" cities of the South and Southwest. Areas with large black populations, these regions have created new administrative centers that provide unprecedented opportunities for black urban firms. The growth of corporate and government administrative activities in central cities induces the development of complementary businesses, such as business services and amenities. Equally important, the skill and capital requirements needed are well within the capacity of today's black entrepreneurs.

The importance of business ownership and management in helping a minority group to achieve pride and influence cannot be overstated. Consider Glazer and Moynihan's description of the benefits amassed by an entrepreneurial community:

> The small shopkeepers and manufacturers are important to a group for more than the greater income they bring in. Very often, as a matter of fact, the Italian or Jewish shopkeeper made less than the skilled worker. But, as against the worker, each businessman had the possibility, slim though it was, of achieving influence and perhaps wealth. The small businessman generally has access to that special world of credit which may give him for a while greater resources than a job. He learns about credit and finance and develops skills that are of value in a complex economy. He learns too about the world of local politics, and although he is generally its victim, he may also learn how to influence it—for mean and unimportant ends, perhaps—but this knowledge may be valuable to an entire community.[64]

That "knowledge may be valuable to an entire community" provides the overarching reason for expanding black business. Once blacks have engaged in the discovery process of the marketplace, the outcome will not simply be increased material wealth, but new opportunities across a wide range of social areas.

Notes

1. Fratoe provides a summary of economic, business management, psychological and sociological approaches in Fratoe, Frank, "A Sociological Analysis of Minority Business" *Review of Black Political Economy,* vol. 15, no. 2, fall 1986, pp. 5–7.
2. Ibid., p. 5.
3. Ibid.
4. Ibid.
5. Foley, Eugene, *The Achieving Ghetto* (Washington, D.C.: National Press, 1968, p. 136).
6. Bates, Timothy, "An Analysis of Minority Entrepreneurship: Utilizing the Census of Public Use Samples" (Fourth progress report on MBDA contract, Burlington, Vermont, 1985, p. 5).
7. Ibid.
8. Du Bois, W.E.B., *The Negro in Business* (New York: AMS Press, 1971, p. 4; first printed in 1899).
9. Ibid., p. 5.
10. Ibid., p. 15.
11. Ibid., p. 47.
12. Washington, Booker T., *The Negro in Business* (Chicago: Afro-American Press, 1969, p. 319; first published in 1907).
13. Ibid., p. 368.
14. Myrdal, Gunnar, *An American Dilemma* (New York: Harper and Brothers, 1944).
15. Ibid., p. 311.
16. Frazier, E. Franklin, *The Negro in the United States* (New York: Macmillan, 1949, p. 407).
17. Ibid.
18. Circula No. 1 issued by Frederick Douglass (U.S. Senate, 46th Congress, 2nd Session, report 440).
19. Lee, Roy F., *The Setting for Black Business Development* (Ithaca: Cornell University Press, 1973).
20. Cross, Theodore, *Black Capitalism* (New York: Atheneum, 1969).
21. Ibid., p. 198.
22. Ibid.
23. Bates, Timothy and Fusfeld, Daniel R., *The Political Economy of the Urban Ghetto* (Carbondale: Southern Illinois University Press, 1984, p. 104).
24. Ibid., p. 223.
25. Stevens, Richard L., "Measuring Minority Business Formation and Failure" (*Review of Black Political Economy,* vol. 12, no. 4, spring 1984).
26. Kotkin, Joel, "The Reluctant Entrepreneurs" (*Inc.,* September 1987).
27. Bates, op. cit., p. 17.
28. Ibid.
29. Stevens, op. cit., p. 71.
30. Ibid.
31. Fratoe, op. cit.
32. Moskos, Charles C., "Blacks in the Army: Success Story" (*Atlantic Monthly,* May 1986, pp. 64–72).
33. Ibid., p. 67.
34. Such as Osborne, Alfred E.,"Emerging Entrepreneurs and the Distribution of

Black Enterprise" in Smilor and Kuhn, *Managing Take-Off in Fast Growth Companies: Innovations in Entrepreneurial Firms* (New York: Praeger, 1986).

35. Bearse, Peter and Johnson, Peter, "Minority and Ethnic Entrepreneurship in the United States—1980—A Comparative Analysis" (Princeton: Peter Bearse Associates, Sept. 1, 1986, p. 57; prepared for the Minority Business Development Agency, U.S.Department of Commerce).

36. Bates, op. cit., p. 25.

37. U.S. Department of Commerce, Bureau of the Census, *Survey of Minority-Owned Business Enterprises* (Washington, D.C.: U.S. Government Printing Office, 1985, pp. 4–7).

38. Swinton, David and Handy, John, *The Determinants of the Growth of Black-Owned Businesses: A Preliminary Analysis* (Washington, D.C.: U.S. Department of Commerce, Minority Business Development Agency, Sept. 1983, p. 85).

39. Bates, op. cit.

40. Swinton and Handy, op. cit.

41. Myrdal, op. cit., p. 308.

42. U.S. Small Business Administration, *The State of Small Business* (Washington, D.C.: U.S. Government Printing Office, 1986, p. 205).

43. Frankel, Pearl, Robert and Matilda, "Composition of Personal Wealth at the Start of the Eighties " (Paper presented at the annual meeting of the American Statistical Association, Cincinnati, 1982).

44. O'Hare, William, "Wealth and Economic Status: A Perspective on Racial Inequality" (Washington, D.C.: Joint Center for Political Studies, 1983).

45. Myrdal, op. cit., p. 318.

46. Division of Research and Statistics of the Board of Governors of the Federal Reserve System, "Bank Portfolio Comparisons for 1971 and 1982" (Washington, D.C.).

47. Cole, Edwards, Hamilton and Reuben, "Black Banks: A Survey and Analysis of the Literature" (*The Review of Black Political Economy*, vol. 14, no. 1, summer 1985, p. 30).

48. Ibid.

49. Boorman, John, *"New Minority-Owned Commercial Banks"* in Bates, Timothy and Bradford, William, *Financing Black Economic Development* (New York: Academic Press, 1979, p. 66).

50. Bates and Bradford, *Financing Black Economic Development*, pp. 85–87.

51. Bates and Fusfeld, op. cit., p. 231.

52. Bates, op. cit., p. 23.

53. Fratoe, Frank, "A Sociological Perspective on Minority Business Ownership: A Synthesis of the Literature with Research and Policy Implications" (Washington, D.C.: Minority Business Development Agency, U.S. Department of Commerce, December 1984).

54. Fratoe has recently elaborated on the dearth of "social capital" among black business owners. Social capital refers to ethnic community and institutional sources of support for businesses. See Fratoe, Frank, "Social Capital of Black Business Owners" *Review of Black Political Economy,* spring 1988, pp. 33–49).

55. Bates, op. cit., p. 32.

56. See the following sources for material on government assistance to black businesses:
    Bates, Timothy, "Impacts of Preferential Procurement Policies on Minority-Owned Businesses" *Review of Black Political Economy,* Summer 1985).

———"Black Entrepreneurship and Government Programs" (*Journal of Contemporary Studies,* fall 1981, pp. 59–70).

Klein, Richard, "The Small Business Administration's Business Loan Program" (*Atlantic Economic Review,* September/October 1978).

Small Business Administration, *1974 Annual Report* (Washington, D.C.: U.S. Government Printing Office, 1975).

U.S.. Comptroller, *The Limited Success of Federally Financed Minority Business in Three Cities* (Washington, D.C.: General Accounting Office, 1973).

Wollard, David, *Small Business Administration Loan Program* (Washington, D.C.: U. S. Government Printing Office, 1974).

57. Interview with Richard Stevens, research director of the Minority Business Development Agency (Washington, D.C., November 1988).

58. Brimmer, Andrew, "The Future of Blacks in the Public Sector (*Black Enterprise,* November 1985, p. 39).

59. Ibid.

60. Kotkin, op. cit.

61. Ibid., p. 85.

62. Freeman, Richard B., *Black Elite: The New Market for Highly Educated Black Americans* (Berkeley: Carnegie Foundation for the Advancement of Teaching, 1976).

63. Jones, Edward W., "Black Managers: The Dream Deferred" (*Harvard Business Review,* May/June 1986).

64. Glazer, Nathan and Moynihan, Daniel P., *Beyond the Melting Pot* (Cambridge: MIT Press, 1963, pp. 30–31).

3

Black Families and Family Firms

In outlining the formation of an entrepreneurial event, Shapero and Sokol make a strong claim for the primacy of family relationships:

> The family, particularly the father or mother, plays the most powerful role in establishing the desirability and credibility of entrepreneurial action for an individual.[1]

The importance of the black family as a mediating structure between individual black entrepreneurs and the larger structures of society will become clear as we turn now to black families, family business, and the need to encourage entrepreneurial values in black culture.

We will begin by describing some of the generalizations that abound concerning the black American family. Keeping our analytical framework in mind, we will discuss the black family as a mediating institution. How do the individual choices of black Americans, based on internalized values and expressed through behavior, interact with the structural frameworks of American society? Do aggregate patterns, exclusive to some or all black Americans, exist? Can assumed patterns in themselves constitute constraints? How can changes take place?

Second, we will look closely at successful entrepreneurial families, not in black culture specifically, but in society at large. How have individuals within these families made their choices? What culturally based values informed those choices? To what degree were external constraints or opportunities important? Can replicable patterns be found?

Finally, the atypical black family business will be examined as an example of variant behavior that might be used as a model for social change.

Black Families: An Ideological Battleground

When attempting to describe black American families from the available research, it soon becomes evident that no objective reality exists. A composite picture includes sentiments varying from a view of the black family as pathological to one that lauds its exceptional strength and resilience in the face of harsh oppression. Across-the-board observers concede that the black family is undergoing a crisis. But determining the parameters of the crisis and how to discuss them leads to vehemently opposed ideologies.

In his article "Black Families in a Changing Society," Billingsley provides one of the most recent statistical updates on black families in America. Among his salient points: *The poverty level is no longer falling as rapidly as in the 1960s.*

Table 3.1 provides a more schematic illustration of this trend. It shows the percentage of black families living on incomes below the poverty level in each given year, starting in 1959 and ending in 1985. The figures are based on a definition of poverty formulated by the census bureau that changes from year to year; currently the poverty line for a family of four is $10,990.

In addition, even black families not living in poverty—the majority of about 70 percent—have fewer economic resources than comparable white families. As shown in Table 3.2, the median income for black families remains far below the median income for white families. Consequently, black families function in the same economic market as white families but with half the income.

Unemployment

Unemployment continues to adversely affect the income levels of black families. Black unemployment, especially for black men and youth, has remained consistently higher than that of the population at large. As indicated in

TABLE 3.1. Black Families Below the Poverty Line[2]

Year	1959	1970	1980	1982	1984	1985
Percent of black families in poverty	55%	32%	31%	36%	34%	31%

TABLE 3.2. Median Income for Black Versus White Families

Year	1960	1970	1975	1980	1982	1985
Black median income as percentage of median white income	55%	60%	62%	58%	55%	56%

Table 3.3, official figures improved between 1982 and 1985 as the American economy moved out of recession. Nevertheless, the rates for blacks continue to be high. As of September 1986, blacks comprised 10.7 percent of the total civilian labor force, but black unemployment was 14.8 compared to 6 percent for whites, or more than twice as high. [3]

Family Structure

The family structure has undergone dramatic changes in recent years. Nuclear families have lost ground in black culture as the number of married couple households has decreased while the number of female-headed households has increased (Table 3.4). Statistically, these changes are reflected by increases in divorce and separation, a prevalence of early death among black men, and increasing numbers of unmarried parents.[4]

Teenage Pregnancy

Teenage pregnancy is a major problem in the black community. Billingsley points out that the rate of births to unmarried black teenagers actually dropped between 1970, when 96.6 out of 1,000 black babies were born to unwed mothers, and 1982, when that figure was 87 out of 1,000. He also notes that

TABLE 3.3. Black Unemployment[3]

Year	1960	1970	1980	1982	1985
Unemployed black men	9.6%	3.7%	11.3%	18.9%	15%
Unemployed black women	8.3%	5.8%	11%	17.6%	13%
Unemployed black youth (18–25 yrs.)	24.4%	24%	35.4%	40%	40%

TABLE 3.4. The Changing Black Family Structure[4]

Year	1960	1970	1980	1985
Percent of married couple families	78%	68%	54%	53%
Percent of female-headed families	22%	27%	43%	44%

black teenage pregnancy is declining faster than among whites.[5] Lest those statistics sound promising it should be added that black American teenagers still have the highest pregnancy rate in the industrial world and that, differential rates of increase and decrease aside, the number of black unwed teenage teenage mothers is still more than four times greater than that of whites. In fact, the rate of decline among both white and black teenage mothers reflects a shrinking female teen population.[6]

Overall, current statistics and trends among black families portend a grim scenario for the future of many black Americans. If they continue, predicts the University of Chicago's W.J. Wilson, "by the end of the century, 70 percent of black families will be headed by single women and 30 percent of black men will be unemployed."[7]

Whatever the figures, emotionally opposed schools of thought underlie many of their diverse interpretations. It would therefore be useful to provide an historical overview of the conflicting perspectives on black families that fire the current debate.

Staples provides a helpful framework for understanding what he poses as four historically rooted "stages of research" on black American families.[8] With others, he maintains that ideas are a function of the political environment in which they flourish. As a result, the history of twentieth century theories on black families reveals that most thoughts on the subject have been shaped by the policy recommendations that preceded or followed them.

Stage One: The Original Studies

Staples begins with the "original studies" of E. Franklin Frazier, Gunnar Myrdal, and Arnold Rose. All three attempted to find a link between the socioeconomic circumstances into which blacks are born and the creation of patterns and norms of behavior that brought about family "disorganization." These studies were produced during the 1940s, an era during which urbanization effected profound changes in the structure of American society. Solutions to the problem of black poverty seemed to lie in the integration of blacks into a white world. Underlying this assumption was another: that the problem of black family disorganization was not a new one, but had roots in both slavery and emancipation.

The introduction of black people into American slavery resulted in a complete break between them and the outside world. A slave was forced into the role of a child absolutely dependent on his father figure, the white master. Masters disciplined their slaves and held their lives in total control. Personal relations among slaves, including those within families, were extremely tenuous.[9] "Slavery undermined the formation of strong marital bonds," explains Myrdal, who continues to attest that during emancipation "mobility was increased, work was not readily available, and there began a migration to the cities with attendant increases in desertion, prostitution and temporary marriages."[10]

Frazier adds that when black couples migrated from rural settings in the South to urban settings in the North, they no longer had the support of their rural neighbors and institutions. Family ties were severed, allowing men and women to "pursue individual impulses and wishes."[11] Thus city life redefined sexual relationships and motherhood for American blacks. "Sex relations tend to acquire a purely hedonistic character and the burdens of motherhood are something to be avoided."[12]

Coincident with these negative developments, Myrdal concedes, the "stability of the Negro family grew because of the strong hold of religion."[13] But unfortunately, "The starting point was so low that the Negro never caught up. Isolation, poverty and ignorance were once again obstacles to acculturation."[14]

Frazier sharply contrasts the differences between black upper and lower classes:

> Among [black] upper class families there is much individualism. Husbands, wives and children insist as a rule upon the right to follow their own interests.[15]

Many wives in upper-class families were employed, enabling the family to maintain relatively higher standards of consumption. Because of standards and values characterized by Frazier as thrifty ambition, "upper class families have few children and there are many childless couples."[16] Frazier considers these families preferred role models for the black community at large, because they provided "a bridge for the complete integration of the Negro in the northern city."[17] "Disorganization of Negro family life," Frazier concludes, "has retarded the socialization of the Negro and lowered his economic efficiency."[18] His policy recommendations emphasized getting black family norms into conformity with those of the white middle class.

Stage Two: Pathology Research

Twenty years later, researchers took up where Frazier, Myrdal, and others left off, using many of the same indices of black family disorganization. Moynihan, in his controversial and hotly debated 1965 report, claimed that weaknesses in the structure of the black family largely accounted for black problems in American society:

> In essence, the Negro community has been forced into a matriarchal structure which, because it is so out of line with the rest of American society, seriously retards the progress of the group as a whole, and imposes a crushing burden on the

Negro male and, in consequence, on a great many Negro females as well.[19]

Here Moynihan appears to assume that male leadership in both private and public affairs defines the stable norm. "A subculture, such as that of the Negro American, in which this is not a pattern, is placed at a distinct disadvantage."[20] Moynihan modified his attack on the matriarchal family by conceding:

> There is no one Negro community. There is no one Negro problem. There is no one solution.

Yet he stresses:

> Nonetheless, at the center of the tangle of pathology is the weakness of the family structure. Once or twice removed, it will be found to be the principal source of most aberrant, inadequate, or antisocial behavior that . . . now serves to perpetuate the cycle of poverty and deprivation.[21]

According to Staples, while this stage of research echoes the conclusions of Frazier, it differs because of three primary factors. First, it took place in the 1960s era of civil rights and affirmative action and had significant impact on the formulation of public policy. Second, most scholars promoting the model were white. Third, it in effect placed the blame for black problems on the black family—more specifically, on black women—without discussing the dearth of social and economic opportunities that presumably contributed, in large measure, to the original pathology.

Stage Three: The Reactive Period

Following Moynihan's indictment of black family structure, an outburst of disclaimers attempted to prove both Moynihan and Frazier wrong. According to Loury:

> By daring to suggest that dysfunctional family behavior among poor blacks constituted an insuperable barrier to economic development, Moynihan elicited an emotional, ideologically-charged response which permanently altered racial discourse in America.[22]

Refuters argued that black families were much like white families, except for their impoverished status. Rather than inherently pathological, the black family was the victim of a long history of racial oppression. Data incorrectly presented in the first place by Frazier had subsequently led to further distortions by Moynihan. Claimed one critic:

A major distortion (of Moynihan) was his singling out instability in the Negro family as the causal factor for the difficulties Negroes face in white society. It is quite the other way around.[23]

According to the "reactive" interpretation, the racial differences in family structure that had so alarmed earlier social scientists were in fact a post–World War II phenomenon. No basis for their existence could be found in historical records, and thus they could be explained by neither slavery nor emancipation.[24] The institution of slavery was not completely disruptive. African heritages brought by slaves to America contained long family lineages and stability, and though these traditions were greatly shaken by the move from Africa and the entry into slavery, the institution of the family was not utterly destroyed. Basic humanity and mutual concern among family members, as expressed in extended kinship, for example, continued to persist. Even under slavery, enough residential stability had existed to permit the development of strong family ties.[25] With emancipation and the destruction of their mostly rural southern life-style, large numbers of black Americans retreated to family and kin for survival, finding in them their major source of economic and social stability. Mass migration, first toward urban centers in the South and later the North, ordinarily involved family units, not footloose individuals.

The reactive school claimed that an examination of census data from the late nineteenth and early twentieth centuries showed that a substantial number of families were intact among the poor of all races. Most of the women who headed families were widows, and the association of female-headed households with poverty could therefore be explained by a higher mortality rate among poor men. The two-parent nuclear family defined the norm among black and white Americans, regardless of class.

Because historical data on the pathology of black families proved otherwise, argued Moynihan's critics, his conclusions could be summarily disregarded.

Stage Four: The Strengths of the Black Family

Following the reactive phase, a different black perspective trumpeted black pride and self-affirmation: "Yes, we are different, and we are proud of it." Admittedly, black family life was structured differently from that of whites, but that was precisely its strength. Explains Staples, the focus on strengths in the black family concurred with a rejection of traditional, middle-class life-styles among large numbers of whites. Hence the women's liberation movement judged the matrifocal black family in a new light, and increased sexual freedom in society at large legitimized premarital sex and common-law marriages.

In the late 1960s, Billingsley described the black family as an "absorbing, adaptive and amazingly resilient mechanism for the socialization of its children."[26] Frazier was criticized as a middle-class and moralistic critic. Female-headed families, acceptance of illegitimate children, more frequent changes of spouse, and more casual discipline were in this view neither morally wrong nor the product of pathological conditions. Instead they were the product of cultural differences—of a different, but no less valuable, personality type. In some respects, goes the argument, the black family is even superior; it does not produce the anxiety over cleanliness and achievement so often fostered among white families.

Staples himself subscribes to this view. In his essay on the "Black Family Revisited," he adheres to a political program among black activists promoting a Pan African vision of black unity: "People of African descent have a common culture as well as a common history of racist oppression that has culminated in a shared destiny."[27] The Afro-American family should therefore be seen in a comparative context that includes black families in the West Indies and Africa. Staples also outlines a model emphasizing political and economic influences on family life. He sees value in combining the two perspectives in a syncretic model that shows how economic forces act on family life, counteracted by cultural adaptations to each event. Staples adds that a third model, defining white colonialism within the United States, would have to be included in the analysis, because "white racism" is "another pre-eminent force in American life."[28]

The focus on black family strengths, growing out of earlier criticisms and reaction, paid far more attention to the unflattering depiction of the black family in urban ghettos than to proposed remedies. In its focus on black strengths and resilience it overlooked very real problems of poverty, illiteracy, and malnutrition. The problems of the black urban poor have considerably worsened in the past two decades, yet any attempt to direct attention to culturally derived explanations for the black underclass have until recently met with outcries of "racism" and "blaming the victim."

Various definitions of "black culture" and the institution of the family within that culture have been forwarded. Valentine, for one, considers that black Americans share "a subcultural status . . . as an ethnic subsociety."[29]

The American Negro people is North American in origin and has evolved under specifically American conditions: climatic, nutritional, historical, political and social. It takes its character from the experience of American slavery . . . emancipation . . . race and caste discrimination, and from living in a highly mobile society possessing . . . an explicitly stated equalitarian concept of freedom . . . .

Its secular values are those professed, ideally at least, by all the people of the United States . . . . This "American Negro culture" is expressed in a body of folk-lore, in the musical forms of spirituals, the blues or jazz; the idiomatic version of American speech . . . .

There is an American Negro idiom, style and way of life, but none separable from the conditions of American society, nor from its general modes of culture—mass distribution, race and intra-national conflicts, the radio, television, its style of education, its politics.

If general American values influence us, we, in turn, influence them—speech, concept of liberty, justice, economic distribution, international outlook . . . our national image of ourselves as a nation.[30]

An ethnic group, according to Billingsley, is a relatively large configuration with a shared feeling of peoplehood. "Ethnic subsociety" reflects some of the variation within an ethnic group. Social class, regional locality, and rural versus urban residence are dimensions catching some of the variation among members of the same ethnic group. Of these, social class has become the most powerful tool for defining the differing conditions of life among black Americans. Nonetheless, class differences do not mean that "middle class Negro families have more in common with middle class white families than they do with lower class Negro families."[31] Within a black American subculture, the different black classes share a sense of peoplehood and a commonality of experience.

Class differences might therefore be a good starting point for constructing a more balanced model of the black family. One obvious flaw in Moynihan's report was his description of social experiences and patterns in which he implicitly included all black families, although he was dealing primarily with blacks living in poverty. According to the data we presented earlier, roughly 30 percent of black families officially live in poverty. How do we account for the remaining 70 percent majority? Reminds Wilson:

It is difficult to speak of a uniform black experience when the black population can be meaningfully stratified into groups whose members range from those who are affluent to those who are impoverished.[32]

Before turning to the differences between blacks who are affluent and those who are impoverished, we need to find an operational definition of class. What determines class? Education? Occupation? Income? Several possibilities exist. Hill mentions three major determinants of social class status—style of life, occupational strata, and family income.[33]

For some, occupational status has been seen as more significant and useful in placing blacks along a class hierarchy within the black community. The occupation of school principal, for example, which is considered middle class among whites, is generally viewed as upper class among blacks. Factors other than purely economic rewards are clearly a factor in the attribution of class—in this instance, varying interpretations of respectability and level of community involvement come into play. On the other hand, family income has more frequently been used to place black families within the class hierarchy of American society at large.

For our purposes, Wilson's general definition appears most useful:

> [Class refers to] any group of people who have more or less similar goods, services, or skills to offer for income in a given economic order and who therefore receive similar financial remuneration in the market place.[34]

Of course, the goods, services, and skills that a person has to offer for income in the marketplace depend in turn on both individual capacity and position relative to social and economic opportunities.

Hill presents data from the U.S. Bureau of Labor Statistics pinpointing classes in American society according to family budget expenditures:

Social Class	Family Budget
"Upper"	$34,317
"Middle"	$20,517
"Lower"	$12,582

While exactly 50 percent of all white family budgets fall in the middle, only 24 percent of black family budgets do.[35]

The Black Underclass

Keeping these definitions in mind, we will move to the main object of the current debate over black families in America: the bifurcation in the black community between the so-called black underclass and the black middle class. We will present the views of the two major streams of argument, realizing that in reality, informed opinions have also ranged somewhere between the two extremes.

One side of the debate focuses again on black families living in poverty, maintaining that in the ghetto, "It appears that the distinctive culture is now the greatest barrier to progress by the black underclass, rather than either unemployment or (dependency on) welfare."[36] Accordingly, solutions to the problems of the underclass should address this destructive yet self-sustaining culture. As described by Lemann and others, a separate culture has emerged largely because the middle class has left the ghetto, creating a moral and leadership vacuum in poor black communities. Left to themselves, the underclass has developed a distinct way of life not shared by middle-class blacks.

The moral values that have in large part accounted for the ascendancy of the black middle class are simply absent in ghetto culture. Family life is unstable and disorganized. Personal ambition and a sense of upward mobility do not commonly exist. In their place, most ghetto residents experience strong feelings of marginality, helplessness, dependency, and inferiority. They demonstrate little ability to defer gratification or plan for the future.

The underclass is self-generating in the double sense that socialization in the typical ghetto family perpetuates both the cultural patterns of the group as well as the psychological inadequacies of individual members. Together, these constraints effectively block escape from the ghetto.

> Out-of-wedlock childbearing . . . is the aspect of life in the ghetto over which people there have the most control, and it will be the last and hardest thing to change. It is today by far the greatest contributor to the perpetuation of the misery of ghetto life.[37]

The debilitating ghetto culture thesis is highly reminiscent of both Frazier and Moynihan. While accounting for pathological behavior through a pathological family structure, it pays little attention to other factors that contribute to social deterioration in poor black communities.

From the opposite side of the debate, the problem of blacks today is put forth in wholly different arguments. Blacks no longer experience a destructive culture fostered by legalized racial oppression, as was the case before the era of civil rights and affirmative action. The major problem for blacks today, especially the underclass, is that the government is not organized to deal with new barriers imposed by structural changes in the economy. The conditions of the black underclass have resulted from these new structural constraints to economic and social opportunities.

The theoretical underpinnings of this end of the spectrum bear little resemblance to those of Frazier and Moynihan. To begin with, although the black lower class possesses distinct subcultural patterns, it also subscribes to middle-class norms in many areas of life.

In his refutation of the "culture of poverty," Valentine argues that although female-headed households may be statistically prevalent among the poor, "this does not necessarily mean that it is culturally preferred. It may be a . . . temporary adaptation to extrafamiliar stresses."[38]

He continues:

> The domestic group may frequently be unconventional in form and process, but both households and kinship are organized . . . in ways that are adaptive to externally imposed conditions.[39]

Stack wholeheartedly supports Valentine in her ethnographic study of poor black, female-headed kinship groups:

> The families in the Flats and the non-kin they regard as kin have evolved patterns of co-residence, kinship-based exchange, networks linking multiple domestic units, elastic household boundaries, life-long bonds to three-generational households, social controls against the formation of marriages that could endanger the network of kin, the domestic authority of women and limitations on the role of the husband or male friend within a woman's kin network.[40]

With Valentine, Stack adheres to the idea of a black subculture, calling the way of life she has described "one dimension of the multivalued cultural system, the value-mosaic of the poor." The black urban poor are "locked into" an ongoing bond with "white culture and white values."[41]

But aspirations to the rewards offered by white culture can only be realized with accompanying economic opportunities. Deprived of meaningful social and economic opportunities, the poor "stretch" their values to cope with poverty. Without abandoning the values of mainstream society, they develop a parallel set of values to cope with the deprivation. The two sets are not mutually exclusive:

> The structural adaptations of poverty described in this study do not lock people into a cycle of poverty preventing the poor from marrying, removing themselves from their kin network or leaving town. But if such opportunities do arise (and they rarely do) these chances are taken after careful evaluation based on both middle class standards and the experience of poverty.[42]

Furthermore, research on black unemployment has shown:

> Poor blacks tend not only to value work but also to feel that self-respect and employment are inseparable. Enduring lack of success in the labor market lowers their self-confidence and promotes feelings of resignation that can lead to abandoning the job search temporarily if not permanently.[43]

In sum, if blacks have low aspirations and do not plan for the future, it is not ultimately the result of different cultural norms, but rather because of restricted opportunities, a future without hope, and the resignation that results from negative personal experiences.[44] Accordingly, behavior described as socially pathological—that is, derived from and perpetuated by pathological family patterns—should not be seen as stemming from a separate culture but as the symptom of differential access to economic opportunities.

We think it possible to construct a model of the black family today that would take into account both its strengths and its weaknesses. Rather than paint a monochromatic set of cultural traits, it would seek to point out the variations in black culture. In our view, both sides of the debate on the black underclass deserve our consideration. Nevertheless, as Valentine describes them, what we need is more than a simple hybrid of the two extremes: on the one hand a model of a "self-perpetuating subsociety with a defective, unhealthy subculture" and on the other an "externally oppressed subsociety with an imposed, exploited subculture." Returning to our own framework of decision-making individuals interacting with opportunities in their environment, our interpretation sees individual behavior among the black poor resulting from internalized cultural norms *in relation to* exogenous opportunity structures. We fully agree with Valentine's general prescriptions:

> Innovation serving the interests of the lower class to an optimal degree will therefore require more or less simultaneous, mutually reinforcing changes in three areas: increases in the resources actually available to the poor; alterations of the total social structure; and changes in some subcultural patterns.[45]

The Black Middle Class

Families not included in the underclass constitute roughly 70 percent of all black American families. They are part of a very different picture than the one painted by Moynihan and Lemann. As Wilson puts it:

> One's economic class determines in major measures one's life chances, including the chances for external living conditions and personal life experiences.[46]

Billingsley has found that the majority of black families avoiding poverty and deprivation live within a family structure composed of husband, wife, and children. Hill's data on the black middle class support this assertion. While 57 percent of all black families were comprised of couples, 82 percent of middle-income black families consisted of two parents. Hill adds that the largest increase in one-parent families during the 1970s occurred among both black and white middle-class families, primarily because of a spiraling divorce rate over the past two decades. The structure of the family in American society at large has thus been undergoing rapid and traumatic change.[47]

A third of blacks have reached middle-class status, while another third is steadily employed in the blue-collar working class. In 1969, married couples with both spouses working—roughly one third of all black families—had 75 percent of the income of similar white families. By 1982, the gap had narrowed to 80 percent. A variety of factors account for the gains, including increased educational opportunity and greater occupational and geographic mobility for many black Americans.[48]

Scanzoni describes the stable black family of the working and middle classes—the strata above the underclass. He makes an important point when discussing the stability of family patterns, using the term in a conventional sense to refer to situations where husband and wife head the family together. Scanzoni considers it a stable configuration because, over time, it has been the predominant family pattern among Western societies. The majority have expressed their value preference by choosing to live in a nuclear family pattern. The one-parent family patterns prevalent in the black underclass are also evolved cultural adaptations to changing environmental circumstances. Scanzoni claims, as others we have cited:

> The main tool for understanding the black family is social class—or level of possession of economic status resources. An adjunct to class is ethnicity, particularly in terms of the definition held and practiced by dominant white society against blacks.[49]

Describing a sample size of 400 households, in which both spouses were black and had been married at least five years, Scanzoni concludes these families hold a status above the black population nationally. The great majority perceived their parents as providing them with ample resources for both economic and social attainments. Most were highly involved in their churches and many had received support from community figures such as clergymen and schoolteachers. Their position contrasts strongly with that of blacks in the underclass, whose involvement in mediating structures, outside of kinship, has been minimal.

In education, job status, and income, it was evident that those surveyed by Scanzoni had made substantial gains over their own parents. Hill has recently substantiated these data. He found that by 1983, 24 percent of all black families with heads twenty-five and older were college educated, while 42 percent of middle-income black family heads had some college education. "Although a majority of heads of black middle class families are not college educated, a growing majority have obtained education."[50] The one area in which the black middle- class majority had declined, however, was in their level of self-employment.

The parents Scanzoni studied encouraged their children to participate in the American Dream. That meant children were encouraged to do well in school and expected to continue their education at the college level.

Scanzoni attributes the major differences between families of the middle and underclasses to a "differential access to the economic rewards of the total society."[51] Our own interpretation is that this differential access has both internal and external factors impinging on it. Black families living in poverty have evolved subcultural patterns and values that include a sense of hopelessness and a disbelief in the institutions of the larger society. Their hopelessness, and the behavior that has evolved from it, cannot be dissolved by placing the blame on "structural inequalities of society."

Scanzoni himself suggests that changes must come from within the ethnic subsociety of blacks:

> Ultimately, the future course of the black family in America is tied to the capability of black society to participate fully in the decisions that effect its own destiny.[52]

He mentions that first steps include phasing out current welfare programs, which are demeaning and dependency-inducing for those who resort to them. Blacks will have to help restructure elementary and secondary schools to meet the particular needs of black children. Black interests will have to be met in local, state, and federal political, legal, and legislative processes. Blacks themselves must take measures that encourage more blacks not only to enter professional and management positions, but to form their own businesses along a variety of entrepreneurial lines. Above all:

> Black self-determination, if it is to be genuinely free from white paternalism, requires the right not only to innovate, but also at times to fail and be able to start over.[53]

Characterization of Family Enterprises

In our introduction, we pointed out that social change begins with individual behavior. What we find interesting are individual actions that vary from regular patterns of collective behavior. From these variations will come the changes that continue to reshape both our social institutions and the values that regulate individual behavior.

To understand the black family as a mediating structure between individuals and society, we will discuss a unique variation from the general norm: the family business. Our focus will be on the action of individuals within two spheres, family and business. Individuals in family businesses make choices that are not purely pragmatic and profit-oriented. Other, and sometimes equally strong, motivations direct business-related decisions. Problems can arise from the overlap, as the family in the private sphere competes for resources with the business in the public sphere. Yet because of their strong mediating potential, family businesses also contain distinct advantages for individual members. To a large degree, the relative mix of advantage and disadvantage will depend on the type of family and the type of business.

Family businesses are commonly regarded as a dying breed. Recent studies demonstrate this is a false assumption. Exact national statistics on the number of family businesses are unavailable, but a common estimate is that more than 90 percent of the 15 million businesses in the United States are family owned (or controlled) and operated within a single family. Although many family businesses are small, a substantial proportion are major corporations, including about 175 of the Fortune 500. Half of the nations's GNP and nearly 50 percent of nonfarm, private-sector employment derive from family businesses.[54]

The general definition of a family firm is an organization whose ownership or management decisions are influenced by its relationship to a family (or group of families). Some controversy exists over whether a business is truly a family business if majority ownership lies within the family yet only one family member remains directly involved in the business. Rosenblatt, for one, stipulates that not only must the family exert control over the business through its ownership, but two or more family members must be directly involved at some time or another.

Donnelley presents a set of specifications that help determine exactly when a company should be considered a family business. He explains that a company can be classified a family business when identified with at least two generations of a family and when this link has had a mutual influence on company policy and the interests and objectives of the family. The presence of one or more of the following conditions indicates this relationship:

- Family relationship is a factor, among others, in determining management succession.
- Wives or sons (or daughters) of present or former executives are on the board of directors.
- The important institutional values of the firm are identified with a family, either in formal publications or in the informal traditions of the organization.
- The behavior of a family member reflects on or is thought to reflect on the reputation of the enterprise, regardless of the individual's formal connection to management.
- The relatives feel obligated to hold the company stock for more than purely financial reasons, especially when losses are involved.
- The position of the family member in the firm influences his or her standing in the family.
- Family members must come to terms with their relationship to the enterprise in determining their own careers.[55]

The goal of most family businesses is to provide a good living for the family and to pass the business on to the next generation. Yet fewer than 15 percent of family businesses remain in the family for more than three generations. The average life expectancy for a successful family business is fifty-five years, after which it either closes or changes hands.

> A family is forgiving, a family is loving. A business is not forgiving; a business is bottom-line oriented. How do you really meld those two together and still have a successful business and a loving family?[56]

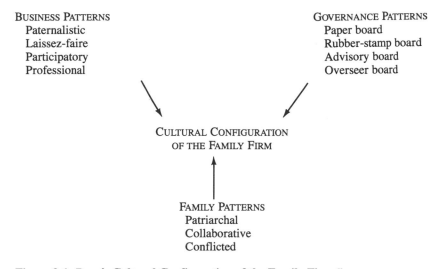

BUSINESS PATTERNS
  Paternalistic
  Laissez-faire
  Participatory
  Professional

GOVERNANCE PATTERNS
  Paper board
  Rubber-stamp board
  Advisory board
  Overseer board

CULTURAL CONFIGURATION
OF THE FAMILY FIRM

FAMILY PATTERNS
  Patriarchal
  Collaborative
  Conflicted

Figure 3.1. Dyer's Cultural Configuration of the Family Firm.[59]

Rosenblatt has devised an answer to the problem. All families, he maintains, have patterned ways of interacting, both within the confines of the family and with the outside world. Problems arise when the family must relate in an enterprise, located in the public sphere, as well as domestically, in the private sphere. Imbalances in the system occur because patterns of interacting in one setting are inappropriate in the other. The two systems may support each other but they also compete for resources. "The interconnection may create problems when one system benefits at the expense of the other."[57]

To further understand the dilemma, Rosenblatt suggests thinking about the problem of combining family systems and business systems in terms of goals. While the enterprise must simply profit to survive, family goals include difficult-to-quantify but no less important achievements; for example, a sense of self-worth and feelings of belonging together. The dissimilarity in objectives means, "It is unlikely that what it takes to keep an enterprise viable is identical to what it takes to keep a family going."[58]

Dyer offers a schematic approach to the issue of family businesses as interconnecting public and private systems. In what he calls a cultural configuration of a family firm, he sketches out patterns of interaction among families, business patterns, and governing bodies (Figure 3.1).

Within each of the three patterns there are broad types of behavior. The final configuration of the family firm depends on which kind of behavior typifies each of the three separate patterns. As we will illustrate, more problems result from the combination of some types than others.

Hartman examines the role of the next generation in three businesses, arguing that a family business by definition is small, confining, and too much work for too little pay. He discusses a number of case studies in which it is clear that the family aspect of the business—its small scale and hands-on approach—acts to restrict what under more rational management could become million-dollar enterprises. By Hartman's own definition, a million-dollar enterprise no longer qualifies as a family firm. Family businesses, à la Hartman, are a nice living but not very glamorous. They are not aggressive in the marketplace, not too ambitious. They are down-to-earth, concerned with traditional ways of doing things, and open to little innovation.

Hartman's view mixes family with business in a pattern corresponding to Dyer's paternalistic business and patriarchal family combination. One problem with the paternalistic–patriarchal model is its ascriptive bias against certain family members. For example, a woman is at a disadvantage in the family business if either her family or the business subscribes to paternalistic–patriarchal views of women. In a number of case histories women are clearly "not expected to get into sales" or any other area related to the business.[60] In many of the companies he studied, Donnelley found that "the firm is currently managed by the eldest son of the former chief executive. Such situations suggest that [male] primogeniture exists in some companies."[61]

In Benedict's discussion of family firms in the Seychelles, an island group off the western coast of India, the cultural setting is somewhat different than the one discussed so far, that of family businesses in the United States. But his contrast and comparison of different ethnic groups have surprising parallels in American culture. Thus his typology of entrepreneurial families may be useful even when taken out of it original cultural context.

Benedict concludes that the growth and success of small family firms in the Seychelles are highly dependent on strong, authoritarian fathers and closely knit cooperative families. Wives and sons must be willing to submit to the father's rule. Their submission is accompanied by an ideology stressing loyalty to the family and hence to the firm.

In the Benedict study, women are confined to a restricted role in the family business. For them, the family is less a mediating than a constraining structure between private and public spheres. Again, paternalistic business patterns combined with patriarchal family patterns represent but one of a number of possible configurations. An entirely different outcome might emerge by combining participatory business conduct with a collaborative family.

Family businesses can offer some distinct advantages, to women and minorities as well as others. Pave tells us, "A lot of enterprise is staying in the family these days" because of changed attitudes and a changing economy.[62] She outlines a number of reasons for the resurgence of the family business:

- *Entrepreneurship*: The business world has rediscovered the satisfactions of creating and building a company. Although the sons and daughters who continue the business did not start the company, they enjoy being instrumental in the decision-making and chances that will determine the company's future.
- *Impatience with bureaucracy*: Within the parameters of a family business it is possible to cut down on meetings "every time you turn around," and tackle risk arbitrage with a minimum of meetings, committee reports, and other formalities.
- *Humanistic values*: Many in their twenties and thirties are repelled by "What they see as the strictly bottom-line approach of most large companies." They place a high priority on setting their own schedules, and like linking their parents to their children at work as well as at home.
- *Economic pressures*: "Corporate life doesn't look as good as it once did." Careers in the corporate world move too slowly.
- *Home-grown opportunities*: As opposed to the slow corporate track, the family business provides opportunity for faster advancement, usually due to the deeply felt sense of purpose spurred by personal sacrifice.[63]

In the same vein, Rosenblatt stresses that in his study of fifty-nine families, the most common advantage mentioned for working in a family business was personal freedom: "Freedom from the controls of others, freedom to do what one wants, freedom from criticism, and freedom to use time flexibly."[64] The fact that freedom is so important seems paradoxical, because the freedom of working in a family business generally involves sixty plus work hours per week.

Among other advantages mentioned are "prestige and pride, creativity, and the capacity to do good things for one's off-spring."[65] At times the resolution of the tensions connected with a family business were seen as a way to improve family relations.

Most studies neglect to mention the advantages for minorities in a family business. Depending on the structure of relationships within the family, women can have a more equal chance in the family business than in an impersonal work world where, in many cases, women still receive less pay than men for similar work. The same holds true for blacks who opt for a family business; although the internal standards and demands may be high, they do not have to face a prejudiced employer.

> It is apparent that families *do* stay in their businesses, and the businesses stay in the family. Thus there is something more deeply rooted in transfers of power than impersonal business interests. The human tradition of passing on heritage, possessions, and name from one generation to the next leads both parents and children to seek continuity in the family business.[66]

According to consultants for family businesses, only 30 percent survive into the second generation, and less than 15 percent survive the third.[67] The problem of transition affects both family and nonfamily members. Insiders as well as those not in the family "have more than a passing interest as a company moves from one generation to the next."[68] Tensions over succession were present in a majority of the businesses studied by Rosenblatt. "Typically, [problems] reflected the senior person's ambivalence about giving up the business, about trusting a successor, or about letting changes occur."[69] Hartman presents a humorous vignette illustrating the potential effect of intergenerational differences in attitudes and values on family business decisions:

> Seymor Siegel, 57, and his son, Jeff, 35, agree that that their 10-year disagreement was probably inevitable. When Seymor was growing up, people were saving tinfoil, and apples were for sale on the street corner, two for a penny. When Jeff grew up, people were saving the whales and Apple was on its way to the Fortune 500.[70]

In most of Rosenblatt's case studies, candidates for succession were more often children of the chief executive officer than of any other relative. Furthermore, he found that, "Socialization from the teen years or earlier to enter the family business was reported commonly by sons of (male) entrepreneurs though not daughters."[71] Men without sons or with sons uninterested in the business worried about succession, but few considered daughters or sons-in-law viable alternatives.

> Perhaps the neglect of daughters as possible successors represents a cultural bias to consider males but not females appropriate in entrepreneurial roles. One can speculate that another reason for discounting daughters as potential successors is that in America most daughters change their surname when they marry.[72]

If a business changes hands between nonrelatives, the legal transition is well documented. Within a family, however, transitions are often blurred. As in other areas of system overlap, argues Rosenblatt, there is "a tendency for parents to continue to parent and for off-spring to continue to live with that."[73] Unwillingness to face the future stalls both family and business transactions, since in one sense the future can only mean the death of the older generation. In addition, entrpreneurs are a special breed; even heads of a family business have most of their identity and sense of self-worth tied up in the business, and find it difficult to give up the reins. Smooth successions occur when the parent is willing to give up control and "at least one child has the competence to take over."[74] Giving up control is easier when less of the original founder's identity and self-worth are at stake, when, for example, other activities besides the family business help define the founder's self-image.

Rosenblatt makes a series of recommendations to help counter possible transition conflicts in a family business:

> Counting daughters as possible successors, planning the succession process. . . , giving a potential successor latitude to choose not to be a successor, giving potential successors appropriate education and opportunity to learn on the job. . . .[75]

Stated explicitly, potential successors need the opportunity to move up through the ranks. Experts consider the age of twelve ideal for getting a successor started at learning the family business. A son or daughter might work for a similar company before joining the family business. Experience elsewhere can teach the next generation how the business world works and give it the requisite skills to enter the family enterprise.

While a transition imposes the strain of generational overlap, another related process occurs as the company grows organizationally. According to Barnes and Hershorn, several points should be mentioned in connection with the transitional stages characteristic of family businesses:

- Organizational growth tends to be nonlinear.
- Periods of organizational development occur between periods of growth.
- A typical management response to transitional strains is a reorganization of the company.[76]

The first stage of a family business is characteristic of an entrepreneurial company with direct management. Dyer calls it "creating the company."[77] New businesses tend to have few employees doing a greater variety of things, which means that work roles are poorly defined. Businesses are more likely to be marginal. With survival as the most pressing need, much time and commitment are required of the persons involved. Initially, the founder may not even think of the business as a family enterprise. The transition from individual to "family" can occur when other members of the family get involved, which usually happens without consideration of the succession problem.

The next organizational stage is a period of growth and development.[78] It is typified by a rapidly growing product line and market situation in which a second level of management operates specialized functions. The founder can no longer manage all facets of the business directly and delegates responsibility to others. As the organization grows, the business usually has more contact with attorneys, CPAs, and tax experts who push for estate and succession plans. If such plans are neglected, the business is unlikely to pass on to a second generation of family ownership.

During the third stage, the family business has divisional operations with a diverse line of products and markets. Typically, this stage involves a looser, more impersonal, collective style of management with the chief executive managing generalists as well as functional specialists. "People with diverse interests" must be brought together "for the common good."[79]

Dyer includes a fourth stage not mentioned by Barnes and Hershorn: "Public ownership and professional management."[80] Few family firms reach this stage, which comes about when the business needs additional capital to continue its operation. Capital is procured by going public, usually concurrent with the introduction of professional management. "Often at this stage the family firm ceases to exist and the company becomes a publicly owned, professionally managed enterprise."[81]

Crossing the lines between stages of growth requires time, new interaction patterns, and awkward periods of overlap. Matters are further complicated by the fact that family transitions and company transitions can occur separately and at different times.

In sum, the family business in the United States is far from being extinct. As of the late 1980s it is both alive and flourishing. It is a peculiar breed of business that can be more clearly understood by keeping in mind the idea of two interconnecting but separate systems. The family and the business are two systems in that the goals, needs, and tasks of each are not identical. Because of the ambiguous nature of the interconnection, problems can and do arise. Methods for sorting out the roles and rules for the two systems need to be consciously developed and understood. Rules of succession, enabling the passing of authority in the business system to someone who is a member of the family system, are especially critical.

The advantages of running a family business are worth reiterating. They bear close resemblance to those voiced by entrepreneurs generally—a feeling of freedom, a provision of income and capital, a sense of creativity. Family businesses can be a satisfying way to provide a living and for family members to feel collectively rewarded for their personal sacrifices. Under the best of circumstances, the family firm can provide a basis for meaningful and enduring family connections.

Black Entrepreneurial Families

On August 10, 1987, the business sections of major U.S. newspapers announced that TLC Group L.S., a Wall Street investment firm, would pay $985 million for Beatrice International Food. With annual sales from Beatrice of $2.5 billion, the acquisition overnight made TLC the largest black-owned firm in America. Renowned for his active, aggressive leadership, Reginald F. Lewis runs TLC, which is controlled by him and his family.[82]

In February 1988 Columbia Pictures distributed the newest production of black cinema Wunderkind, Spike Lee. Lee, thirty-one, wrote, produced, and directed "School Daze"—a black musical portraying a controversial view of cultural conflict among black college students—with considerable help from his family. His aunt, a pianist, was assistant music director. His sister, Joie, was a cast member. Two of his brothers worked on the film crew. His father wrote the musical score. Lee's first hit, "She's Gotta Have It," made on less than $175,000, pulled in $7 million. In the *New York Times Magazine*, Mieher wrote that "for an independent shoestring production by a black man about black people, it was astounding."[83]

Members of black families who also share a family firm are innovators within black culture. In varying degrees, they have been able to create new combinations of economic resources from their surrounding social and economic environments. They constitute a special breed of family within a cultural pattern in which business participation is much lower than in other ethnic groups.

The disparity between the level of black business participation and that of other ethnic groups has been attributed to a number of causes, including the relative absence of positive entrepreneurial role models, the low status of business ownership in black communities, and a lack of both business knowledge and capital. Some black families, however, have successfully managed to overcome these constraints.

We conducted in-depth interviews with family members of six family businesses in two different regional locations. Our purpose was to discover how the behavior patterns of these families differed from the majority of black American families.

Three of the businesses were small to medium-sized funeral homes. Two were realty firms of very different size serving distinctly different markets. One business was a bank. All six had been in the family for at least fifty years, meaning present company leadership represented third-generation family involvement in the firm. All but one were started by men. The exception was founded by a combination of an older sister and two younger brothers. Three companies currently had women presidents, each of whom had inherited her position from her father. All were originally started to serve the black community in the highly segregated society of fifty years ago. The three funeral homes continued to serve primarily black customers, although they occasionally worked with white families. One realty firm had expanded into a larger market of integrated condominiums in a predominantly white part of town; the other realty firm dealt solely with real estate in the black community. The bank held onto its long-standing reputation of serving blacks and did not actively seek a new clientele.

Although six cases hardly constitute a sample base for statistical averages, they can begin to shed light on family entrepreneurship in black culture. In what ways are these black families in business for themselves different from the average black family (regardless of class)? Here we need to keep in mind the generalized characteristics of both family enterprises and black families.

Evidently, because these are family businesses, the concern for the welfare of the family is the overall value, as predicted by the material on family enterprise in general. Founders usually married, stayed married, and had between one and six children. Among subsequent generations, numbers of children varied between one and two.

The importance of education for economic advancement is a prevailing attitude among the black middle class. In every case, education played a major role for both founders and their descendants. In the funeral home started by three siblings, the two brothers had finished high school, while the older sister's education ended with elementary school. In all the other businesses, at least one of the founders had some college background or specialized degree, in mortuary science or real estate, for example. Education continued to be a highly valued resource among following generations. Usually this meant private primary and secondary schooling before going off to prestigious colleges and universities. Among them were Amherst, American University, Dartmouth, and Wharton as well as the black "name" colleges of Spelman and Morehouse.

All but one of the current presidents had heir apparents in training. The one exception had had a son in the business as a legman, but he had died before reaching a takeover position. In this aspect, the firms were unusual compared to family businesses in general. With two exceptions, the third generation of management stood ready to pass over the reins of company leadership to a fourth generation. Only one had no heir. In one case—the large realty consultant firm—the heir was a business colleague with no relationship to the family.

Presidents stressed that the children groomed for takeover learned the business from the bottom up. No pressure other than parental enthusiasm for the business had been applied to encourage the next generation to get involved in the family business. One characteristic of family firms pointed out by Donnelley seemed to hold true: Family members had to come to terms with their relationship to the family enterprise in determining their careers.[84]

In our general discussion of family businesses we mentioned the problem of "systems-overlap" between the family and the business. There did not appear to be any special problems connected with the overlap between family and business among those we interviewed, or at least none willingly shared with an outsider. One possible conclusion is that these families were not representative of black family businesses. Another is that these families were, because of the traditional strength of family and kinship networks in black families, better able to integrate the goals of family businesses. During interviews with two of the businesses, explicit mention was made of the importance of frequent family reunions with members who had moved to distant parts of the country.

These black families differed significantly from the statistical average in their propensity to consume and invest. They looked to the future, both in terms of the business and in terms of the family. The latter was strongly manifested by their concern for the education of their children.

To a large degree, the family business proved advantageous to the next generation. They had a secure place of employment in a racially biased society. Although sons and daughters did not start the company, and in that sense did not play the role of a founding entrepreneur, they were instrumental in the decision-making and possibilities that would determine the company's future. As successful businessmen and women, they were able to serve as entrepreneurial role models for their children at a time when few blacks had access to those roles. Hence, their family goals of achieving self-worth and feelings of belonging together were intimately connected with their business goal of making a profit.

Rosenblatt claimed, "It is unlikely that what it takes to keep an enterprise viable is identical to what it takes to keep a family going."[85] In our cases, the small scale of all but one gave the family an overriding importance in deciding the bottom-line issues. The large black realty company had expanded to the point of becoming a racially mixed consultant firm. A nineteen year-old daughter was employed as a secretary, but the heir apparent was not a family member.

This brings us to a discussion of the growth stages in family firms. Most of the six businesses were moving into the second stage outlined by Barnes and Hershorn.[86] That is, although the business had been in existence for at least three generations, work roles were still poorly defined—a characteristic of the first stage—but outside bookkeeping had become standard—a characteristic of the second stage. Only the realty consultancy firm had reached the third stage of divisional operations and diverse product lines. The president acknowledged that his business was well on its way to moving out of the family altogether and into Dyer's fourth stage of "public ownership and professional management."[87]

In terms of family patterns and business system overlap, or in Dyer's words, "the cultural configuration of the family firm,"[88] the six businesses were either participatory or professional and the family patterns collaborative. Thus they did not distinguish ascriptively defined roles for family members. Women as well as men could move between private and public spheres with plentiful support from both the family and the family business.

Members of the businesses we interviewed had a high level of involvement with and strong commitment to their surrounding communities. All were actively involved in their churches as well as in various other associations—the

NAACP, Urban Business League, YMCA, black bank boards, and local
neighborhood groups. They were aware of their special responsibilities as
leaders of the community, not in any political sense but as "outstanding citizens" with valuable experiences and resources. "Entrepreneurship is important for blacks," said one female informant. "It says something about character, that you're not afraid to work." The businessman who no longer
considered himself the president of a family business sat on the board of the
Urban League and Africare. It is important to "take care of your own," not
only in the sense of family, but also in the broader sense of a common community. "We must learn to share, just like other ethnic groups," said one
female informant who represented the second generation of her family
business.

Family members expressed concern over the double standards they felt
were applied to black businesses. They believed the survival and expansion of
black business hinged on their moving beyond exclusively black markets into
a fully integrated marketplace. Even so, said two female presidents, "Integration has been a double-edged sword" for many black businesses. They expressed ambivalence about supporting a black business solely because it was
black. "It used to be that a black business could be a greasy spoon in the
ghetto, and that was the only place I could go as a child, but I wouldn't be
caught dead in a place like that today."

As was true of the values held by family business members generally, our
families emphasized personal sacrifice and the satisfaction of earning and
appreciating "something that is yours." Like other entrepreurial families,
they enjoy the creativity, feeling of freedom, and good living provided by the
family business. They were skeptical of blacks who shunned starting a small
business and preferred employment in a big corporation like IBM. "Should
they ever be in a difficult economic situation, they won't know how to make it
on their own."

In our study of six family businesses we have tried to apply the framework
suggested in our introduction. We have focused on the action and behavior of
individuals within the spheres in which they operate. As we have shown, the
spirit of entrepreneurship becomes less a matter of mythic individualism and
more collective as family members gather up their resources as a family in the
private sphere and put them to collective use in the public. Their sense of
collectivity extends not only to other family members but to the black community at large.

It would be interesting in the future to compare black family businesses
with black businesses in general. Do members of family businesses show a
greater concern for issues affecting the black community at large? Does a
higher level of trust and accountability exist both within the business and
among businesses because families are involved?

As we have noted in our position on the black family, the ability of individuals to perceive and act on entrepreneurial opportunities rests on both external opportunities and an internal predisposition to do so. Black culture has within it comparatively few examples of the entrepreneurial family. The cultural values of the majority of black families, though stressing improvement, do not generally translate into entrepreneurial behavior. Even black middle-class families who have access to economic and social opportunities do not choose entrepreneurship as a means of providing for their families' well-being.

Any advantages or disadvantages experienced by blacks who have opted for a family business should be presented within the context of black culture. Historically, black Americans have been set apart, socially and economically, because of their race. Regardless of their distinctive role as black business leaders, those families we interviewed nourished a keen sense of belonging to a wider community in the midst of a unique and difficult struggle for a more rewarding life in America.

Notes

1. Shapero, Albert and Sokol, Lisa in Kent, Sexton, and Vesper (eds.), *Encyclopedia of Entrepreneurship* (Englewood Cliffs, New Jersey: Prentice-Hall, 1982, pp. 78–79).
2. Billingsley, Andrew, "Black Families in a Changing Society" in *The State of Black America 1987* (New York: National Urban League, 1987, p. 99).
3. Ibid., p. 100.
4. Ibid., p. 100. See also Black Enterprise Board of Economists, "Economic Perspectives" (*Black Enterprise,* vol. 17, January 1987).
5. Ibid.
6. Dash, Leon, "At Risk: Chronicles of Teenage Pregnancy" (*Washington Post,* January 26, 1986).
7. Cited by McGrory, Mary in "Moynihan was Right Twenty-One Years Ago" (*Washington Post,* January 26, 1986).
8. Staples, Robert, *The Black Family: Essays and Studies* (Belmont), California: Wadsworth, 1978).
9. Frazier, Franklin E., *The Negro Family in the United States* (Chicago: University of Chicago Press, 1939). See also Moynihan, Daniel P., "The Negro Family: The Case for National Action" in *The Moynihan Report* (Washington, D.C.: Howard University Press, 1965).
10. Frazier, op. cit., p. 631.
11. Ibid., p. 632.
12. Ibid., p. 633.
13. Myrdal, Gunnar, *An American Dilemma* (New York: Harper and Brothers, 1944, p. 931).
14. Ibid.
15. Frazier, Franklin E., *The Negro in the United States* (New York: Macmillan, 1957).
16. Ibid., p. 325.

17. Ibid.
18. Ibid., p. 637.
19. Moynihan, op. cit.
20. Ibid., p. 29.
21. Ibid., p. 30.
22. Loury, Glenn C., "The Family, the Nation, and Senator Moynihan" (*Commentary*) vol. 81, no. 6, June 1986, p. 22).
23. Billingsley, Andrew, *Black Families in White America* (Englewood Cliffs, New Jersey: Prentice-Hall, 1968, p. 199).
24. Figures cited in Loury, op. cit., p. 22. Taken from Gutman, Herbert G., *The Black Family in Slavery and Freedom: 1750–1925* (New York: Pantheon, 1975).
25. Adams, Bert N., "The Black American Family" in *The Family: A Sociological Interpretation* (Boston: Houghton Mifflin, 1980). See also Loury, ibid.
26. Billingsley (1968), op. cit., p. 33.
27. Staples, op. cit., p. 15.
28. Ibid.
29. Valentine, op. cit., p. 124.
30. Ibid.
31. Billingsley (1968), op. cit., p. 8.
32. Wilson, William Julius, *The Declining Significance of Race* (Chicago: University of Chicago Press, 1980, p. x).
33. Hill, Robert B., "The Black Middle Class: Past, Present and Future" in *The State of Black America 1986* (New York: National Urban League, 1986).
34. Wilson, op. cit., p. 47.
35. Hill, op. cit., p. 47.
36. Lemann, Nicholas, "The Origins of the Underclass" (*Atlantic Monthly,* June and July 1986, p. 35).
37. Ibid., p. 67.
38. Valentine, op. cit., p. 138.
39. Ibid., p. 132.
40. Stack, Carol, *All Our Kin* (New York: Harper and Row, 1974, p. 124).
41. Ibid.
42. Ibid., p. 126.
43. Wilson, op. cit., p. 107.
44. Wilson, W.J., *The Truly Disadvantaged* (Chicago: University of Chicago Press, 1987, p. 14).
45. Valentine, op. cit., pp. 141–143.
46. Wilson, op. cit., p. ix.
47. Billingsley (1987), op. cit. and Hill (1986), op. cit.
48. Ibid.
49. Scanzoni, John H., *The Black Family in Modern Society: Patterns of Stability and Security* (Chicago: University of Chicago Press, 1977, p. 13).
50. Hill, op. cit., p. 48.
51. Scanzoni, op. cit., p. 81.
52. Ibid., p. 328.
53. Ibid., p. 329.
54. Rosenblatt, Paul C., de Mik, Leni, Anderson, Roxanne M., and Johnson, Patricia A., *The Family in Business* (San Francisco: Jossey-Bass, 1985). See also Dingle, Derek T., "Passing Down the Family Business" in *Black Enterprise* (vol. 14, June 1984) as well as Dyer, W. Gibb, Jr., *Passing Down the Family Business*

(San Francisco: Jossey-Bass, 1986).
55. Donnelley, Robert G., "The Family Business" (*Harvard Business Review*, July/August 1964).
56. Ibid., p. 24.
57. Ibid., p. 19.
58. Rosenblatt, op. cit., p. 7.
59. Dyer, op. cit., p. 22.
60. Nelson, Sharon, "Strategies for Family Firms" (*Nation's Business*, vol. 74, June 1986, p. 26).
61. Donnelley, op. cit., p. 104.
62. Pave, Irene, "A Lot of Enterprise is Staying in the Family These Days" (*Business Week*, July 1985).
63. Ibid.
64. Rosenblatt, op. cit., p. 15.
65. Ibid., p. 16.
66. Barnes, Louis B. and Hershon, Simon A., "Transforming Power in the Family Business" (*Harvard Business Review*, July/August 1976).
67. Dingle, op. cit.
68. Ibid., p. 106.
69. Rosenblatt, op. cit., p. 14.
70. Hartman, Curtis, "Taking the 'Family' out of Family Business" (*Inc.*, September 1986, p. 73).
71. Rosenblatt, op. cit., p. 171.
72. Ibid., p. 175.
73. Ibid., p. 178.
74. Ibid., p. 187.
75. Ibid., p. 195.
76. Barnes and Hershon, op. cit.
77. Dyer, op. cit., p. 3.
78. Dyer, op. cit., p. 4.
79. Ibid.
80. Ibid., p. 5.
81. Ibid.
82. "Black-Owned Firm to Buy Beatrice Unit" (*Washington Post*, August 11, 1987).
83. Mieher, Stuart, "Spike Lee's Gotta Have It" (*New York Times Magazine*, August 9, 1987, p. 39).
84. Donnelley, op. cit.
85. Rosenblatt, op. cit., p. 24.
86. Barnes and Hershon, op. cit.
87. Dyer, op. cit., pp. 41–42.
88. Dyer, op. cit., p. 35.

4

Education and Entrepreneurial Values

Introduction

According to popular mythology, successful entrepreneurs frequently have little or no formal education. As with many a misconception of the entrepreneurial genre, the myth does not match the reality. Recent evidence shows that not only do entrepreneurs have, on average, higher levels of formal education than the rest of the population, but that the educational gap is increasing.[1]

Sorting out how, rather than whether, education affects entrepreneurial performance has proved a more complicated task. In general, the higher the levels of technology involved and the bigger the firm, the greater the positive influence of education on the entrepreneur. Level as opposed to type of academic preparation appears the more important criterion for running a successful business. In a study of high-technology firms, for example, while advanced education correlated positively with firm growth, no discernible differences in business performance emerged between entrepreneurs with management degrees and those with technical backgrounds. On the other hand, a study of 153 firms with fewer than 30 employees discovered no significant correlation between the educational level of entrepreneurs and firm growth rates. The same study found business majors less successful as entrepreneurs than nonbusiness majors.[2]

Among minorities, Bates stresses that entrepreneurial ability correlates positively with both education and income. If economic development programs aimed at low-income areas want to succeed, they must concentrate on attracting young, better-educated minorities into inner-city businesses. After all, says Bates, "It is the viable firm that creates jobs."[3]

Outside the family, the school, public or private, is the mediating institution most frequently encountered by black Americans. Over the years, schools have played an increasingly important role in socializing and educating black children. But to what degree have they fostered entrepreneurial achievement among blacks?

In the present chapter, we will look first at the general state of black education in America. Have blacks made significant advances in quality as well as quantity of formal education? To what degree has education led to economic rewards? Has school desegregation succeeded in improving the educational status of black Americans? How do blacks perceive educational opportunities in the 1980s and what are they doing to take advantage of or expand them? While taking external influences into account, we will focus our attention on the ways in which black education affects the condition of other institutional structures within the black community.

Next we will explore the relationship between entrepreneurial values and American culture. What kinds of values do entrepreneurs have and how do they acquire them? How do Americans view entrepreneurs and entrepreneurial values? Do the values entrepreneurs actually espouse mesh with public perceptions of them? If discrepancies exist, how do they affect the entrepreneurial culture and overall economic development of American society?

Finally, we will attempt to analyze black entrepreneurial values. As with the previous section, we will begin by looking at what black entrepreneurs value and why. How and to what extent do black Americans, as a group, value entrepreneurship? Our discussion culminates with data from our own survey of black youth attitudes in Washington, D.C. and Baltimore.

All of our arguments concerning education and entrepreneurial values rest on the underlying assumption that entrepreneurship derives from culturally relevant and acquired behavior patterns.

The State of Black Education

Learning, in the words of Greenfield and Strickon,

> refers to the continuous process by which new behaviors are added to the repertoires of the individuals constituting a population or community. As new behaviors are learned or added, others previously performed may be discarded.[4]

Most of us think of learning as something that primarily takes place in our lives between the ages of five and twenty-five in the hallowed halls of formal institutions known as schools. In fact, learning is a lifelong process that occurs in every facet of our lives.

Entrepreneurial learning is a continuous process of adaptation between the economic and social circumstances of individuals and the larger social and economic processes to which they have access. Entrepreneurial societies, says Drucker, continuously challenge the habits and assumptions of schools and learning.[5]

With these tenets in mind, we want to consider how formal education relates to the larger entrepreneurial learning processes of American blacks. Our purpose is straightforward: Are education and experience providing the next generation of black American leaders with entrepreneurial resources?

Attainment Versus Achievement

In no other area have black Americans so conspicuously advanced as in levels of educational attainment. Since World War II, the rise has been dramatic and widespread. By 1982 the median level of education for black adults was 12.0 years, slightly behind the average of 12.5 years for white adults.[6] High school dropouts had declined and the number of black college students held steady at just over one million, or nearly 20 percent of the black college-age population.[7] Equally important, statistical indicators revealed that lower-class blacks had not fallen further behind upper-class blacks in levels of educational attainment. Concludes Farley:

> The black population is becoming more homogeneous with regard to educational attainment . . . . Blacks at both the top and bottom of their educational distribution are becoming more like whites who have similar positions in the white educational distribution.[8]

But figures for black educational attainment, measured by numbers of years of school, have not necessarily corresponded with the figures for black educational achievement, based on performance. Says Wilhelm:

> *The quality* of education by race leaves much doubt for claiming [black] educational accomplishments amount to a resounding victory.[9]

Between the mid-1960s and the 1970s average achievement scores for black elementary and high-school students fell dramatically. In 1973 twice as many 16-year-old blacks as whites were one or more grade levels behind. In 1975, a federally funded literacy test found 42 percent of all 17-year-old black students functionally illiterate. Along with 12 percent of their white compatriots, the blacks "could not read labels from two dog food cans to determine which contained the most proteins."[10] In 1979, the published results of Florida high-school competency tests disclosed a 42 percent failure rate among minorities, compared with 8 percent among whites.

Similarly discouraging results were reported at the college level. In the late 1970s, black college graduates taking a clerical exam to apply for government jobs failed eight times more often than whites. Compared with 80 percent of whites, a mere 3 percent of would-be black lawyers with college grade-point averages of 3.2 received 600 plus scores on law school admission tests. In the state of South Carolina, 83 percent of all black applicants for teaching jobs, but only 17.5 percent of whites, failed to pass teacher competency tests.[11]

Although greater numbers of blacks enrolled in college throughout the 1960s and 1970s, fewer blacks than whites completed their college educations. Furthermore, explain Brown and Stent:

> While there are a large number of blacks attending college in the United States, the *selectivity of institutions attended is lower* than for the population in general. For example, at the university level only 3.9 percent of the student population is black; 8.7 percent is enrolled in four-year colleges, while 8.3 percent is enrolled in four-year and two-year colleges and underrepresented in universities and graduate centers.[12]

More ominously, since the early 1980s fewer blacks have attended college and fewer still entered graduate school. The decline has been sharpest among young black males, whose college attendance has dropped, relative to both whites and black females, even in traditionally male-dominated fields like science and engineering. Some are lured away from college or graduate studies by the money and status of a well-paying job. More frequently, young blacks, especially males, facing a combination of lower income, greater economic hardship, and rising entry standards, simply opt against college altogether.[13]

Education and Reward

Following emancipation, the eagerness of blacks to obtain an education frequently surpassed all other practical considerations. According to one moving eyewitness account from the Reconstruction period:

> When the collection of the general tax for colored schools was suspended in Louisiana by military order, the consternation of the colored population was intense. Petitions began to pour in. I saw one from the plantations across the river, at least thirty feet in length, representing ten thousand negroes. It was affecting to examine it, and note the names and marks (x) of such a long list of parents, ignorant themselves, but begging that their children might be educated; promising that from beneath their present burdens, and out of their extreme poverty, they would pay for it.[14]

Between 1866 and 1884, black public school enrollment burdgeoned from 91,000 to more than one million. In some areas, black school enrollment rates exceeded that for whites, even in places where blacks were less numerous. In

Florida, for example, blacks represented 30 percent of the population, but not until 1888 did white students outnumber blacks in the public schools.[15]

The flowering of black educational opportunities during Reconstruction, forged by a remarkable combination of missionary zeal, individual state initiatives, and black self-help efforts, was both dramatic and short-lived. At the same time as general education spread rapidly throughout the United States of the late nineteenth century, black education underwent a series of resounding setbacks. Black political power in the South eroded as whites regained political and economic hegemony. Court rulings on school segregation promoted the idea that blacks had different educational needs than whites, for which funding could be distributed differently. As an outcome, blacks received the less expensive, substandard, segregated educations white southerners agreed befitted the lower position of blacks in society. Lieberson summarizes:

> The growing white educational needs, the weak economic resources of the South, a decline in black political power, and a basic lack of sympathy among many whites for quality black education was extraordinarily damaging for black education.[16]

Setbacks notwithstanding, Lieberson records that in 1910, black students enrolled in postcompulsory school programs in the North outnumbered the children of first and second generation white immigrants. Even as late as 1930, blacks living in the North and West remained more literate than foreign-born whites. Lieberson suggests that deterioration in the quality of black education, along with a differential access to economic rewards, eventually widened the educational gap between native-born American blacks and immigrant groups. Whatever the subsequent state of black education, and the relative desire among blacks to obtain it, "There is no indication that blacks were initially any less interested in education, or less willing to sacrifice to achieve it, than were other groups on average."[17]

Although Lieberson's findings are noteworthy in that they indicate the high value black Americans have traditionally placed on education, the fact remains that the vast majority of blacks were historically ill-placed to exercise their educational preferences. Well into the twentieth century, black children in the South—and the majority of blacks lived in that region—were less likely than white children to attend school. In 1910, about 85 percent of the nation's white children, but only 60 percent of black children, were enrolled in school.[18]

By the time Myrdal undertook a comprehensive study of what he called "the American dilemma" in the early 1940s, black confidence in their ability to raise themselves by education had begun to show signs of serious erosion. On the one hand, observes Myrdal:

As self-improvement through business or social improvement through government appeared less possible for them, Negroes have come to affix an even stronger trust in the magic of education.[19]

While on the other, concurring with Lieberson, Myrdal notes:

It is true that some Negroes may lately have lost their faith in education, either because the schools available to them—in the South—are so inadequate, or—in the North—because they achieve education but not the things they hoped to do with it.[20]

Bates offers a concise sketch of the preparation received by the majority of American blacks for the twentieth-century urban life most of them now experience. More than two thirds of the black population migrated out of the rural South between 1900 and 1960 to industrialized cities of the North and West. In addition to poverty and ill-health, the South bequeathed them an abysmal quota of formal education. Bates describes the average educational setting for black residents of the cotton belt, circa 1934:

Black schools in rural areas typically convened in dilapidated buildings provided by the government, or in churches and lodge halls when school buildings were unavailable. Teachers were poorly trained and underpaid, classrooms were overcrowded, and students often lacked such basic necessities as desks.[21]

In Georgia, the average level of attainment for blacks was third grade.

As in most migratory cycles, the better educated left first. Many moved initially to small towns in their own states, which became important centers for acculturation into nonrural education and job markets. Until World War II, interim residence in towns provided many blacks with a critical transition point between life in the country and life in the city. By contrast, blacks who left during periods of mass migration—the two world wars and the final wave out of agriculture in the 1950s—frequently skipped this interim link. Moving directly from the underdeveloped South to the industrialized North, they were ill-prepared—by education, acculturation, or experience—for modern urban life.

Ogbu maintains that U.S. schools exist primarily to recruit people into the job market:

Schools recruit people by teaching children beliefs, values and attitudes that support the economic system; teaching them the skills and competencies required to make the system work; and credentialing them to enter the workplace.[22]

If educational attainment between the races has decreased to a marginal difference, employment discrepancies—pointedly those between black and whites males—have not. Between 1969 and 1983, participation rates in the civilian labor force for black males sixteen or older fell from 75 to 69.5 percent. The percentage for white males also dropped, but from an initial high of 78.7 to a low of 76.2 percent. In addition, although black males at the upper end of the educational spectrum—those holding college degrees— have closed much of the income gap with their white cohorts, those with less education and fewer skills have lost ground. Between 1953 and 1981, black male income as a percentage of white male income fell from 74 to 66 percent in the North and West. While black females have fared considerably better, they, too, lost relative income ground between 1959 and 1981.[23]

The striking divergence between the occupational-cum-educational status of black men and women forms a critical element in understanding the broad patterns of recent economic development among black Americans. The ratio of college-educated black women to college-educated black men has traditionally been high. In 1929, black women comprised nearly half of the student population at the seventy-nine black colleges then in existence.[24] Today, black females outnumber black males on a number of campuses, particularly in graduate-level programs.[25]

As black women, since the 1950s, have steadily gained employment in white-collar jobs, black males have continued to cluster in blue-collar manufacturing jobs. In particular, black women have made inroads into expanded clerical and professional opportunities offered by government and inner-city banking and administrative centers. Meanwhile black men have faced increasingly fewer, and relatively lower-paying, jobs in a shrinking and highly cyclical manufacturing sector.[26] By 1984, the median income for black males was $9,540 compared with $16,160 for black females. The relatively high salaries of black women have become an increasingly critical factor in the upward mobility of black American families. By 1987, one half of black families would have fallen below the poverty line if forced to rely solely on male income.[27]

The persistence of double unemployment figures for black men, despite educational gains and social and legal changes intended to reduce occupational segregation, have been ascribed to a variety of causes. Farley outlines four of the most frequently offered explanations:

1. A mismatch between educational skills and job opportunities.
2. Government programs, including welfare, that discourage men from working.
3. Migration of jobs to the suburbs, away from the inner-city residences of the black male majority.
4. Higher selection standards for black workers among employers.[28]

We will concentrate here on the first explanation, since it deals specifically with education and with black male perceptions of the relationship between education and employment.[29]

In 1983, 55 percent of black males aged sixteen to twenty-one who were not in school were also not at work.[30] It seems that for this age group, advances in educational attainment may have a perverse effect on rates of employment. Inner-city black youths want jobs, but not those attached to low pay and low status. They believe their high-school diplomas should qualify them for better jobs than those provided by their immediate surroundings—car washing, package delivery, floor washing. They see older men in their communities working in the same dead-end jobs they started in at twenty.[31] Frequently they perceive the get-rich-quick schemes of the street as more attractive employment prospects. In a survey conducted by the National Bureau of Economic Research (NBER), ghetto youth were asked to compare their potential earnings on the street with those from a regular job. Thirty-two percent saw greater opportunities on the street. According to conservative estimates, ghetto youth derive one fourth of their total income from illegal activities. Concludes the NBER study:

> Crime and employment are alternatives. Poor employment opportunities (or attractive criminal opportunities) can lead to participation in crime, which further reduces success in the legal job market.[32]

However lucrative, street earnings and the life-style they perpetuate often lead to disastrous consequences. In 1979, the homicide rate for black males was six times higher than that for whites. Nationwide, black youth account for 52 percent of the arrests for violent crime. Not surprisingly, a bleak and angry perception of the link between education and occupation typifies the mindset of a young ghetto entrepreneur. Put succinctly by a twelve-year-old hustler from Chicago's South Side:

> Why should I waste my time going to school so I can end up with a $13,000 a year job at the post office? Hell, man—I can *steal* that much.[33]

Currently one out of every two black, Hispanic, and poor teenagers quits school before obtaining a high-school diploma. For individuals and for society as a whole, the price paid for dropping out is enormous. During their lifetimes, dropouts from a single graduating class in a large urban school district will earn $200 billion less and cost society $60 billion in foregone tax revenues. They will be twice as likely to lose their jobs as high-school graduates, four times more likely than college graduates. In positive terms, each year of high school reduces the chance of being on welfare by 35 percent, and a high-school diploma decreases the likelihood of arrest by 90 percent.[34]

Among older, chronically unemployed black men, Liebow found that low levels of skill coincided with low expectations for successful employment. Like their fathers before them and their present-day peers, Liebow's street-corner denizens expected to fail sooner or later in the job market.

> They understood that no matter how competently they worked, employers would pay them as little as possible and lay them off as soon as work slackened.[35]

Consequently, they held off from working for as long as they could.

Desegregation

> It was not the Fair Employment Practices Committee (FEPC), the poll tax, segregation in interstate transportation, fairness in elections, segregation in the military, "white primary" or "higher education," etc., that fired the deepest public emotional involvement and the most violent public confrontation around the theory and practice of "racial democracy." It was racial democracy in public education at the primary and secondary levels that was the catalyst.[36]

On October 26, 1957, the nation watched as National Guard troops presided over the federally mandated integration of a public high school in Little Rock, Arkansas. On October 18, 1987, the thirtieth anniversary of that event, American television viewers observed the continuing turmoil over school desegregation in Little Rock.[37]

Following the 1957 incident, whites fled to the suburbs, leaving behind inner-city schools to what quickly emerged as an overwhelmingly black constituency. Over time Little Rock's inner-city school district, populated by blacks, became increasingly unequal to the three outlying suburban school districts, populated by whites. In 1986, school desegregation planners decided the solution to the problem was to merge all four school districts into one large district. Translated into action through a combined sharing of resources, the plan relies heavily on teacher trading and student swapping to meet its integration quotas. White and black students from elementary school through high school endure long bus rides far away from their homes and neighborhoods to attend schools neither they nor their parents have selected. Judging from the interviews conducted for the news report, black and white recipients of this solution appear equally outraged. So far only the planners claim satisfaction with the results. A white lawyer for the desegregation planning committee stated flatly that the days of the neighborhood school were gone for good and that *white* families were simply going to have to get used to the idea. After all, he declared, desegregation is a white, not a black problem.[38]

Therein, for an increasingly large number of blacks, lies the heart of the problem with forced public school desegregation. As enacted, it has imposed largely white solutions for what has been perceived as a largely white problem on a largely black—and presumed passive and helpless—population. Speaking generally of minority education in America, Ogbu claims:

> The dominant group's epistemology, their view of how things are and why, usually determines the type of schooling that minorities receive and the remedies for minority group problems.[39]

Across the political spectrum, a growing number of black community leaders seriously question whether forced legal integration—or put in reverse terms, desegregation—has ever addressed the crux of black educational problems. From civil rights activist Daniel Bell to black historian Harold Cruse, blacks wonder aloud whether, by focusing so much effort on overcoming the legal barriers to equality, they may have given away the store.

Bell concedes that the civil rights movement of the 1960s concentrated almost exclusively on integration "to eradicate all the bad things."[40] The black community gave up more than it should have, and in the process lost thousands of small businessmen, teachers, and the social structures which undergirded them. According to Bell, the few black middle-class professionals who have made it are largely marginalized and powerless within the system. Meanwhile, bereft of middle-class role models and internal leadership, the black masses struggle less and less successfully against poverty, crime, and family disintegration. What blacks must concentrate on today, says Bell, is putting the internal social structures of the black community—lost over the past twenty-five years—back into place.

More than thirty years have passed since the U.S. Supreme Court decreed an official end to racial segregation in public schools. Aside from acknowledging its symbolic importance as a benchmark victory for the American civil rights movement, the jury remains out as to whether or not *Brown versus Board of Education* has improved the quality of black education. "It is impossible to conclude," says Farley, "either that the school integration efforts and litigation of the past thirty years were very successful or that they were failures."[41]

Its most enthusiastic proponents believe public school desegregation has significantly improved the quality of education, for black and white Americans alike. Willie, writing for the National Urban League in 1987, asserts:

> While it is difficult to isolate totally the impact of school desegregation within the total context of social change, a reasonable assessment of school desegregation efforts confirms that school desegregation has contributed to the enhancement of education in this nation more than any other experience in recent years: it has

resulted in changes that have been beneficial to the nation as a whole, white America as well as black America.[42]

As proof, he cites the high levels of educational attainment reported for all Americans in a 1982–1983 survey by the census bureau, and the impressive gains in black educational levels since 1950. Furthermore, nationwide public opinion polls have found that blacks prefer integrated to segregated learning environments and that more than two thirds of whites also support racially balanced schools. Pointing to high attainment and enrollment by members of all races in public schools, he concludes that Americans continue to manifest a resolute faith in the value and efficacy of public education.

Nevertheless, Willie acknowledges a growing ambivalence toward school desegregation, among blacks as well as whites. In part he believes the skepticism reflects a major shift to the right in American politics, but that it has deeper roots in the standard procedures by which schools have been desegregated. The big problem, stresses Willie, is the *implementation* of desegregation, not desegregation per se:

> What has discouraged blacks and could affect their future support of desegregation is the unjust and inequitable way that desegregation has been implemented.[43]

Busing policies have guaranteed white children the major benefits of desegregation and left most black children in racially segregated schools. The planning bodies for school desegregation have consisted largely of white, middle-class, middle-aged males. Gerrymandering of school districts and at-large elections have insured white control over school boards in areas with dwindling white populations. To counter these blocks to effective school desegregation, Willie recommends multiracial planning bodies and representative district, rather than at-large, school board elections.

Regardless of their misgivings about how desegregation has taken place, black Americans, says Willie, "are not about to risk a return to separate facilities sanctioned by a state, even if promised that separate schools will be more effective."[44] For those ambivalent about "the real accomplishments of school desegregation and whether the successes have been and continue to be worth the effort," he cautions:

> The national memory tends to forget what the nation was like before *Brown*—a segregated system of unequal opportunity.[45]

Current realities of the American public education system lead many Americans, black and white, to dismiss such warnings as irrelevant. Within the stark confines of many inner-city schools, blacks outnumber whites in proportions equal to if not greater than at midcentury. Robinson, in an article published with Willie's in *The State of Black America, 1987,* reports that over 80 percent of black children in the United States are educated in less than 4 percent of the nation's school districts.[46] Most live in large cities, with more than a third crowded into fewer than ten urban centers of the North and Northeast.

> The 1980 census reported that 34 percent of all blacks resided in just seven urban centers: New York, Chicago, Los Angeles, Philadelphia, Detroit, Baltimore and Washington, D.C.[47]

Between 1970 and 1980 residential segregation among the nations' twenty-five central cities with the largest black populations decreased by six points on a one-hundred point scale. But the overall picture was mixed:

> In three cities the scores did not change, and in Philadelphia and Cleveland residential segregation apparently increased. Despite decades of racial change and numerous civil rights laws, Chicago, St. Louis and Cleveland were almost as segregated as they would have been if a law mandated that all blacks live exclusively in black blocks and whites in exclusively white ones.[48]

Urban residential segregation, created largely by an outflow of whites and affluent blacks to the suburbs, has translated into de facto segregation in inner-city public schools. For the black majority who attend such schools, educational quality—despite three decades of political rhetoric and legal maneuvering around the desegregation issue—has deteriorated.

Washington Post reporter Althea Knight spend most of the 1986–1987 school year at McKinley High School sitting in on classes, attending faculty meetings, and interviewing students and teachers about the problems confronting today's urban high schools.[49] McKinley was chosen because, on the basis of standardized test scores and percentage of college-bound graduates, it represents an average Washington, D.C. public high school.

Housed in an imposing Georgian structure on a hill overlooking the nation's capitol, McKinley lays claim to a prestigious past. During the 1960s, its renowned science, engineering, and music departments attracted top students from around the District. Many graduates joined the vanguard of a rising black middle class by becoming outstanding nurses, doctors, lawyers, educators, administrators, and business executives.

Over the past twenty years, McKinley's reputation as "Tech"—the inner-city school where gifted blacks could successfully pursue their dreams along a variety of career paths—has been badly tarnished. The majority of its shrinking population of 1,200 students, less than half the student enrollment of 1967, comes from black poor and working middle-class neighborhoods. Many attend school on a part-time basis in order to maintain part-time jobs.

Being good at school is not considered "cool." Explains principal Bettye Topps of her honor roll students, "They want to do well, but they don't want to be identified as people who do well."[50] Irwin Kenny, an eleventh-grade honor student, does his best to camouflage his talents:

> I hang around with people who aren't smart. People see me in the hall a lot. I'm loud in class . . . I make a lot of noise. But I get my work done.[51]

Discipline problems abound, from low attendance, chronic tardiness, and poor academic performance to general misbehavior in and out of the classroom. They contribute substantially to a pervasive atmosphere of student indifference to learning and corresponding teacher malaise. Having given up on most of their students, many teachers concentrate their efforts on the few students who show some promise for academic success. Although currently undergoing its first major rennovation in fifty-nine years, the deteriorating physical condition of the building also conveys a strong sense of neglect, misuse, and decay.

Recent attempts by principal Topps to get parents jointly involved with teachers, students, and school administrators in reviving the academic spirit at McKinley have largely fallen through. Attendance remains low and standardized test scores dropped over the school year. Regularly scheduled PTA meetings drew fewer than 100 parents. Many teachers failed to cooperate in an "action plan" for decreasing tardiness and absenteeism. When, at the end of the 1986–1987 academic year, Topps gathered her faculty to relay the discouraging results of her "Renewing a Legacy" campaign, no one feigned surprise. But Topps, a tough administrator and a long-term survivor of inner-city schools, refuses to give up. As she urges her students, parents, and faculty to do, she has taken head-on a personal responsibility for the quality of education at McKinley:

> Unfortunately, the responsibility of getting a child to school is not in the home anymore. That responsibility now lies with the principal. What is going on in this building should be so stimulating that the children will want to leap forward and come to school. We have to get some challenging programs for our children.[52]

As reflected by the ongoing concern and efforts of administrator Topps, not all the news coming out of McKinley is negative. She receives substantial support from parents like Betty Thomas, parent of a tenth grader and the 1986–1987 PTA president. Even though she has failed to recruit more parents into the PTA over the past school year, Thomas continues to believe in McKinley, its principal, and its good teachers. "We don't show enough appreciation of our teachers, " she regretfully admits. "It seems like a thankless job."[53] Marge Johnson Kelly, a 1961 McKinley graduate and an active member of the alumni association, planned to put a mentor program into place at the beginning of the next school year. She hopes the added attention and encouragement for students on an individual basis will help fill a critical void:

> Children in 1987 are striving to feel comfortable in the world that surrounds them, a confusing world. Often, the requirements for their learning surpass their abilities or the time the family has to work with them.[54]

Topps maintains that the key to a good school is the quality of its teaching:

> The best teachers—the ones who can motivate the least interested students—are the ones who are knowledgable, well-prepared and creative.[55]

Three of the best at McKinley are ROTC "Master Gunny" Washington, social studies teacher Leroy Swain, and French teacher Vernon Williams. Although they share little in terms of personality or teaching style, their teaching methods have much in common. Summarizes Knight:

> They are well-prepared and organized. They rarely come to class late, they start working as soon as the bell rings, they hand out homework assignments and never fail to collect them, grade them and hand them back . . . . They are blunt and willing to give their students realistic evaluations . . . . Frequently, they take a personal interest in their students . . . . They take little for granted, least of all their relationships with their students.[56]

It is perhaps neither surprising nor coincidental that these three "best" teachers in a chronically flagging inner-city school are men. They provide strong role models for youth too often deprived of consistent male authority at home. Says teacher Swain of his McKinley students:

> They're good kids. They are just begging for help. They all want discipline. They all want guidance. It's up to us to do it.[57]

As more career opportunities have become available for black college graduates, fewer have chosen to go into teaching. The present shortage of minority teachers could become a critical dilemma for the rapidly increasing population of minority students. If current trends continue unchecked, by the year 2000 minority teachers will have shrunk to less than 5 percent of the public school teaching force, while the number of minority students will have grown to 38 percent.[58]

Black college graduates cite low pay and prestige as the primary factors that have discouraged them from teaching. A number had parents who were teachers, and have thus experienced up close the advantages and disadvantages of a teaching career. Many will readily admit that having black educators as role models had a decisively positive influence on their own academic success. Explains one young man:

> We had a black lady principal who held herself up as being number one, being very respectable, being very much a lady, very professional. And up to this time, I hadn't really seen that.... I didn't question it, but I hadn't seen anyone.... In your mind it makes an impression; hey, there are black people who are making it.[59]

But when asked whether or not such an educational role model might encourage black students to become principals themselves, the student responded:

> No. They give you the inspiration to say that you can. So it's not so much becoming a teacher, but saying that you can.[60]

Robinson summarizes the chronic problems of inner-city black schools as fewer resources—including a shrinking black teaching force—and low academic achievement, in conjunction with alarmingly high rates of teenage pregnancy, drug use, and crime. Taken together, she concludes:

> The pregnancy rates of young black females and the "social drop-out" rates among black males pose real threats to the hope of a stable black community. But it is this lack of hope, not potential, which is most debilitating to today's black youth.[61]

Rejuvenating the System

During the 1980s, black Americans have once again rallied under the banner of education. This time, however, they are looking within rather than beyond their own communities for the political and economic resources to carry out their objectives. To address the education crisis, exhorts Robinson:

> Black America must reunite and organize a political coalition which transcends economic status, geographic residence and other distinctions that may separate one black person from another.[62]

Bringing black parents back into the center of action, especially the parents of children with the greatest risk of failure, has become the number one priority. In the context of Robinson's community-based action formula:

> These parents are potentially the most explosive and powerful component.... They could become the vanguard of one of the most significant movements in American education. Though black parents care deeply about the educational issues affecting their children, they have largely been ignored.[63]

Private Alternatives

Increasingly, disaffected black parents are taking matters into their own hands. In many low-income, urban areas they have been primarily responsible for a groundswell of privately funded and administered black schools.

According to the Institute of Independent Education 220 such schools now exist, the vast majority serving poor families in inner-city neighborhoods. These schools are characterized by their emphasis on academics and discipline and are staffed, attended, owned and operated almost entirely by members of minority groups. Academic achievement runs higher than in most schools.[64]

One highly touted example is the Ivy League school in Philadelphia. Ivy League, which began with 17 prekindergartners in 1965, now has over 700 students from kindergarten through eighth grade studying at four different locations. Course offerings range from state-of-the-art computer and science programs to the humanities, vocational training, and hands-on business experience. Through one project coordinated with the National Center for Neighborhood Enterprise in Washington, D.C., Ivy League eighth graders sold $16,000 worth of smoke detectors to the residents of low-income Philadelphia neighborhoods.

Ivy League schools are funded entirely by tuition fees and private fundraising efforts. Even so, their tuition fees equal about half those of comparable private schools in the area. Parents actively support the cause with a significant measure of independent fund-raising. Low-income parents have been hired as staff to allay tuition expenses for sons and daughters.

The hard work and perserverance of parents, administrators, teachers, and staff has paid off. Eighth-grade graduates of Ivy League are sought after by the best high schools in Philadelphia. Many have obtained full scholarships to nationally recognized private academies.[65]

Public Reforms

Figures for black enrollment in private elementary through high schools indicate that, however heartening the progress of a successful few, privately run alternatives to public schools cannot begin to meet the urgent demand for higher-quality black education.

In the fall of 1985, 301,000 out of a total of 4,872,000 black Americans—6.2%— were enrolled in private kindergarten, elementary and high schools in the U.S.[66]

If black parents and educators are to gain greater control over the education of black children, most of them will have to concentrate their efforts on taking charge of the public schools in their own communities. Several around the country have already done so.

In March 1987, the MacNeil/Lehrer Newshour aired a special report by correspondent John Merrow on the remarkable transformation of East Harlem School District in New York City. Explained Merrow in his introduction:

> By and large, public schools don't offer choice. Children go where they're told. . . . Only those who can afford private school have a choice. Under those conditions, there's really a monopoly. Public schools have become standardized. They're pretty much the same no matter where you live. But in other areas of our lives we pick and choose: the clothes we wear, the food we eat, the cars we drive. Yet, when it comes to one of the most important decisions of all—how our children will be educated—most of us are left with no choice at all.[67]

East Harlem represents a dramatic example of what can happen when choices are introduced into the public school system. Over half the families of the 12,000 students who attend East Harlem schools fall below the poverty line. In 1964, out of thirty-two schools districts in New York City, East Harlem ranked last in reading and mathematics. Reasoning they had nowhere to go but up, the district school board and superintendent decided to introduce "theme schools" into its junior high school system. Each junior high school was encouraged to develop a different educational program, among which parents and children could then select. One school specialized in the performing arts, another in the sciences and humanities. Still others organized their curriculums around communications, sports, and environmental sciences. Over thirteen years, three schools closed down because of low attendance; they reorganized around themes and successfully reopened. By 1987, twenty-one junior high schools in East Harlem had converted to theme schools, while only two remained "standardized" public schools.

Results have been phenomenal. The numbers of students who read at or above grade level has gone up from 15 to 64 percent. Previously number thirty-two, the district has moved in its overall academic ranking to position sixteen. Student, teacher, and parent high morale has become the rule rather than the exception. Even the dilapidated conditions of some of the school buildings does not deter enthusiasm. Manhattan East Junior High School, which has the best academic reputation among district schools, is housed on the fifth floor of a run-down building without elevators. Plaster has fallen or hangs in places from ceilings and walls. Still, says one loyal student, "I don't really notice it at all . . . . When you're focusing on what you're here for, you don't."[68]

And another:

> I think the condition of the school adds a human element. . . . It makes it more of a
> comfortable environment to be in. You know, if everything's perfect, you feel kind
> of alienated. But this has more of a relaxed tone to it.[69]

In fact, Manhattan East has such an attractive educational environment parents are taking their children out of private schools to send them there.

Part of the success of East Harlem's "theme" schools can be attributed to their small size, on average 200 students per school. But most of it, claims district administrator Fliegel, has to do with the healthy effect of choice and the competition it engenders.

> If you have kids who've selected your school and their parents selected your school
> and the teachers selected that school, there's a sense of ownership. That school's
> going to do better than a school where you had to go or had no choice.[70]

Asked whether he is trying to make public schools like private one, Fliegel retorts:

> I have a standing rule. I've always felt what's good for the children of the wealthy I
> will almost automatically accept for the children of East Harlem. Without question,
> if it's good enough for rich kids, I think we can impose it upon our poor kids. It just
> makes sense.[71]

Fliegel warns that the success of East Harlem in introducing choice may not be easy to replicate elsewhere. For the system to work, he points out, "There's got to be a grassroots movement to support it."[72] Apparently, the parents of East Harlem, their children, and their schools have made a choice that works for them.

Providing Leaders

The same hard necessity sparking grass-roots efforts to improve the quality of community schools also drives a renewed vigor in black higher education. A large number of historically black American colleges fell by the wayside in the wake of desegregation. Faced with rising costs, low endowments, and in some cases a critical shortage of students and teachers, many more are expected to fold over the next few years.

Morehouse College, in Atlanta, stands first among those slated to survive. For decades, Morehouse has played a seminal role in shaping the future of black America. From its ranks have come a disproportionate share of the nation's top black leaders in business, academia, and the professions. While Martin Luther King is indisuputably the most famous, other prestigious alumni include multimillionaire businessman Marion Greene, Connecticut banking commissioner Howard Brown, and New York attorney C. Vernon Mason. Comedian Bill Cosby's son enrolled there in 1988.

An all-male school, Morehouse takes pride in its high academic standards and rigorous, disciplined atmosphere. From the day students walk in the door, they are taught that "the essential qualities of a Morehouse man are self-discipline, self-confidence and above all, strength."[73] Addie Mitchell, who for thirty-three years has taught a basic reading course to entering freshmen, "informs laggards that there are two ways to exit from her classroom: the door or the window." "You may leave by whatever means is most convenient," she says.[74] One senior recalls his indoctrination by the college dean:

> Look to your right. Look to your left. One of those gentlemen won't be here when you graduate.[75]

Since Morehouse graduates about half as many candidates as it enrolls each year, the dean's forecast contained the ominous ring of truth.

Founded by the American Home Missionary Society in 1906, for many years Morehouse was "little more than a sleepy Bible school teaching the 3Rs to teachers and preachers."[76] Then, in 1940, Benjamin Elijah Mays arrived to assume the presidency. Mays, a trained theologian and a powerful, charismatic leader, set out to transform both the quantity and quality of a Morehouse education. He recruited top scholars and faculty from all over the country, and located financing to subsidize graduate and overseas studies. He instituted a "compensatory" program to bring talented but underqualified high-school graduates up to par. Individual tracking and frequent testing monitored their progress. Students who failed repeated courses until they had satisfactorily passed them. Sometimes students took six to eight years to finish at Morehouse. Says long-time professor Robert Brisbane, "The aim was to take a sharecropper's son from Mississippi and prepare him for Harvard. . . . We did it more than once."[77]

The well-rounded college graduate—a kind of modern Renaissance man— was the ideal envisioned by Mays. He expected his students to do well not only in but beyond Morehouse. The best were encouraged to pursue graduate and professional studies; meanwhile, all were inculcated with a sense of personal responsibility for upholding the school's growing reputation. At his graduation, recalls the present chancellor of the Atlanta University Center, Charles Meredith, "[Mr. Mays] asked me if I understood that if I didn't succeed in chemistry at Berkeley, no other Morehouse man would be allowed in."[78]

The high academic and moral standards that emerged under Mays' direction prevail at Morehouse today. In contrast to the narrow specialization promoted by many college and university programs, Morehouse students must take courses in a wide variety of subjects, including philosophy and religion. Outside regular classes, they attend mandatory lectures on subjects ranging from black history to etiquette. Comprehensive exams are administered at the end of the sophomore and senior years. Before graduation, every student takes the Graduate Record Exam or its equivalent in his major field of study.

Since the retirement of Mays in 1967 and his subsequent death in 1984, one major change in the Morehouse tradition has taken place. Like many middle-class blacks of his generation, Mays held a general disdain for business as a career. In the words of one alumnus, "You always got the feeling that he didn't believe it was good enough to be just a businessman—you had to be a PhD."[79] Among ambitious young blacks, increased opportunities and the realities of the marketplace have combined to place a growing value on business education. One third of Morehouse students now major in business.

If that news might incur the displeasure of Mays, he would be gratified to learn that so many of his original aims and programs continue to flourish. For his part, recently appointed president Leroy Keith, Jr., has every intention of maintaining the Mays legacy. But first he must expand the relatively small private endowment vested to support the college. As in the past, the tightly knit clan of Morehouse alumni are expected to come through. Given their awareness of the critical need for ever more well-equipped intellectual and cultural black leaders, they may even come through with a vengeance.

Bridging Caste and Class

In his fictionalized version of an elite black college campus, film impresario Spike Lee directs an ongoing feud between the "Wannabees," well-to-do light-skinned students, and the "Jigaboos," who are poorer, darker students. Wannabees want to be—and be treated as—white, while the revolutionary Jigaboos are bent on making inroads into previously sacrosanct bastions of Wannabee privilege. Lee's rendition of "School Daze" is but a faintly disguised testimony to his own years as a Morehouse undergrad. Says Lee:

> The people with the money, most of them have light skin. They have the Porsches, the BMWs, the quote good hair unquote. The others, the kids from the rural South, have bad kinky hair. When I was in school, we saw all this going on . . . . I remember thinking, some of this stuff has to be in a movie.[80]

Morehouse had originally given Lee permission to work at the college. After a few months of uneasy alliance, however, school officials decided they didn't like what the film was saying and kicked Lee and his film crew off campus. Grumbled (then) Morehouse President Hugh Gloster about Lee's portrayal of caste differences: "This just isn't true, and it's never been true. I don't see anyone around here wanting to be white."[81] As the differences of opinion between Spike Lee and the status quo suggest, color lines remain a touchy and controversial issue for blacks. Even so, the fact that Lee and others are beginning to make taboo subjects the occasion for a public laugh by blacks about themselves demonstrates a healthy move toward self-acceptance and change.

Lee's claim that blacker blacks have a lower status and less upward mobility than lighter blacks has received historical corroboration. In 1940, Frazier spoke of the effect of differential treatment, based on color, on the personality development of black students:

> Definite evidence . . . indicates [black] teachers often discriminate against the darker pupils . . . . The great mass of low-class pupils of dark complexion are made conscious of their inferior status. Only the upper-class pupils appear to experience a full opportunity for success in school adjustments.[82]

Having said that, Frazier noted that caste differences among blacks were less strong than in times past.

In 1944, Myrdal also observed class and caste structures in the process of change. According to his analysis, two distinct systems of caste and class, one based on a stratification of whites and blacks, the other on an internal black hierarchy, had developed in American society. As opposed to class, caste was predicated on values beyond an individual's control—namely, ancestry and color—and thus arbitrarily restricted individual efforts to advance. Members of the lowest caste and class in both systems had to rely on either wealth or education for self-promotion. Because wealth, although theoretically possible to obtain, was actually a remote possibility, education, which was within reach, was the most highly sought-after socioeconomic opportunity among poor, dark, but ambitious blacks.[83]

The history of black business development provides an apt illustration of how the educational institutions available to blacks have been shaped by internal class relations, too often to the detriment of the community as a whole. Black bourgeois educational values were patterned after prevailing mores of the antebellum white South. Newly released slaves did not flock into business, but centered their ambitions on learning Greek and Latin, holding public office, or becoming preachers.[84] Blacks who had the "know-how" and skills to pursue craft-related enterprises, fields they had dominated both before and right after the Civil War, lost out to machinery and white competition during Reconstruction.[85] At either extreme of the black class system, business held very little promise of social prestige and economic reward.

A dearth of capital, business traditions, and experience, in combination with a racially obstructed marketplace, have probably meant that black more than white entrepreneurs have depended on formal education to obtain business-related skills. Pierce's path-breaking study of black business education in the 1940s bears out this observation:

> On the average, [black] enterprises operated by persons who took business educa-
> tion in college have been established longer, employ more persons and have larger
> volumes of business than those operated by persons with no business education.[86]

As we have noted, economic exigencies and new opportunities are rapidly overcoming the historical "value" deficiencies of pursuing a business career. More young blacks than ever before are enrolled in business courses or working in business-related fields. If many of them have begun as employees of established businesses, a fair number are now ready and restless to move out on their own.[87]

Although the caste system, based on ancestry and color, may be dying a slow death, class differences within the black community are alive and well and rapidly growing. As a group, blacks have attained the peculiar distinction of both outperforming and underperforming their white counterparts; in 1978, nationwide school test scores indicated more blacks than whites were performing above as well as below grade level.[88] Still, the majority of those who are making it come from that privileged, "talented tenth," coined by Du Bois. What blacks must strive for is a better balance between the relatively few overachievers at the top and the decisively large group of underachievers at the bottom.

No credible black leader believes overcoming the divisions within the black community will be an easy task. Yet perhaps more than ever before, most realize the need for blacks to unite around internally based and directed community action. As in the past, schools will provide an important locus for the new movement. The black middle class, which has traditionally dominated black education, has begun to recognize its responsibility toward the blacks it has left behind.

Some blacks believe the gains of the black middle class over the past twenty-five years have been made at the expense of the struggling masses.[89] Not all agree. Loury, for one, maintains that middle-class progress has reaped positive benefits for all blacks.[90] He points out that class, not race, has become the more important dividing line between the haves and have-nots in American society. But he also acknowledges race as a dominant factor of black life. What blacks must do now, he says, is return to a tradition of self-reliance and cooperation within their own communities. They must recognize that only by maintaining—and in some cases, rebuilding—their own institutional bases will they succeed in bridging the development gap between middle and underclass blacks.

Entrepreneurial Values and American Culture

—So this is the chemical company that's paying Hagen to dump its waste.

—Yeah, big business, fast bucks and all highly illegal.

Clip from prime-time T.V. series, "The A-Team"[91]

Business magnates, as portrayed by America's most popular fictional medium, television, frequently embody character types the average American would not want a son or daughter to emulate. "Hollywood's Favorite Heavy," a public television documentary broadcast in 1987, focuses on the extent to which Hollywood scriptwriters and producers have tarnished the image of American business. Reports host, Eli Wallach:

> On prime-time T.V., businessmen commit more crimes than any other occupational group. A majority of the heads of corporations break the law. By the age of 18, the average kid has seen businessmen on T.V. attempt over 10,000 murders.[92]

Illegal dumpers and inside traders notwithstanding, real-life businessmen rarely resort to murder to achieve their objectives.

Maligning big business has deep roots in American popular culture. Until the late 1960s, however, first the movies and then television reflected both positive and negative attitudes toward business. If Lionel Barrymore as Potter, the heartless banker of Frank Capra's classic "It's a Wonderful Life," was only too willing to turn hapless mortgagers and their families out on the street, he was effectively countered by the selfless son of a rival banker, played by Jimmy Stewart. In a dramatic confrontation between the two, the Stewart character castigates Potter with an image of his own father's altruistic way of doing business:

> Why, in the 25 years since he and Uncle Billie started this thing, he never once thought of himself. Ain't that right, Uncle Billie? He didn't save enough money to send Harry to school, let alone me. But he did help a few people get out of your slums, Mr. Potter. And what's wrong with that? Why, you're all businessmen here. Doesn't that make them better citizens, doesn't it make them better customers?[93]

For most of four decades, Hollywood heroes in the Stewart mold generally prevailed over profit-obsessed villians. Why the change? Makers of "Hollywood's Favorite Heavy" cite the Vietnam War, Watergate, and environmental crises as having shaken America's faith in its basic institutions. The antiestablishment culture that arose in the late 1960s became deeply entrenched among Hollywood and television image-makers. Television writers, in particular, have perceived the majority of their audience as simple-minded working-class people who readily accept big business, the military, and the government as common enemies. At the same time, because of increased sensitivity to ethnic stereotyping, traditional "bad guys" such as the Mafia are no longer safe targets. These two elements have combined to make "the wild bias" of Hollywood against business both expedient and profitable. As one T.V. writer put it:

> If you go into a network and say, "I want to do a show on the spiritual side of man," they will say, "Well do a documentary." Spiritual values are just not saleable, I think.[94]

A *Wall Street Journal* critic points out that "Hollywood's Favorite Heavy" fails to address several pertinent issues. For one, it omits one of the most interesting speculations from Ben Stein's book, *The View from Sunset Boulevard,* on which it draws heavily for material. Stein suggests Hollywood's antibusiness bias derives at least in part from differences in culture between "creative Hollywood types" and "the pin-stripe, ratings-obsessed businessmen" who run the networks.[95] For another, says the *Journal,* the "bad" businessmen and women of prime-time soaps have become more complex than the stock establishment "heavies" of the late 1970s and early 1980s. Most go through "bad" phases but then return to moral, upstanding behavior. Even everybody's favorite villain, Dallas oilman J.R. Ewing, has his countervailing force in "good" brother businessman, Bobby Ewing.[96] Perhaps, at the end of the Reagan era, business has returned to center stage in American melodramas *because* of its acknowledged importance to the American way of life.

Al Burton, the executive producer of Universal Studios, considered Stein's suggestion for a T.V. series with the businessman as hero. Finally, he said, the real business of business may simply be too dull for the average T.V. viewer or network producer to swallow as entertainment.[97] In *The Capitalist Revolution,* Peter Berger analyzes the issue from a scholarly perspective. He observes that, as an institutional arrangement, capitalism-qua-capitalism remains peculiarly devoid of inspirational power. The "mythic deprivation" of the capitalist paradigm contrasts sharply with the legitimating myths of Marxism, which, during the modern era, have moved entire populations to sacrificial frenzy. Explains Berger:

> The mythic deprivation of capitalism is, very likely, grounded in the fact that capitalism is an economic system and nothing else (by contrast, socialism is a comprehensive view of human society). All economic realities are essentially *prosaic,* as against the poetry that inspires, moves, and converts human minds.[98]

How then has the nonpoetic, prosaic "business of business" continued to dominate as the principal paradigm of modern economic development? Precisely, says Berger, because it works. That scientifically demonstrable fact continues to fire the engines of capitalist development around the world. For moral legitimation, capitalism allies itself with "other, noneconomic legitimating symbols" such as traditional religious systems and the ideals of progressive democracy.[99]

As we have noted, in the United States the capitalist model appears to face a high level of hostility from the popular myth-makers of television and film. But the extent to which the American public has internalized these negative images remains open to debate. To understand whether and how Americans value "the business of business" requires understanding the values of American entrepreneurs.

American Entrepreneurial Values

Perhaps the best-known popular myth of American entrepreneurship derives from the rags to riches tales of Horatio Alger. Horatio Alger was a failed mid-nineteenth century schoolteacher and preacher, who between 1850 and 1900, successfully consoled himself by producing over 100 best-selling boys' novels. The basic plot of each consists of a youth born into dire poverty who eventually makes good through a combination of luck, pluck, and innate moral superiority. According to one synopsis, the Alger tale:

> inevitably located an impoverished but ingenious lad, often an orphan, in a hostile environment, usually the city. There, possessed of those virtues which have become synonymous with the Alger myth—optimism, ambition, thrift and self-reliance—the lad matured toward an adulthood of power, affluence and respectability.[100]

At least some important elements of the Horatio Alger myth appear to hold up under scientific scrutiny. A study of "living innovating entrepreneurs" conducted in the early 1960s revealed that "many subjects . . . had experienced childhood poverty and disrupted family lives which stimulated strong motivations for personal achievement."[101] A follow-up 1978 analysis of yet another group of entrepreneurs obtained similar findings. Over half came from "disadvantaged" backgrounds in terms of relationships with their fathers and deprived economic circumstances. Sarachek, the study's author, defines "disadvantaged relationship with fathers" as various traumatic deprivations of positive father figures during childhood, whether through death, separation, rejection, or paternal incompetence. The early disadvantages of Sarachek's entrepreneurs fit many of the Horatio Alger "rags to riches" stereotypes:

> Their backgrounds involved modest income or actual poverty. The entrepreneurs typically began to work at earlier ages than other businessmen, and they frequently

benefited from association with some older male "sponsor" at some point in their careers.[102]

Nondeprived entrepreneurs of the Sarachek study displayed what many researchers have identified as the "characteristic profile" of American business elites. That is, they were "predominately native born, urban, better educated than the general population and originated disproportionately from higher economic classes."[103] According to Sarachak, they also began their entrepreneurial careers later and depended on their own fathers for sponsorship.

Whatever the relationship of real-life entrepreneurs to the Alger myth, the research of Sarachek and others reconfirms the principal values and characteristics attributed to successful entrepreneurs. Above all, successful entrepreneurs suffer from what de Charms has called "the achievement syndrome" or "the disposition to strive for satisfaction derived from success in competition with some standard of excellence."[104]

In the late 1960s McClelland and Winter refined the achievement disposition of entrepreneurs. "*n* Achievement," as they called it, involves four principal traits:

1. Moderate risk-taking as a function of skill, not chance.
2. High levels of activity and/or instrumental behavior.
3. The assumption of responsibility for personal behavior.
4. A desire for a knowledge of the results of decisions.[105]

Earlier, McClelland had identified what he considered the key psychological factors responsible for the development of *n* Achievement.[106] According to his model, family structure plays a predominant role in determining which individuals develop high degrees of *n* Achievement. Having restricted his study of *n* Achievement to males, McClelland asserted that in an entrepreneurially positive family paradigm, sons receive warmth, high standards of excellence, and low father dominance. Although the pattern may vary somewhat among different cultures, theoretically ideal mothers of high *n* Achievers provide warm, nurturing environments in which early self-reliance and problem-solving are encouraged. Ideal fathers set high standards of excellence and promote personal initiative, in large part by refraining from taking over their sons' responsibilities and decisions.

From McClelland on, applied *n* Achievement learning models have produced substantial evidence that the entrepreneurial disposition of *n* Achievers can be acquired later in life by motivated individuals. Those wishing to seed entrepreneurship among currently low performance groups should take heart from the apparent fact that entrepreneurial characteristics "are not fully innate—rather they are to an extent acquirable, learnable and teachable."[107]

McClelland paved the way for subsequent attempts to create workable models for stimulating entrepreneurial behavior. Many, including McClelland, concentrated on factors that stimulate *n* Achievement and applied the results toward improving individual entrepreneurial performance. Achievement motivation added a significant new psychological dimension to the exclusively managerial and business skills approach of earlier programs.

Achievement motivators proposed to alter typical "thought patterns" of individuals toward business. Instead of perceiving success in business as controlled by fate or chance, individuals learned to see their business successes as within their own control, as indeed dependent upon their own abilities and behaviors. In practical terms, program evaluators found that as a result of their motivation training, recipients worked longer, planned more, hired more employees, and participated in a wider range of business activities.[108]

The most successful entrepreneurial training programs have combined achievement motivation with management development (skills) training. Timmons and Durand, among others, maintain that only a combination of motivation and skills training can sustain long-term positive changes in entrepreneurial performance.[109]

In addition to discovering how *n* Achievement operates together with practical skills and experience, researchers have also analyzed the learning styles of successful entrepreneurs. A 1987 study by Bailey found that "high-yield" entrepreneurs were more systematic and scientific in acquiring knowledge than previously supposed. "Low performers," on the other hand, tended to use ad hoc and intuitive learning methods. As a group, high-performing entrepreneurs exhibited abstract rather than concrete thought patterns, used every situation to seek new opportunities, and viewed education and training as important contributors to their success in business.[110]

Observations such as these suggest that the entrepreneurial drive to succeed rests upon a strongly pragmatic set of personal values. Using the Personal Values Questionnaire (PVQ) developed by England, Watson and Simpson conducted a comparative study of the values of black and white owner–managers of small American businesses. The PVQ permits two types of analyses—a "general personal values orientation" to determine whether respondents fall into pragmatic (successful), ethical–moral (right) or affect (pleasant) categories—and a "by-concept analysis" to discover the likelihood of stated values translating into behavior. The forty black and forty white owner–managers studied shared thirty-one out of sixty-six pragmatic, operationally likely value concepts. They differed most over values that both groups intended but did not consider imperative for success, and over those rated by both as unimportant. Thus black and white owner–managers ranked competition, aggressiveness, profit maximization, and organizational efficiency as highly important operative values, while concepts such as liberal-ism, compromise, compassion, and conformity received different ratings from the two groups, but were not likely to be acted on by either.[111]

If businessmen, regardless of race, tend to perceive and act on shared values, American public opinion of entrepreneurial values is less straightforward. Over the past several years, the Roper organization has tracked American attitudes toward business. Although only seven in ten Americans express a moderately favorable opinion of large businesses—an improvement from a decade ago—nine out of ten Americans view small businesses favorably. Furthermore, while fully one quarter of the public has an unfavorable view of large businesses, only 4 percent rate small businesses unfavorably.[112]

O'Neill has looked closely at the image problems facing large American companies. "Going beyond," he says, "the overall view of the large corporate forest and taking a look at some of the individual trees, some flaws emerge."[113] In the first place, Americans rank corporations by type more strongly than by size. The tobacco and liquor industries receive consistently low ratings, while those for retail chains, computers, and food processing are consistently high. Moreover, the public believes too few large companies control major segments of the country's economy, a conviction probably strengthened by the recent rash of corporate mergers. Opinion polls also show that Americans have little confidence in the ethics of big companies and their leaders. In order of trust and confidence, among seventeen American institutions posed, large companies came in twelfth, and among eighteen American occupations, corporate executives ranked fifteenth in ethical, moral behavior. The public believes corporations routinely rake in huge profits at the expense of both individual workers and national well-being. Few Americans seem to understand the relationship between company profits and economic growth; for example, most say profits should go to increase worker salaries and benefits rather than to pay dividends to stockholders. Bigness, impersonality, ruthlessness, and greed combine to form an image of big business as at best insensitive and at worst dangerous in the eyes of many Americans. Their negative perceptions have been reinforced by the apparent antibusiness bias of the American media.[114]

Jackson's 1986 study of American entrepreneurial and small-business culture reveals an interesting anomaly between American perceptions of big and small businesses and how business size actually affects national economic development. Consistent with the Roper data, Jackson's figures show Americans view small businesses much more favorably than big corporations. Nevertheless, they continue to believe that big companies provide more economic opportunities than do small entrepreneurial types:

> Thus, contrary to much of the empirical evidence provided by Birch and others, the public rates entrepreneurs as being least important in creating economic oppor-

tunity—and perceives large companies as being the most important.[115]

Despite the bad press and some persistent negative images, businesses, large and small, retain a high level of support from the American public. If Americans want big companies better regulated in some cases and more socially responsible in others, the vast majority still consider business a vital, even progressive institutional force. A recent Roper poll found that nine out of ten concur with the idea that "large companies are essential for the nation's growth and expansion."[116] From a purely economic standpoint, Americans view business as an essential provider of wealth and jobs. But they also see business ownership as a way to move up socially, and as an important means for people to gain greater control over their lives. Many appear to have the basic risk-taking propensities necessary to start a business, and most would approve sons or daughters taking on an entrepreneurial challenge.[117]

The social values Americans attribute to business ownership may be of particular importance in garnering support for future entrepreneurial initiatives. As Jackson observes, "People are far more receptive to public policies seen as promoting social values than they are to policies perceived primarily as aid for particular economic interests."[118] In addition to increasing the public's general understanding of and respect for the real "business of business," the task remains to inform Americans of the vital role played by entrepreneurial enterprises in the economy.

Black Entrepreneurial Values

> In stressing the relationship between individual and group advancement, contemporary black businessmen are not only challenging "the myth of Negro business" but also, in some sense, the larger myth of American individualism.[119]

Although McClelland demonstrated society and culture as causes of entrepreneurial behavior, he restricted his examination of effects to individual psychology. Together, increased motivation and a better understanding of business mechanics have helped individuals succeed as entrepreneurs. But studies of n Achievement and entrepreneurial techniques have done little to explain how entrepreneurs, as a group, influence and are influenced by society and culture. Anthropologists Greenfield and Strickon caution that:

> Studying entrepreneurs isolated from their social contexts is like studying animals independent of their natural habitats, an activity not without some value, but one

that misses the complex interaction upon which the evolutionary process depends.[120]

Here we are specifically concerned with the interaction between black entrepreneurs, as a group, and the larger evolutionary processes of social and economic development.

An early proponent of the "social group" school of minority business development, E. Franklin Frazier hypothesized blacks lacked "a tradition of enterprise." In the late 1950s he stated, "Although no systematic study has been undertaken of the social causes of failure of the Negro to achieve success as a businessman, it appears from what we know of the social and cultural history of the Negro that it is the result largely of the lack of traditions in the field of business enterprise."[121] Even without systematic analysis, Frazier's sweeping generalization that black Americans entirely lacked experience in "buying and selling" bears no resemblance to reality. From their arrival, black Americans participated, as buyers and sellers, in the larger business culture. Frazier might more appropriately have proposed the degree to which black Americas have participated as businessmen in the American economy as well as the kind of business traditions they have developed.

Myrdal's monumental 1948 study, *The American Dilemma,* devoted scant pages to black enterprise. His brief summary is self-explanatory: Other than as undertakers and life-insurers, blacks retained a small and tenuous hold in the American business community. Whereas black undertakers and insurers benefited from enforced segregation, black bankers, retailers, and the handful of black manufacturers remained crippled by their exclusive reliance on impoverished ghetto clienteles. Myrdal further noted that what he called "shady occupations"—from relatively innocent numbers games to small-time pimping and bootlegging to big-scale racketeering—siphoned off an undetermined amount of black entrepreneurial energy.[122]

His 1940s description of black underlife bears a frightening resemblance to the conditions portrayed as commonplace among today's underclass. Underprivileged blacks then, as now, experience exclusion, isolation, and a fatalistic sense of not belonging to the larger society. High unemployment strengthened antisocial tendencies in neighborhoods bereft of strong black leadership and positive community endeavors. Crime thrived where social disorganization and lawlessness offered ideal locales for the well-organized and highly profitable activities of illicit entrepreneurs.[123]

Even though he drew, in painstaking detail, the many social, political, and economic distinctions among them, Myrdal referred to American blacks as members of a distinct community. His view of what he considered basic black institutions and cultural patterns was fundamentally negative:

In practically all its divergences, American Negro culture is not something independent of general American culture. It is a distorted development, or a pathological condition, of the general American culture.[124]

Thus black family instability, inadequate black education, the "emotional-
ism" of the black church, and the "excessive cultivation of the arts" (to the
exclusion of other fields, such as business) all produced evidence of the social
pathology of black culture. Deficient black institutions, concluded Myrdal,
resulted from a racially imposed and inferior caste status.[125]

Myrdal considered black enterprise yet another flawed institutional mirror
of the larger American culture. In his brief discussion of them, the black
businesses Myrdal spoke of were either illegal, small and struggling, or, as in
the case of insurance and undertaking, designed to fleece the very people they
served.

As noted in our discussion of the black family, Myrdal's depiction of black
culture as perverse and pathological has been shared by other prominent
scholars, including Frazier and Moynihan. While it may have been easier in
the pre-civil-rights era to see the black community as an indivisible entity and
black culture as perverse, then as now such interpretations fail to adequately
address the reality of black diversity.

One of the most difficult concepts an observer of black American culture
must grapple with is the extent to which *a* black American community can be
said to exist. Again, as we have observed, although blacks do share some
distinct patterns as an American subculture, they are also highly differenti-
ated. If not already in 1948, in 1988 many black Americans are more distinct
from one another then they are from other American subgroups. In discussing
entrepreneurial values and culture, three important cleavages to consider are
class, occupation, and country of origin. Frequently cutting across one another, these lines of segmentation draw sharp entrepreneurial distinctions between members of various black groups.

Class Differences

Class is a major determinant of black entrepreneurial behavior. By status, if
not by income, irregular and illicit entrepreneurs of the ghetto occupy the
bottom rung of the ladder. According to Bates and Fusfeld, ghetto irregulars
provide unconventional, partly legitimate services—such as car repairs, welfare information, and soul food—that would otherwise be too expensive or
unobtainable in the ghetto. In positive terms, irregular entrepreneurship ac-
crues significant income and provides important services to ghetto residents.
It also creates an outlet for entrepreneurial abilities among people generally
considered low in entrepreneurial initiative and skills. Negatively, the flexi-

ble, informal nature of the irregular economy may lead to lax, irregular work habits that are incompatible with the standards of the regular economy.[126]

The rewards and costs of criminal entrepreneurship are considerably higher. Bates and Fusfeld divide the bulk of criminal ghetto business activities into four areas: numbers, loan-sharking, drugs, and prostitution. The numbers racket and loan-sharking are widespread and closely linked. Profits from policy (numbers) games fund a banking system for loan sharks who charge clients up to 20 percent weekly interest. In 1968, 75 percent of all teen and adult slum residents of New York City spent $3 to $5 a week on the numbers game; $150 million annually in Harlem, the South Bronx, and Bedford-Stuyvesant.[127]

Even twenty years ago, when the narcotics industry was much smaller than other areas of the ghetto crime economy, it was also much more lucrative. In 1968, revenues from the narcotics business in the three major ghettos of New York City totalled between $120 and $250 million.[128]

The criminal landscape of American inner cities has changed dramatically since 1968. Narcotics far exceeds numbers and loan-sharking as the principle illicit ghetto industry. A comparison of New York City Police Department arrest records for the crimes of drugs, gambling, robbery, and prostitution in 1968 and 1987 reflects the enormity of the changes.[129]

	1968	1987
Drugs	22,428	79,189
Gambling	13,292	5,127
Robbery	9,420	23,572
Prostitution	7,094	15,033

As loan-sharking is linked to the numbers racket so prostitution and theft have traditionally been tied to the narcotics trade. Girls and women sell themselves as prostitutes, and boys and men steal to support expensive drug habits.[130]

Crack, a distilled and highly addictive form of cocaine that appeared on the drug scene only four years ago, has become the fastest growing segment of the underground economy. In 1987 the NYPD and other New York City law enforcement agencies seized 3,500 pounds of cocaine, including crack cocaine. In 1988 the same groups confiscated 10,350 pounds of cocaine and crack in New York City.[131] One estimate places the total revenue from 1988 illicit narcotics sales in New York City at between $1 and $2 billion.[132]

Those in control of today's drug culture are well armed and routinely violent. Palley and Robinson report that "whereas murder in a holdup was frowned on and avoided by participants in ghetto criminality thirty years ago, today 'murder is in style.' "[133] If most of the profits of illegal entrepreneurship end up outside the ghetto, the vast majority of damage occurs within. In addition to skyrocketing homicide rates—more black males were murdered in 1977 than died in nine years of fighting in Vietnam—the high-stakes crime culture has created a powerful lure for many of the disaffected and otherwise unoccupied ghetto young.[134]

For obvious reasons, reliable data on irregular and illegal ghetto businesses are difficult to obtain, and it is therefore impossible to give exact figures for their dollar contribution to black entrepreneurship. Suffice it to say that the amount has long been considerable and in many locations appears to be rapidly growing.

The bulk of the black entrepreneurial middle class has traditionally consisted of small retail services—beauty shops, restaurants, grocery stores—located in black neighborhoods. Over the past several decades, their numbers have steadily declined. At the same time, so-called "emerging" black entrepreneurs have risen to replace them. If the overall rate of black entrepreneurship has increased only modestly over the past fifteen years, a significant number of blacks have begun to do business on a wholly different scale. Emerging lines of business in areas such as professional and business services, finance, and manufacturing hold tremendous promise for black business development. Most of the traditional middle-class black businesses profiled by Myrdal were small establishments started by people with little income or education. These kinds of black enterprises were and are prone to failure. Emerging businesses, whose proprietors have capital or access to it, good educations, and mainstream business experience, create larger firms that are much more likely to stay in business, grow, and create new jobs.[135] As important as the evolution in quantity and type of middle-class black entrepreneurs are the changes in underlying entrepreneurial values. Emerging entrepreneurs take greater risks than their predecessors but they also yield greater returns. They are more ambitious and willing to invest new resources in their businesses. They are pragmatic in assessing their progress and able to set realistic goals for reaching long-term objectives.[136] Success breeds success. As more black businesses prosper, more talented young blacks will be drawn to entrepreneurial careers. And as black entrepreneurship expands, so will the independent financial base and other wealth-producing resources of black communities.

The positive relationship between the success of black middle-class entrepreneurs and the economic development of black Americans as a group plays a central role in our argument. One way to look at this connection involves comparing, once again, the personal value profiles of black and white entrepreneurs. While it is true that black and white business owners appear to share a majority of basic, operative values, the few in which they differ may also be significant. In the Watson and Simpson study, black owner–managers place employees and blue-collar workers at the top of value concepts they consider highly important and vital to their success. White owner–managers, on the other hand, rate employees as an intended value, but not one vital to success. Furthermore, they rank blue-collar workers as of average importance with little influence over their activities. To white owners, organizational stability and obedience take precedence, whereas black owners, who intend organizational stability, are not inclined to act on it, and consider obedience a value concept of average importance and low behavioral relevance.[137] These differences suggest key differences in the business activities of black and white entrepreneurs. In fact, black firms are more likely to create jobs for black blue-collar workers in or near black neighborhoods.[138] Black businessmen also evidence a strong commitment to the progress of all black Americans. Observes Boneparth:

> Implicit in their attitudes is the belief that individual success in business cannot be meaningful outside a context of group advancement, both because individual business successes can do little to ameliorate group conditions and because an inferior group status carries with it built-in limitations for individual success.[139]

Perhaps more than any other occupational group, black entrepreneurs have a vested interest in developing the economic and social bases of their communities.

From a negative perspective, Collins maintains that black middle-class businesses remain overwhelmingly dependent on a segregated black market, in combination with public subsidies and government-mandated contracts, for their advancement. She maintains that the entire black middle class has progressed, socially and economically, on a fragile political base that has seriously eroded since the early 1980s. Asserts Collins, "The lack of a large business and capital base means that middle-class blacks have a limited ability to form self-help groups."[140] While agreeing with her analysis of the tenuous political base of the black middle class, we emphatically disagree with her conclusions as to the connection between black businesses and self-help groups. We would argue, on the contrary, that self-help groups have most often been formed to overcome the individual weaknesses and deprivations suffered by members of particular groups. From informal savings networks to labor unions, America's underprivileged and set-upon have forged communal ties to take on their economic crises with united strength.

Occupational Differences

As with black and white owner–manager values, the view of black Americans, as a group, toward entrepreneurship is similar to that of white Americans. Both groups give favorable ratings to entrepreneurs and rank big companies as more important than small businesses to the economy. However, blacks give small businesses a much lower ranking than do whites, and significantly higher marks to union leaders, executives, and federal workers. These findings are consistent with the large percentage of black workers in blue-collar and government jobs. As a group, public-sector workers are less likely than others to see business ownership as a way for people to improve themselves.[141]

Another American occupational group exhibiting strongly negative entrepreneurial values is educators. Not only do educators, black and white, appear more risk-averse in that they are less likely to use savings or borrow money to start a business, but they are also more inclined to see starting a business as difficult, especially for blacks.[142] The negative entrepreneurial propensities of many people who staff America's educational institutions may have serious implications for black entrepreneurship. A large number of black professionals are educators, and thus may have a disproportionately negative influence over the growth of more positive entrepreneurial values in black communities, particularly in black children and youth. Black or white, the dim view taken by American educators toward entrepreneurship, and especially toward the prospects for black entrepreneurship, may reinforce or inculcate damaging beliefs among blacks about their entrepreneurial abilities.

Country of Origin Differences

Black Americans also evince distinct cleavages along intra-ethnic lines, particularly by country of origin. Caribbean blacks have long filled important political and economic leadership roles in the United States, from Marcus Garvey to Stokely Carmicheal to former Brooklyn congressional representative Shirley Chisholm. Recent waves of immigrants from Jamaica, Haiti, Guyana, and Panama, as well as from a number of African countries, strongly challenge many of the entrepreneurial stereotypes attached to native-born American blacks. Reports Jim Sleeper in an article for the *Washington Post:*

> Committed to professional and entrepreneurial mobility in the liberal pluralist framework, many Caribbean blacks are imitating white immigrant models by emphasizing ethnic gains over broad social reforms meant to redress old wrongs. As their ethnic activism departs from traditions of the civil rights and anti-poverty movements of the '60s, it blunts native American black leaders' claims to speak for a "unified black agenda" based in past struggles for welfare rights and community controls of schools and poverty programs.[143]

As do their counterparts from Asia and Latin America, the new entrepreneurially inclined black immigrants depend heavily upon their families and communities for support. Like countless generations of ethnic groups before them, they tap their personal networks for money, advice, moral support, and free labor. Together, they have added thousands of new small businesses to inner-city American neighborhoods.[144]

While the entrepreneurial successes of Caribbean and African blacks have already had a distinctly positive effect on the black business climate, differences between the entrepreneurial values of the new immigrants and native-born blacks are not likely to disappear soon. When challenged as to why they, too, do not find small businesses a meaningful route to upward mobility, many native black Americans quickly point out that they have been here as long as most white Americans. They are far less inclined than immigrants to do what they consider "the dirty work" of making it up the ladder through "mom and pop" type businesses. Among both lower and middle-class native blacks runs a uniform perception of blacks as less able in business, and a strong conviction that although black individuals may occasionally succeed as entrepreneurs, blacks as a group have few prospects for success in business. Many lack the step-by-step concrete understanding of how entrepreneurial goals are achieved.

From without, the entrepreneurial values of native-born blacks have been further assailed by government programs that have decreased, rather than increased, their personal initiative and sense of self-worth. The American private sector has remained generally indifferent and frequently hostile to the specific needs of black businesses. Finally, and not insignificantly, instead of challenging the extant legal and social barriers to black economic development, the majority of black politicans continue pouring water over the ashes of long dead civil rights fires. If many of the perceived barriers to the advancement of black Americans have already been eliminated, others, never perceived, have yet to be addressed. To do so, more blacks must first become aware of the real remaining barriers, among which are their lingering misperceptions about the value of and their own capacity to attain entrepreneurial success.

Entrepreneurial Values of Black Youth

A recent episode of Berke Breathed's "Bloom County" cartoon strip features a besuited social worker type, pencil and pad in hand, accosting an inner-city black youth street vendor. Muffled by a head scarf, he stands behind a small kiosk with a sign reading: "Illegal Cat Sweat Scalp Tonic: $12,000 a Bottle."

"Hello young underclass youth," she begins, "I'm from the government. We'd like to know why you prefer a life of crime making $20,000 a week selling scalp tonic when you could be working honestly at McDonald's."

"Allergic to french fries," he replies.

"Oh!" she chirps, "we have a program for that!"[145]

The illegal tonic sold by the underclass youth comes from a formula devised by Bloom County regular and black scientific boy wonder, Oliver. Oliver's "hair-raising" experiments periodically panic and bewilder his respectable middle-class father. Together, Oliver and the hair tonic salesman capture the widening gulf between ghetto underachievers and upwardly mobile overachievers. At the same time, their connection connotes the continued social and economic interdependence of middle and underclass blacks. What is missing in the comic strip scenario, and too often in reality, is a pragmatic, hard-headed black entrepreneur to link the resources of the two extremes in legitimate social and economic enterprises.

The real entrepreneurial proclivities of black youth have received little systematic attention. Most of the existing evidence must be inferred from evaluations of government programs and studies concerning the psychosocial development of black children.

For example, a recent evaluation of government job-training programs for black youth unearthed several interesting clues.[146] It found that black youth from families on welfare did far worse in the job market that those from nonwelfare families with similar incomes. Black youth in public housing do less well than those in private housing. Black youth who have other working family members are more likely to be employed. Evaluators conclude that welfare households and the attendant atmosphere of low-income public housing "exacerbate" the problem of high black youth unemployment, either because of their effect on contacts and information or general attitudes toward work. The degree to which crime appears a more attractive alternative than legitimate employment depends upon perceptions of risk:

> The youths who felt that the chances to make money illegally were pretty good and who saw little chance of being penalized tended to commit crimes. More often than not, they tended not to be employed, not to be in school, not to spend their time productively, and to be involved with drugs or gangs. Furthermore, when they held jobs, those engaged in criminal activity tended to perform poorly on the job.[147]

A number of psychological studies help fill in the background on black adolescent behavior. In striking contrast to white family patterns, a consistent finding about black children is that their mothers, not their fathers, most often play the role of significant other in motivating them to succeed.[148] Significant others, by definition, are the people who influence youngsters to acquire the attitudes, values, and behaviors they need to function competently.[149] Black fathers more often contribute to their children's welfare by taking care of their physical needs, providing them with male sex role models, and helping them adapt to the larger world.[150] Male children from low-income black families are particularly dependent on their mothers for positive support:

> In a study of factors which aided lower class minority males in achieving social mobility and escaping the ghetto, Ross and Glaser found that each person studied had an important significant other who set standards and guided his aspirations. In most instances, this was his mother.[151]

Occupationally, black male youngsters look first for inspiration to people holding the jobs they want and second to their mothers.[152]

Between the ages of ten and eleven, many low-income black males are also highly susceptible to the influence of their peers. According to Perkins, "It is this group which seems most influenced by peer group and 'street culture' to commit themselves to unacceptable approaches to obtaining success."[153] At worst, the standards of behavior adopted by streetwise children contradict and undermine the value preferences of their parents and surrounding communities.

Black children at all economic levels have in common a strong mother influence in shaping their life goals. Compared with whites, they tend to choose careers that appear open rather than those they would prefer.[154] Whether as residents of inner-city ghettos or largely black suburban neighborhoods they frequently experience a lack of recognition and respect from the wider society. When blocked from participating in cultural traditions with which they can identify, black children frequently adapt by accepting the limitations of existing institutions and finding creative outlets elsewhere.[155] Depending on the opportunity structures in their immediate environment, those choices may be healthy or perverse.

Some of their most negative early social encounters occur at school. Fordham and Ogbu note that black students have enormous ambivalence about doing well academically, in the first place because they are expected to do less well and in the second because they have internalized the expectations.[156] A common "defensive" reaction among black students is to gang up on kids who get good grades and follow the rules. As a result, "not acting white" by "not succeeding in school" has become the norm in many schools with large black populations. Abdul-Jabbar recalls his first days at school:

> It was my first time away from home, my first experience in an all-black situation and I found myself being punished for doing everything I'd ever been taught was right. I got all A's and was hated for it; I spoke correctly and was called a punk. I had to learn a new language simply to be able to deal with the threats. I had good manners and was a good little boy and paid for it with my hide.[157]

A Survey of Black Youth Attitudes

The state of black youth motivations to succeed, entrepreneurially or otherwise, is of critical importance to our predictions as to the future of black entrepreneurship. Given the dearth of first hand information on the subject, we decided to conduct a survey of black youth attitudes. Our sample consisted of 104 black youths between the ages of fifteen and twenty-five from two lower and two middle-class neighborhoods in Baltimore and Washington, D.C. The sample size and brevity of the interview process preclude taking our findings as general truth. However, the information we obtained does provide some useful, if preliminary, insights into the entrepreneurial values and expectations of individual young blacks in four distinct urban neighborhoods.

Description of Communities

The neighborhoods targeted for research were selected on the basis of census data as well as suggestions from city planning officials and community organizations. Each exhibited certain characteristics that we believed would offer the most valuable contribution to our study.

Riggs Park. Riggs Park is a middle-class neighborhood located in the northeast section of Washington, D.C. Situated within the city's largest industrial corridor and in close proximity to Fort Totten, this community of detached and semidetached homes has become a stable, middle-income residential area. Much of its affluence can be attributed to the growth of surrounding industries during the 1970s.

New Northwood. Also a middle-income area, the Baltimore neighborhood of New Northwood shares many physical characteristics with its Washington, D.C. counterpart. Most of the 5,600 residents are black. To the outside observer, it appears a picture-perfect neighborhood of manicured lawns and tidy single-family dwellings.

Kenilworth Parkside. As the 1980s began, occupants of Kenilworth Parkside, a low-income public housing development in northeast Washington, D.C., were suffocating under the combined pressures of poverty, crime, drug abuse, and the highest level of unemployment in the District. Neglected by managers, the 2,900 residents of the twenty-five-year-old project had been left without heat or hot water for three years. In 1982, fed up with the condition of their community, a group of tenants successfully organized to take over the management of the project.

Efforts by the residential management corporation have made substantial progress in ameliorating the lives of community residents. In 1982, three fourths of Kenilworth Parkside residents were on welfare. Today that figure has dropped to less than half. Teen pregnancies are also down. With the help of a community program called "College Here We Come," many youngsters have been able to attend college. Nevertheless, the high incidence of female-headed households remains a major problem. In a 184-unit complex, 75 percent of the households are headed by women. Moreover, 85 percent of the community's residents are under eighteen years of age, while about 5 percent are over sixty-four, leaving a narrow margin of working-age members to sustain the community.

Park Heights. Park Heights, an economically depressed, low-income area in northwest Baltimore, has long been plagued with sanitation problems and high crime rates. In 1980, the unemployment rate for the 55,000 residents of greater Park Heights reached 35 percent. It is now the city's largest urban renewal area. The community receives much of its aid through the Park Heights Community Corporation, a city-sponsored agency providing housing advice and other social services.

Interviewer Comments

Our ten interviewers were themselves fifteen through twenty-five-year-old residents of the four target neighborhoods. They were selected with the help of community leaders on the basis of their community activities, communication skills, interest in the project, and demonstrated self-motivation. Over a two-day period in mid-July 1987, they spent an average of twelve hours apiece administering our survey among young residents in their neighborhoods.

The weekend before the survey was taken, we conducted a training session for the interviewers. We began by giving them basic information about how to find respondents and present questions. In addition to recording factual responses, we asked them to observe people's emotional reactions to the survey. When they turned in their questionnaires, they were asked to complete a form about and then discuss their impressions of the survey. The following summary combines information from both sources.

The two interviewers from Kenilworth Parkside expressed disappointment but not surprise at the answers they received, especially concerning future goals and aspirations. One young woman, a twenty-three-year-old Virginia State University senior, lamented, "There are too many black people who don't want to do anything with their lives; they don't want to go to college." The other interviewer, also a Virginia State student, said the survey results were not surprising:

> When you ask them what they want to do, you find out that they don't want to do anything. They tell me, "My mother didn't do anything, my brother didn't do

anything, so why should I?"

The second interviewer went on to explain what she saw happening to many of the young people in her community:

> The younger people of the community need someone to motivate their parents as well as themselves; so they can know what they want to do with life in the future, instead of selling drugs. They are too materialistic. All they want to do is have gold jewelry and a big car. . . . They just don't know what to do.

A lengthy discussion with a sixteen-year-old interviewer in Park Heights, the other low-income neighborhood, provided a good deal of insight into her own feelings about life as well as her impressions of her peers. She pointed out several neighborhood youngsters in her age group and analyzed their fortunes:

> See that girl over there. We went to school together, and now she is pregnant with her third child. I'm glad I don't have any children.

According to this summer camp counselor and high academic achiever, too many of her peers are in the same situation and seem to have no ambition. A supportive and stable family life appears to have contributed substantially to her own very different outlook on life.

An eighteen-year-old female interviewer in middle-class New Northwood said:

> I found the questions interesting, and the answers received were a revelation about what is really going on in the heads of young people. I know this survey made me think and take notice of my life and where it's going.

A freshman at Morgan State University, she was stunned by the number of interviewees who were interested in using drugs or selling them to make money, as well as by the fact that many of them had made no concrete plans for the future. A male interviewer from the same middle-class neighborhood complained that survey questions were too difficult for many young people to understand.

What We Found

To analyze results, we clustered survey responses into seven topics: background and personal information, goals and aspirations, work experience, financial practices, starting a business, awareness of and attitudes toward government-sponsored business programs, and finally, experiences with and attitudes toward black and other businesses.

Background and Personal Information. Reponses to "Who was the most important influence over the kinds of jobs you expect to have?" indicate that black parents and other family members remain the strongest role models for the youth we surveyed. More than half attributed their job aspirations to parents, while another third listed grandparents, siblings, aunts, and uncles. As had their parents and relatives, the great majority intended to make a living in nonprofessional service work. Although some parents were doctors, nurses, or teachers, most were employed in blue- or white-collar service jobs: postal workers, special police, custodians, steelworkers, secretaries, and bank clerks.

Most wanted to return to or continue their educations, yet very few were currently enrolled in college and only four had completed college degrees. The largest single group of nine who did not plan to continue their educations beyond high school came from Kenilworth Parkside, the low-income public housing project in the District of Columbia.

A small number, all of them in the twenty to twenty-five age group, were married at the time of the survey: none from Riggs Park, four from New Northwood, two from Kenilworth Parkside, and three from Park Heights. Almost all of those not yet married planned to in the future. While only one Riggs Park resident had children, a total of fifteen residents from the other three neighborhoods were already parents. When asked what they wanted their children to do for a living, their most common responses, in order of frequency, were:

- Whatever makes them happy.
- Doctors/lawyers.
- Something successful.

On the whole, parents and would-be parents displayed a nonchalant attitude about the kind of life they expected to provide for themselves and their children. Few had more than a vague notion of what they wanted for their children or how they planned to support their goals.

Goals and aspirations. One of the main purposes of our survey was to gain information about the future plans, hopes, aspirations, dreams, and goals of black youth. We began by posing the following question: "All of us want certain things out of life. When you think about the purpose of your life, your goals and what makes you happy, what would you like to be doing in ten years?" Young people under age twenty were asked to comment on a five rather than a ten-year span.

Answers revealed interesting differences as well as similarities among the four neighborhoods. Similarities, in particular, seemed to cut across class lines, while differences appeared to be a strong function of both family income and geographic location.

Washington, D.C.'s Riggs Park residents commonly expected to join the ranks of young black urban professions. As "buppies," the black equivalent of yuppies, they looked forward to having a family and home and the good jobs certain to follow graduate, law, or medical school. Several mentioned owning their own businesses, but for most, starting an enterprise was way down on the list of desirable futures.

By contrast, Baltimore's New Northwood group, also from middle-income families, placed owning a business or working in a skilled trade at the top of their future priorities. They most frequently mentioned trucking, carpentry, mechanics shops, or the beauty business as potential lines of work. The majority expected to have homes and families and to work steadily and hard to support them. Nevertheless, more than a few looked forward to being "laid back" in condominiums, or being rich enough not to have to work at all. Many considered their own chances for success greater than that of their peers.

The proportion of young people who wanted to own their own businesses was much higher in the two lower-income neighborhoods. Eight Kenilworth Parkside residents rated it their top future priority, while twelve focused on completing their educations. In all but one case, "finishing education" meant receiving a high-school diploma. About one third wanted to work for someone else after finishing high school. A handful hoped to be rich, laid back, and not working. Only two had no ideas about the future.

In Park Heights, fifteen out of twenty-five interviewees wanted to run a business. Four placed a family and home in first place and still others mentioned having good jobs, or again, being rich, living the good life, and not having to work for a living.

We also asked what most of their friends would be doing in five or ten years. By far the most consistently optimistic responses came from Riggs Park, where almost all expected their friends to finish college, marry, and obtain secure, well-paying jobs. Although a majority in New Northwood thought their friends would be settling down into jobs and families, three anticipated they would be unemployed and two that they would be dead from drugs or alcohol. Responses from Kenilworth Parkside and Park Heights were even more disturbing—almost one third from each of these lower-income areas predicted friends would be pregnant and on welfare, unemployed, on drugs, in jail, or dead. In the stark words of one teenage girl from Park Heights, "The girls will be on welfare and the boys will be in jail." Many could not picture their friends' futures and simply answered "don't know." Several other answers ranged from the wildly optimistic, "rich and successful basketball player," to the cautiously hopeful, "trying to finish college or get a job." Less than half had a sure sense that their friends would enter adult life with intact educations, families, and jobs.

Work Experience. We designed a series of questions revolving around the question of work-related experiences. The overwhelming majority of teens and young adults we surveyed had had a job at one time or another. From 100 percent of Riggs Park to close to 90 percent of New Northwood and Park Heights to a noticeably lower 67 percent of Kenilworth Parkside residents, part- or full-time employment records were the norm. Well over half of those who had worked were employed in full-time positions. The length of time jobs were held varied considerably, with the older age group dominating the category of working a year or more.

Recent employment histories were not encouraging. In Riggs Park a majority of resident still held jobs, but in New Northwood, Park Heights, and Kenilworth Parkside almost two thirds of those surveyed were currently unemployed.

Across all four areas, 12 percent said they had worked for relatives while another 16 percent had worked for friends. Most of the jobs were located outside the neighborhoods; only a fraction of Riggs Park, New Northwood, and Kenilworth Parkside residents reported working close to home. Lower-income Park Heights in Baltimore was the exception, with ten residents working in the neighborhood; even here, however, more than half of all workers commuted elsewhere. A slight majority worked for organizations or businesses with between eleven and twenty-five employees.

Financial Practices. In order to determine whether or how our sample might finance a business, we asked a number of questions about borrowing money.

Less than one fifth of the youth in our survey had ever borrowed money; five from each of the Riggs Park, New Northwood, and Park Heights areas and two from Kenilworth Parkside. Thirteen out of the seventeen were between twenty and twenty-five years old. More than half had borrowed from a bank or a credit card and the rest from family or friends.

The most common reason given for borrowing money was to provide transportation to and from work, although school tuition and car purchases were also frequently mentioned. Other included paying for clothes, buying a keyboard, and making up for a shortage of cash. All those who had borrowed used the money for the purpose originally intended. Only one Riggs Park resident, who had borrowed money for a car, had not yet paid back the full amount of the loan.

Most of those who had borrowed said they would borrow again. Their reasons varied, but generally included covering such long-term purchases as houses or cars as well as seeing themselves or their families through an unexpected crisis. Those who did not want to borrow again either disliked the pressure of having to pay back a loan or preferred the greater independence of paying for items by themselves.

Among those who had never borrowed, a majority would borrow for some purposes. As with the experienced borrowers, most gave transportation as their number one reason. In three out of four neighborhoods, well over half indicated they would borrow for work-related reasons; from buying a car to get to work, to paying for an education to get a job, to opening a business. By contrast, nearly two thirds of Kenilworth Parkside residents stated they would not borrow for any work-related reason. Of the one third who would, most would use the money for transportation, school loans, or food. Only two said they would use loans to finance their own businesses.

New Northwood and Kenilworth Parkside residents were more inclined to borrow from friends or relatives, while Riggs Park and Park Heights inhabitants considered banks and credit cards the more likely loan sources.

Starting a Business. As opposed to what they anticipated doing, a majority of young people from all four neighborhoods thought they would like to own and run businesses. Park Heights, which also had the highest number of individuals who expected to become entrepreneurs, came in first with close to 80 percent positive. Two thirds of New Northwood and Riggs Park residents agreed, while those in Kenilworth Parkside who said "yes" to business ownership represented exactly 50 percent. Given the opportunity to indicate uncertainty, 35 percent of Kenilworth Parkside residents—at least twice as many as in any of the other neighborhoods—said they did not know whether they would want to run their own businesses.

Residents of New Northwood, Kenilworth Parkside, and Park Heights decidedly preferred businesses in the small retail services category—clothing stores, beauty salons, barber and manicure shops—all of which are traditional lines of black business. By contrast, Riggs Park opted for real estate firms, restaurants, law firms, and sporting goods stores. If two of these—restaurants and sporting goods stores—could generally be characterized as small retail services, they have a greater likelihood than clothing or beauty and barber shops for expanding into larger-scale enterprises.

Asked who they would go to for advice or where they would go for information on how to start a business, families were once again the most frequently cited resource. School or college teachers were also mentioned. In Kenilworth Parkside, where the tenant management organization has received widespread recognition for its support of small-scale enterprise development, several residents referred to its president as an important source of business information. Finally, the Better Business Bureau, government job services office, libraries, and black or small business associations were variously listed as potential business resources.

A majority of our prospective entrepreneurs said they would be willing to work the more than forty-hour week it generally takes to keep a small business operating. Park Heights indicated the greatest willingness to invest extra time and energy, and Kenilworth Parkside the least.

The question "What kinds of characteristics does a successful business owner and manager have?" received responses strongly reflective of both class and geographic location. Open-ended answers clustered into four principal areas, listed here in descending order of overall frequency:

- Good personality or attitude (including customer relations skills, cooperativeness, and kindness).
- Education/degree (a generic category in which type or level was frequently not specified).
- Keen knowledge of or talent for a particular business.
- Patience.

The two middle-class neighborhoods, Riggs Park and New Northwood, placed an almost equally high emphasis on attitude and education. Out of all four areas, only Riggs Park considered specialized knowledge (or talent) a very important trait. While many middle-class participants listed the quality of patience, no one from either lower-income area did. Park Heights, more than any other group, would rely on attitude; Kenilworth Parkside on education.

Responses as to the kind of training or education that best prepares an individual for business were more consistent, with a college degree by far the most common choice. Similarity was greatest between classes in the same geographic location. Two thirds of Riggs Park and one half of Kenilworth Parkside (Washington, D.C.) opted for college degrees, in contrast to New Northwood and Park Heights (Baltimore), which, although a sizable number chose college, tended more to vocational training or hands-on experience.

The overwhelming majority thought they could, if they so chose, get started in such programs: over 90 percent of Riggs Park, New Northwood, and Park Heights and 60 percent of Kenilworth Parkside. The frequent appearance of "sign-up" or "enroll" in response to the question of "how to go about it" seemed to indicate that most believed business training and education programs were readily available and easy to get into. Respondents also mentioned asking their teachers, talking to businesspeople, calling different schools and programs, doing library research, reading newspapers, listening to the radio, enlisting in the military, and getting related job experience as potential methods for getting started in a business.

Almost all of the young people in our survey had some business skills, most commonly typing, using a computer, or accounting. A majority would like to obtain more, particularly in the areas of computer programming, accounting, and business management. They believed these skills would be useful not only in starting and running their own businesses but in helping them to find better-paying jobs.

Finally, we asked participants to rate owning and running their own businesses against other career options; specifically being part of another organization or company, working for the government, or being a teacher. A majority in all four neighborhoods thought running their own businesses was preferable, but a sizable number saw no difference or left the question unanswered. Youth in Riggs Park and Park Heights—middle-income Washington, D.C. and lower-income Baltimore—indicated their friends wanted to run businesses, while those in New Northwood and Kenilworth Parkside stated business ownership was not the goal of most friends. Business options of friends closely paralleled their own preferences for beauty and barber shops, clothing stores, real estate, and restaurants.

Awareness of Government Programs. We wanted to know whether our respondents were aware of any government programs to help black businesses and, additionally, whether they thought such government programs were successful.

Differences in answers to the question of program awareness were sharply divided along class lines. Nearly two thirds of Riggs Park and New Northwood residents were aware of specific government programs, in contrast to one quarter of those in each of the lower-income neighborhoods. Specific programs that received more than one mention included:

- Blue Chip In.
- Small Business Administration.
- Manpower Services.
- Student loans.
- Social Services/Unemployment Office.
- Kenilworth Parkside Day Care Center.
- College Here We Come.

The last two programs, based in Kenilworth Parkside, receive government funding.

The amount of misinformation about specific programs was also revealing. Young people in both cities mentioned Urban League initiatives as the most common "government programs," and several brought up the National Association for the Advancement of Colored People (NAACP). Their incorrect identification of the Urban League and the NAACP as government-sponsored organizations indicates a high degree of ignorance about the difference between private- and government-sector programs.

Other than three Riggs Park residents, an overwhelming majority of participants thought government programs helped blacks. One person from Riggs Park who said otherwise explained that due to a lack of publicity, such programs failed to reach the people who needed them. Nevertheless, preponderantly positive responses indicated a strong commonality of beliefs and feelings among the young people we interviewed. Their responses generally fell into one of three categories:

- Blacks were given a chance they would not otherwise have had.
- People were gotten off the streets and into jobs.
- Young people were able to get an education.

Several believed government programs needed to go much further in helping blacks. Their general logic was that because blacks as a group were more depressed than other groups in their cities, they should be given special chances to make something of themselves. One Park Heights resident suggested that government programs are helpful only to a degree because interest on loan payments is too high and loans take too long to repay. His recommendation: "Blacks should be given free loans, considering how we have been cheated in the U.S."

We asked whether government programs over the last twenty years have done more to help blacks than those which preceded them. In terms of jobs, the answers were largely positive from all four geographic areas, but noticeably more so in the two Washington, D.C. neighborhoods. Business programs, however, were viewed more favorably by those in Baltimore; while over half of residents in both Baltimore neighborhoods responded affirmatively on the role of government aid to black businesses, less than a third in either Washington, D.C. neighborhood did so.

Questioned as to whether different levels of government—city, state, and federal—should be more, less, or about the same to help blacks get jobs and start businesses, most of the neighborhoods responded "more" for every level. The noticeable exception was Kenilworth Parkside, which, although residents thought more should be done by the city in terms of both jobs and businesses, believed the federal government should do about the same in terms of aiding black businesses, and the same or less to help blacks get jobs.
Experiences with and Attitudes Toward Black Business. Among those who acknowledged having at least one black business and one owned by another ethnic group in their neighborhood, we asked which businesses they used and why. Fewer middle-income residents used all the neighborhood businesses. Choices were based almost entirely on the location of a business and the variety of products or services it offered.

Several answers provided information as to why some ethnic groups receive more business than others in a particular area. In New Northwood, two individuals patronized businesses of nonblack groups because they were closer and more numerous. Two others in the same neighborhood went to a black bank because it was black-owned and operated. In lower-income Kenilworth Parkside and Park Heights, ten and three residents respectively said they used only the black-owned businesses in their neighborhoods, while one refused to use a store owned by a Chinese family. Although most gave no reasons for their preferences, two Kenilworth Parkside residents expressed a belief in group solidarity—"supporting my brothers and sisters" and "the other stores have attitudes about blacks."

In all four neighborhoods, most considered the black-owned businesses they use successful. We provided a list of possible answers as to why some black businesses were successful and others not. Most respondents took advantage of the opportunity to give more than one response. Under "reasons for success," convenient location, pleasant disposition of the employees, cooperative attitude of owners, and the impact of friends and family on shopping habits were most frequently selected. Seven mentioned product and service variety, while six in each neighborhood considered "a sense of security doing business there" important. Other responses given more than once were the amount of business handled by a particular establishment, the fact that a business had other branches, and the fact that a business was the only one of its kind in the neighborhood.

Reasons as to why black businesses were not successful were equally varied. Across the neighborhoods, poor selection and presentation of merchandise was the most common response, followed by an uncooperative or unpleasant attitude on the part of owners and employees. Inconvenient location, lack of security, and the fact that relatives or friends seldom went there also came into play.

In addition to comparing successful and unsuccessful black businesses, we asked our participants to compare black with other ethnic businesses. Here the differences split along class lines. More than half of middle-income participants thought black business owners performed at about the same level as those in other ethnic groups, with about one fourth indicating they performed less well, and fewer than one eighth better. Half of those in the two lower-income groups believed black owners were more successful in their neighborhoods, with one fourth choosing about the same, and another fourth choosing less.

The young people of these four neighborhoods gave the following advice for improving black business performance, listed in order of frequency:

- Improve location and appearance.
- Improve products and prices.
- Stick together, stop being jealous of one another.
- Hire better workers.
- Maintain a positive attitude.
- Seek loans or assistance from investors to expand.

• Advertise and expand to include the white community.

Only three participants, one each from Northwood, Kenilworth Parkside, and Park Heights, considered that it was unimportant for blacks to be good in business. According to the eighteen-year-old from New Northwood, "Blacks are just like anyone else, so it makes no difference whether or not they are good in business."

The majority who believed it was important for blacks to be good in business were practically unanimous in their reasoning: blacks have been oppressed, denied respect and opportunity, and it is through business that they will prove themselves to the world, especially to white Americans. More than 70 percent of residents from Riggs Park, New Northwood, and Park Heights agreed with this rationale, joined by 20 percent from Kenilworth Parkside. Once again demurring from the majority, most of the residents of Kenilworth Parkside stated that making more money was the best reason for blacks to be good in business.

In light of the fact that most considered business an important means for black advancement, we asked why more blacks were not in business for themselves. Participants were given the following list of responses, from which they could choose as many as they thought relevant:

• Lack of money.
• Other career opportunities.
• Lack of education.
• Perception that black businesses often fail.
• Lack of skills.
• Other.

Answers were very consistent across all four neighborhoods; lack of money (83 percent), lack of education (68 percent), lack of skills (52 percent), and the perception that black businesses often fail (38 percent). In New Northwood, a much larger proportion of residents (38 percent) than in any of the other areas thought blacks were taking advantage of other career opportunities.

Our final question on attitudes concerned black American leaders. When we asked which black leaders have historically been most important for black advancement, the two names most frequently given were Dr. Martin Luther King, Jr. and the Rev. Jesse Jackson. In addition to King and Jackson, inhabitants of both Riggs Park and Kenilworth Parkside in Washington, D.C. included figures ranging from Frederick Douglass and George Washington Carver to Bill Cosby and Marion Barry. Baltimore residents seemed much less aware of other blacks who have contributed to the progress of black America. Three out of four neighborhoods believed in the existence and strength of current black leaders. Park Heights in Baltimore disagreed. If well over half of residents in the other areas considered some blacks as their present leaders, 53 percent of Park Heights respondents said there were no black leaders today.

Our Conclusions

To reiterate, 104 black youths in two East-Coast cities does not constitute a large enough universe from which to draw firm conclusions about black youth attitudes toward entrepreneurship. Nevertheless, our sample provides an opportunity to look at some of the ways in which education and experience have affected entrepreneurial perceptions among youth from four black lower- and middle-income communities.

Shapero and Sokol note that negative "pushes" more than positive "pulls" are likely to propel an individual toward starting a business: "It takes a powerful force in a new direction or the accumulation of many detracking forces before an individual is pushed to or consciously opts for a major change of life path."[158] It is readily apparent that many of the negative conditions that drive individuals to create businesses exist among the youth of our survey. Firings, insults, anger, boredom, and being out of work or school were common to residents of all four neighborhoods.

As expected, comments from Park Heights and Kenilworth Parkside indicate that the most powerful negative stimuli to go into business exist in low-income black communities. A large number of individuals from these two areas stated owning a business as a principle life goal. By contrast, fewer middle-income youngsters, especially those from Riggs Park, have experienced the same level of negative displacement and most do not anticipate pursuing entrepreneurial careers.

In addition, although perceptions of entrepreneurial desirability are high among both lower- and middle-income groups, middle-class youngsters have many more opportunities to choose from. New Northwood youngsters readily admitted that most of their colleagues were drawn toward the less risky avenues to middle-class success offered by white-collar professional jobs. Riggs Park residents, even though many would like to own businesses, generally do not expect to, nor, if they are right, will their friends. On the other hand, many Park Heights and Kenilworth Parkside youths both wanted and expected to start their own businesses.

Kenilworth Parkside, among the four groups, was consistently the outsider. It is interesting to speculate on the reasons. First, it has the weakest inherent institutional structures—an artificially high number of single mothers and young children living under what have been, until recently, uniformly dismal conditions. Second, over the past three years, the community has experienced a rapid change in opportunity structures. Self-management has led to a whole host of new possibilities, from getting a college degree to starting a business. Previously nonexistent entrepreneurial role models have begun to infuse the community with a galvanizing spirit of risk-taking, initiative, and self-reliance. Obviously, the changes are far from complete. If one third see their futures in terms of successful day care centers and beauty shops, and another third as job-holding high school or college graduates, a final third has yet to see beyond a future of poverty, welfare dependency, and social dislocation.

Finally, with the possible exception of Park Heights, even if many of the young blacks we interviewed would like to start their own businesses, most do not believe they will actually do so. For middle-class participants, the opportunity costs are still too high, and among the lower-income blacks, a lack of money, education, and skills remain formidable obstacles. Thus a majority of Kenilworth Parkside residents, who believe college educations provide the best background for business ownership, do not aspire beyond high-school educations and steady jobs. They have the fewest financial resources, and are the least inclined to borrow money for work-related expenses. Even more tellingly, the almost universal emphasis on improving attitudes among black business owners and employees suggests that the general culture of business inside black communities remains weak. Both middle- and lower-class youngsters recognize that legitimate business careers offer rewards, not only to themselves as individuals, but to their communities. However, positive as well as negative incentives are needed to entice young black Americans into entrepreneurship. As yet, all too few role models exist within their immediate spheres of influence. As Sokol and Shapero's paradigm suggests, "Exposure to those near oneself is more important than exposure to great successes."[159] Until and unless more young blacks are exposed to the real step-by-step, day-to-day process of making it in business, they are unlikely to perceive business ownership, however desirable, as feasible.

Notes

1. Gasse, Yvon, "Elaborations on the Psychology of the Entrepreneur" in Kent, Sexton, and Vesper (eds.), *Encyclopedia of Entrepreneurship* (Englewood Cliffs, New Jersey: Prentice-Hall, 1982, p. 64).
2. Ibid., pp. 64–65.
3. Bates, Timothy, "An Analysis of Minority Entrepreneurship: Utilizing the Census of Public Use Samples" (Fourth progress report on MBDA contract, Burlington, Vermont, 1985, p. 15).
4. Greenfield, Sidney M. and Strickon, Arnold in Aubey, Strickon, and Greenfield (eds.), *Entrepreneurs in Cultural Context* (Albuquerque: University of New Mexico Press, 1979, p. 341).
5. Drucker, Peter F., *Innovation and Entrepreneurship* (New York: Harper and Row, 1985, p. 264).

6. Bates, Timothy and Fusfeld, Daniel R., *The Political Economy of the Urban Ghetto* (Carbondale, Illinois: Southern Illinois University Press, 1984, p. 104).
7. Ibid.
8. Farley, Reynolds, *Blacks and Whites: Narrowing the Gap?* (Cambridge: Harvard University Press, 1984, p. 178).
9. Wilhelm, Sidney M., "Black/White Equality: The Socioeconomic Conditions of Blacks in America, Part II (*Journal of Black Studies*, December, 1983, p. 156).
10. Ibid., p. 157.
11. Ibid.
12. Ibid., p. 159.
13. Ibid., pp. 159–161. See also "Graduate Schools Losing Out" (*Washington Post*, October 12, 1987).
14. Du Bois, W.E.B. (ed.), *The Negro Common School* (Atlanta: Atlanta University Press, 1901, p. 5). In Lieberson, Stanley, *A Piece of the Pie: Black and White Immigrants Since 1880* (Berkeley: University of California Press, 1980, p. 139).
15. Lieberson, Stanley, *A Piece of the Pie: Black and White Immigrants Since 1880* (Berkeley: University of California Press, 1980), p.140.
16. Ibid., p. 141.
17. Ibid., p. 252.
18. Farley, op. cit., p. 16.
19. Myrdal, Gunnar, *An American Dilemma* (New York: Harper and Brothers, 1944, p. 884).
20. Ibid.
21. Bates and Fusfeld, op. cit., p. 63.
22. Ogbu, John U., "Schooling the Inner City" (*Society*, November/December 1983, p. 75).
23. Bates and Fusfeld, op. cit., pp. 109–115.
24. Cruse, Harold, *Plural But Equal* (New York: Morrow, 1987, p. 181).
25. *Washington Post* (October 12, 1987), op. cit.
26. Bates and Fusfeld, op. cit., p. 122.
27. Glasgow, Douglas G., "The Black Underclass in Perspective" in *The State of Black America* 1987 (New York: National Urban League, 1987, p. 136).
28. Farley, op. cit., pp. 52–55.
29. Government disincentives and job migration are considered at some length in Chapters 1, 2, and 6.
30. Freeman, Richard B. and Holzer, Harry J.U., "Summary of Findings" in Freeman and Holzer (eds.), *The Black Youth Employment Crisis* (Chicago: University of Chicago Press, 1986, p. 3).
31. Anderson, Elijah, "Some Observations of Black Youth Employment" in Anderson and Sawhill (eds.), *Youth Employment and Public Policy* (Englewood Cliffs, New Jersey: Prentice-Hall, 1979). In Farley, op. cit., pp. 52–55.
32. Freeman and Holzer, op. cit., p. 29.
33. "Black Youth: A Lost Generation?" (*Newsweek*, August 7, 1978, p. 30).
34. Cannon, Angie, "What Dropouts Cost Society" (*San Francisco Chronicle*, November 18, 1988).
35. Liebow, Elliot, *Tally's Corner* (Boston: Little, Brown, 1967). In Farley, op. cit., p. 53).
36. Cruse, Harold, op. cit., p. 19.
37. "Report on Desegregation Efforts in Little Rock, Arkansas" (MacNeil/Lehrer Newshour transcript, October 16, 1987).

38. Ibid.
39. Obgu, op. cit., p. 75.
40. Bell, Daniel, "Twenty Years After Kerner" (*"All Things Considered,"* cassette transcript of National Public Radio Broadcast no. 870805, 1987).
41. Farley, op. cit. p. 32.
42. Willie, Charles V., "The Future of School Desegregation" in *The State of Black America, 1987,* op. cit., p. 37.
43. Ibid., p. 41.
44. Ibid.
45. Ibid., p. 37.
46. Robinson, Sharon P., "Taking Charge: An Approach to Making the Educational Problems of Blacks Comprehensible and Manageable" in *The State of Black America, 1987,* op. cit., p. 34.
47. Bates and Fusfeld, op. cit., p. 111.
48. Farley, op. cit., p. 34.
49. Knight, Althea, "Pursuing the Legacy" *Washington Post,* September 13, 1987).
50. Ibid.
51. Ibid.
52. Knight, Althea, "Pursuing the Legacy: Lack of Follow-Through Thwarts Principal's Year-Long Campaign" (*Washington Post,* September 15, 1987).
53. Ibid.
54. Ibid.
55. Knight, Althea, "Pursuing the Legacy: Three Teachers Who Make a Difference" (*Washington Post,* September 16, 1987).
56. Ibid.
57. Ibid.
58. Merrow, John, "Help Wanted" (MacNeil/Lehrer Newshour transcript, September 7, 1987).
59. Ibid.
60. Ibid.
61. Robinson, op. cit., p. 33.
62. Ibid., p. 35.
63. Ibid.
64. Ibid.
65. Woodson, Robert L., "Ivy Leaf School" in Woodson, Robert L. (ed.), *On the Road to Economic Freedom* (Washington, D.C.: Regnery Gateway, 1987, pp. 104–107).
66. Census figures gathered by the Office for Civil Rights (Center for Education-/Statistics Office for Educational Research and Improvement, Washington, D.C., October 1987).
67. Merrow, John, "Shopping for Schools" (MacNeil/Lehrer Newshour transcript, March 23, 1987, p. 11).
68. Ibid., p. 13.
69. Ibid.
70. Ibid.
71. Ibid.
72. Ibid., p. 14.
73. Williams, Linda, "Molding Men: At Morehouse College, Middle Class Blacks Are Taught to Lead" (*Wall Street Journal,* May 5, 1987).
74. Ibid.

75. Ibid.
76. Ibid.
77. Ibid.
78. Ibid.
79. Ibid.
80. Mieher, Stuart, "Spike Lee's Gotta Have It" (*New York Times Magazine,* August 9, 1987, p. 39).
81. Ibid.
82. Frazier, E. Franklin, *Negro Youth at the Crossways* (New York: Schocken, 1967, p. 111).
83. Myrdal, op. cit., p. 1129.
84. Young, Harding B. and Hund, James M., "Negro Entrepreneurship in Southern Economic Development" in Epstein and Hampton (eds.), *Black Americans and White Business* (Chapel Hill: University of North Carolina Press, 1964), pp. 112–157.
85. Ibid.
86. Ibid., p. 243.
87. Hymowitz, Carol, "Taking a Chance: Many Blacks Jump Off the Corporate Ladder To Be Entrepreneurs" (*Wall Street Journal,* August 2, 1984).
88. *Newsweek,* (August 7, 1978), op. cit., p. 30.
89. Bell, Daniel, "Twenty Years After Kerner," op. cit.
90. Loury, Glen, ibid.
91. "Hollywood's Favorite Heavy: Businessmen on Prime Time T.V." (*Manifold Productions,* Transcripts, March 25, 1987, p. 4).
92. Ibid., pp. 5–6.
93. Ibid., p. 9.
94. Ibid., p. 15.
95. Bayles, Martha, "T.V.: Big Bad Businessmen" (*Wall Street Journal,* March 23, 1987).
96. Ibid.
97. "Hollywood's Favorite Heavy," op. cit., p. 2.
98. Berger, Peter L., *The Capitalist Revolution* (New York: Basic Books, 1986, p. 196).
99. Ibid., pp. 207–209.
100. Lohof, Bruce A., Synopsis of Horatio Alger (*Reader's Biographical Dictionary,* 1986).
101. Sarachek, Bernard, "American Entrepreneurs and the Horatio Alger Myth" (*Journal of Economic History,* vol. 38, June 1978, p. 439).
102. Ibid., p. 456.
103. Ibid., p. 439.
104. De Charms, R., *Personal Causation and Internal Effective Determinants of Behavior* (New York: Academic Press, 1968, p. 181). Cited In Durand, Douglas E., "Effects of Achievement Motivation and Skill Training on the Entrepreneurial Behavior of Black Businessmen" (*Organizational Behavior and Human Performance,* vol. 14, no. 197, 1975, p. 77).
105. Ibid.
106. McClelland, David C., *The Achieving Society* (Princeton: Van Nostrand, 1961, pp. 373–376).
107. Carsrud and Olm, "Entrepreneurs—Mentors, Networks and Successful New Venture Development: An Exploratory Study" in Ronstadt, Hornaday, Peterson,

and Vesper, *Frontiers of Entrepreneurship Research, 1986* (Wellesley, Massachusetts: Babson College, 1986 p. 242).

108. Durant, op. cit., p. 87.
109. Ibid., p. 89.
110. Bailey, John E., "Learning Styles of Successful Entrepreneurs" in Ronstadt, Hornaday, Peterson, and Vesper, op. cit., p. 209.
111. Watson, John and Simpson, Leo, "A Comparative Study of Owner–Manager Personal Values in Black and White Small Businesses" (*Academy of Management Journal,* vol. 21, no. 2, June 1978, pp. 313–319).
112. O'Neill, Harry, "The Business Climate" (*Forethought,* vol. 1, no. 1, 1988).
113. Ibid.
114. Ibid. O'Neill mentions that a recent study found that 75 percent of business journalists consider "keeping high ethical standards" a major corporate responsibility, while only 6 percent think most large American companies are achieving this goal.
115. Jackson, John E., "The American Entrepreneurial and Small Business Culture" (Institute for Enterprise Advancement, 1986, p. 5).
116. O'Neill, op. cit.
117. Jackson, op. cit., pp. 32–34.
118. Ibid., p. 33.
119. Bonaparth, Ellen, "Black Businessmen and Community Responsibility" *Phylon,* vol. 37, March 1976, p. 26).
120. Greenfield and Strickon, op. cit., p. 17.
121. Frazier, E. Franklin, *Black Bourgeoisie* (New York: Macmillan, 1957, p. 135).
122. Myrdal, Gunnar, *The American Dilemma* (New York: Harper and Brothers, 1944, pp. 304–317 and 330–332).
123. Ibid., pp. 330–332.
124. Ibid. p. 928.
125. Ibid.
126. Bates, Timothy and Fusfeld, Daniel, op. cit., pp. 164–166.
127. Ibid., pp. 166–167.
128. Ibid., pp. 167–169.
129. Arrest figures obtained from New York City Police Department, Office of Management, Analysis and Planning, February 21, 1989.
130. Bates and Fusfeld, op. cit.
131. Figures obtained from Narcotics Analysis Division of New York City Police Department, February 21, 1989.
132. Estimate of Bruce Johnson, director of research on the economics of drug selling at the Narcotics and Drug Research Company, New York City. February 21, 1989.
133. Palley, Howard A. and Robinson, Dana A., "Black on Black Crime" *(Society,* vol. 15, no. 5, July/August 1988, p. 60).
134. Ibid., pp. 59-60. For a recent ethnographic account of youth drug culture in New York City see Williams, Terry, *The Cocaine Kids* Reading, Massachusetts: Addison Wesley, scheduled publication April 1989).
135. Bates, op. cit. p. 23.
136. Bowser, Georgia W., "A Note on Success Criteria for Minority Business" (*Review of Black Political Economy,* spring 1980, pp. 312–313).
137. Watson and Simpson, op. cit., p. 317.
138. Bates, op. cit., p. 39.

139. Boneparth, op. cit., p. 42.
140. Collins, Sharon M., "The Making of the Black Middle Class" (*Social Problems*, vol. 30, no. 4, April 1983, p. 380).
141. Jackson, John E., op. cit., pp. 13 and 24.
142. Ibid., pp. 24 and 30.
143. Sleeper, Jim, "The Caribbean Black Challenge" (*Washington Post*, August 1986).
144. Sagavara, Sandra and Tucker, Elizabeth, "The New Immigrants: The Entrepreneurs; Fortunes Intertwined" (*Washington Post*, December 16, 1987).
145. Breathed, Berke, "Bloom County," cartoon strip (*San Francisco Chronicle*, October 12, 1988).
146. Holzer, Harry J. and Freeman, Richard B., "Young Blacks and Jobs— What We Now Know" (*Public Interest*, vol. 78, winter 1985, p. 31).
147. Ibid., p. 29.
148. Shade, Barbara J., "The Social Success of Black Youth: The Impact of Significant Others" (*Journal of Black Studies*, vol. 14, no. 2, December 1983, pp. 138–139).
149. Ibid., p. 137.
150. Ibid., pp. 142–143.
151. Ibid., p. 140. See also Ross, H. and Glaser, E., "Making It Out of the Ghetto" (*Professional Psychology*, vol. 3, 1973, pp. 347–355) and Scanzoni, J., *The Black Family in Modern Society* (Boston: Allyn and Bacon, 1971).
152. Ibid., p. 138.
153. Ibid., p. 145. See also Perkins, E., *Home is a Dirty Street: The Social Oppression of Black Children* (Chicago: Third World Press, 1975).
154. Parham. T.D., "Black Job Expectation: A Comparative Analysis" *Journal of Black Studies*, vol. 8, no. 3, March 1978, p. 305).
155. Sommes, Clovis E. and Makalani, Jabulani K., "Minority Status and the Problem of Legitimacy" (*Journal of Black Studies*, vol. 15, no. 3, March 1985, pp. 259–275).
156. Fordham, Signithia and Ogbu, John U., "Black Students School Success: Coping with the Burden of Acting White" (*Urban Review*, vol. 18, no. 3, 1986, pp. 176–179).
157. Ibid., p. 177.
158. Shapero, Albert and Sokol, Lisa in Kent, Sexton, and Vesper (eds.), *Encyclopedia of Entrepreneurship* (Englewood Cliffs, New Jersey: Prentice-Hall, 1982, p. 79).
159. Ibid., p. 87.

5

Community-Based Entrepreneurship

Trodding a well-worn path to social mobility, first-generation Asian, Hispanic, Greek, Cuban, West Indian, and Jewish immigrants to the United States have typically started small independent businesses. Kin groups and other voluntary forms of association have provided the great bulk of moral and financial support for these entrepreneurial ventures. In striking contrast, black Americans have not often used similar informal structures to support their small business activities.[1]

Historically, the lack of business participation by black Americans has been traced to racial discrimination in the lending practices of financial institutions and to racial barriers in education and employment. In addition, restricted residential choice, threats of violence, and other subtle forms of social control have perpetuated the disadvantage of blacks relative to other American subgroups. But these explanations, to whatever degree valid, obscure the fact that other racial subgroups—Asians and West Indians in particular—have also faced and managed to overcome similar, externally imposed obstacles to entrepreneurship.

Why the difference? As our chapters on black families and education have emphasized, we believe the answers to problems confronting black Americans in the post-civil-rights era lie as much within as without. Accordingly, our hypothesis as to why blacks have participated less in business rests in part on the dearth of voluntary associations, inside black communities, with a specific orientation toward business development.

In this chapter, we will examine three indigenous voluntary associations formed to benefit different segments of the black American community during the past twenty years. The Majestic Eagles, the Pittsburghers, and the Coalition of Black Professionals have attempted, in different ways, to encourage both economic progress and group solidarity among black Americans. Although each has provided community-based economic support for other blacks, only the Majestic Eagles has focused specifically on black business development. As a consequence, the Majestic Eagles will provide our central focus, with the other two organizations serving as contrasting variants of black voluntary behavior.

The Social and Economic Role of Voluntary Associations

Voluntary mutual aid associations have facilitated entrepreneurship in societies at every stage of economic development. By providing informal social and economic support, they encourage individuals to accept obstacles as a challenge rather than as an occasion for defeat. In America, the mutual aid function of voluntary associations has long-standing links with the social mobility of Asian and European immigrants.[2] Voluntary associations have also played a well-documented role in the successful adaptation of rural Peruvian and West African migrants to urban centers.[3]

In contrast to traditional social groups formed on the basis of kin, clan, or lineage, individual choice determines membership in voluntary associations.[4] The motivation to participate stems from a shared interest, such as the need of rural migrants to adapt to urban life and a broader host culture. One common type among many immigrant groups, the rotating credit association, serves to raise large sums of money for specific individual or community goals.[5] In one important respect, voluntary associations constitute flexible social entities— they are easily founded and easily disbanded.

Historically, the formation of voluntary mutual aid associations has been connected to social change in urban areas. Most are formed and joined by new arrivals on the basis of town, village, or region of origin. In American society, identification with country of origin frequently occurs a decade or more after arrival, if at all. First-generation immigrants generally identify themselves by town, region, or provincial dialect. An important marker of assimilation into the national culture is a perception of one's place of origin along national lines.[6]

In Lima, Peru, migrants from rural areas move near relatives or people from the same village or region and frequently join several regional associations.[7] The regional association promotes socialization to an urban way of life—help in finding a job, speaking a different dialect, and adopting new ways of dress and behavior. Meetings, sports events, and other social gatherings provide a retreat from the rigors of urban life and a haven in which to enjoy native foods and customs. Members have an obligation to help one another, and often exchange labor, lend small amounts of money, and care for the sick. Membership in a regional association gives new migrants access to persons of higher status—lawyers, doctors, politicians—whose resources and influence can solve problems related to urban life. Higher-status persons often become godparents to children of new migrants. In some cases, the regional association lobbies government agencies for improved health, housing, and other neighborhood services. Last but not least, the regional association offers an important network in which to forge new friendships, one of the most important and enduring adaptations to urban life.

In the modern West African cities of Freetown, Accra, and Lagos, colonial powers have established centers of commerce, administration, and industry.[8] Young industrial workers form a large proportion of migrants from rural areas. Frequently, migrants join mutual aid voluntary associations based on tribal or religious affiliations. The association teaches new migrants about standards of dress and behavior and helps with finding jobs. Members also receive financial assistance when unemployed or sick and, in addition, can rely on the organization to sponsor funerals and fund burial plots. Part of regularly collected dues go to assist families in the tribal home area. Traditional feast days and sports events solidify an association's basis for communal identity by reworking traditional forms of social organization into the urban context.

In nineteenth- and twentieth-century America, mutual aid voluntary associations have encouraged successful adaptation to American society while perpetuating selected elements from native areas—retaining, for example, forums for language, food, music, dance, theatre, humor, newspapers, and radio and television programs from various home cultures. Each member contributes annual dues to cover the expenses of mutual aid. Traditionally, voluntary funds have purchased cemeteries, organized funerals, and provided a modicum of sickness benefits and aid to orphans and widows. Not a radical invention, voluntary associations often derive from existing forms of community aid that functioned in native societies. The Jewish Family Circles and Cousins Clubs, for example, originated from eastern European benevolent family and village mutual aid associations.[9] The same holds true for Chinese-American, Japanese-American, and other recent immigrant groups.[10] In the new urban context, members have shared information and advice, and used their power and influence to help one another find jobs. Young people often meet future spouses at association events. Thus, in reality, mutual aid voluntary associations operate both to promote social change and adaptation and to conserve and reinforce traditional behavior patterns.

Voluntary associations based on mutual identification of purpose and shared morality can also serve important economic functions. Light has documented the ways in which some groups have used the rotating credit association as an informal type of collective savings institution.[11] At specified intervals, usually once each month, members who want to participate put an agreed-upon amount of money into a general fund. Each member in turn receives the total sum.

In urban West Africa, subgroups of tribal associations unite, often along occupational lines, to form a rotating credit association. Called "esusu" in

Yoruba, the association helps small entrepreneurs—both men and women—to join funds in order to invest in their individual business ventures. In traditional China, the hui (village association) sponsored small loan groups among a limited number of families. For ten months, ten families contributed a specified amount to the general fund. Once each month, one family sponsored a feast and received the entire fund for that month. When the Chinese immigrated to the United States, the loan societies continued to function, reorganized along lineage and regional lines. As informal "savings and loan" associations, they helped start many small businesses. Jewish-American regional associations, Family Circles, and Cousins Clubs functioned similarly. Light points out that in America, first-generation immigrants use informal cash-pooling systems, while the second generation prefers impersonal credit unions or banks.[12]

In rotating credit associations, members enter both as individuals and as representatives of a larger group. The kin or regional ties among a group of individuals generate the bonds of good faith that form the basis for a moral community. Because it involves mutual obligation and benefit, shared trust serves as collatoral on loans. It also functions as an informal source of social control. Asian, Greek, and Jewish immigrants, who can identify with a larger tradition of religion and values, have evolved additional trust in a new and unfamiliar environment.

In American society, foreign-born and uneducated persons have found self-employment a successful survival option. For those willing to work long hours, at low pay, and with the help of unpaid family labor, a small retail business can support the family while the children get an education and become assimilated. Consumer demands for an ethnic enclave—shops that provide special food, retail goods, and interactions in the native language—have created a protected market for the small-business owners of some ethnic groups. Light argues:

> The relative success of black-owned service establishments [appliance repair, beauty and hair, insurance and undertaking businesses] suggests that black-owned retail businesses would have been considerably stronger had they, too, been protected from outside competition as were the retail trades of the foreign born.[13]

Light mentions the well-documented fact that black Americans have had a difficult time getting loans to finance small-business ventures. Loans are often approved on the basis of personal relationships, and most black Americans have not had a "personal banker." A shared anecdote from a member of the Pittsburgh Club illustrates this common dilemma. In the 1950s, he became the first member of his family to graduate from college. Howard University had granted him a degree, but he couldn't find a bank willing to lend him the money to start his dental practice. For over a year, he borrowed $100 each month in small-business loans from one bank in order to establish a "personal relationship."[14] However, as Light and others remind us, institutional loans do not provide the "start-up" capital for most small business ventures. The majority use loans from family, friends, or other informal credit associations.[15]

The economic resourcefulness of West Indian blacks in American cities has often been held up as a model for the economic development of the black American working class. Although they share a common color and ancestry, the two groups have experienced distinctly different historical and cultural circumstances. During the West Indian plantation era, black slaves produced their own subsistence items and traded in local markets. They maintained many of their African cultural practices, including the rotating credit pools known as "esusu." When West Indians migrated to the United States, the "susu" groups helped open small groceries, tailor shops, and various other small retail businesses. Larger pools, established after the migrants had been in the United States for a decade or more, contributed to the financing of college educations or buying homes. Accounts of the period record that native-born American blacks in 1920s Harlem resented the economic success of the new immigrants and regarded their thrifty habits as stingy.[16]

As an agency for the District of Columbia, the Minority Business Opportunity Commission provides minority firms with technical assistance on marketing and government contract procedures. It also monitors a sheltered market program, under which selected D.C. contracts are reserved for competitive bidding among minority firms. During the course of our investigation into local businesses, we interviewed two black, West Indian employees of the agency. One of them, describing his experiences with black American businessmen, observed:

American blacks are less threatened by West Indians; they don't see us in competition with them. When I took classes at Howard I noticed a preconception—American blacks believe they can't get together and do anything. I think they need to see examples of success to counter the stereotype...and maybe the Majestic Eagles and John Raye are doing that.[17]

He contrasted the typical black American situation with Caribbean black business organizations in the D.C. area:

Currently, 50 people from the D.C. Council of Caribbean Businessmen are giving $50 each month for 50 months. The group hasn't decided what it will do with the eventual $125,000, but we will meet quarterly to decide.[18]

In a quote from a *Wall Street Journal* article on the problems of small business development in the black American community, Fred Rasheed, economic development program director for the NAACP, observes:

> Ironically, advances in racial integration over the past 20 years have also led to the demise of many black enterprises. Many of us started to go downtown and spend our money with the white establishments and the black businesses dried up.[19]

In the same article, economist Walter Williams comments on the economic basis of a growing tension between some segments of the American black population and recent immigrant groups:

> New immigrants aren't likely to set up shop in affluent suburbs because [the cost of] the land and the housing is very high relative to ghetto neighborhoods. Black neighborhoods thus constitute an economic invitation.[20]

The logical question to follow, says Williams, is why haven't black Americans accepted the same circumstances as an invitation to entrepreneurship? He notes a further problem: Middle-class black Americans don't patronize black-owned businesses and don't seem to have a "business ownership ethic." As new immigrant groups pool their wages in informal credit unions and borrow additional capital for small enterprises from family or regional savings associations, tension between black Americans and new arrivals continues to rise. Concludes Davidson:

> There are limited efforts in several cities to stimulate black business ownership. "Buy Freedom" (sponsored by Tony Brown) calls on black consumers to make half their purchases from black companies and the other half from non-black companies that create jobs for blacks. Like Jesse Jackson's "Operation Push," the NAACP has a program to urge corporations to do business with black owned companies to encourage the development of black owned franchises.[21]

The economic underdevelopment of black Americans has historical roots. In the first place, the plantation economy of the American South differed greatly from the conditions experienced by black slaves in the West Indies. Black Americans were numerically fewer, separated from one another, and generally not allowed to provide for themselves. Given the lack of occasion to use them, it is hardly surprising that practices like "esusu"—the rotating credit association that functioned as "susu" in the West Indies—appear to have completely died out of the cultural repertoire of black Americans.[22]

Furthermore, changing conditions in the larger economy and society did not favor the economic advancement of blacks. Mullings describes how free blacks worked as artisans and skilled craftsmen in southern and northern cities, but after 1820 began to lose out to an influx of skilled and unskilled white immigrant labor. Prior to the 1850s, a group of occupations considered "black"—longshoremen, coachmen, stablemen, bootblacks, barbers, and waiters—gave blacks an almost exclusive access to certain niches of the urban job market. Particularly in the North, the arrival of huge numbers of unskilled Irish after the 1847 famine undercut the pay scale for these jobs.[23] In the South, the relative advantage of freed master workmen before and right after the Civil War fell victim to new technical requirements and the purposeful monopolization of skilled labor positions by whites.[24]

Industrialization, the growth of cities, and increased European immigration in the late nineteenth century relegated blacks to the bottom rung of the economic ladder. Mullings contends that by 1919, Italian and Green immigrants had replaced blacks as barbers and bootblacks, French and Germans as cooks and waiters, and Swedes and Germans had appropriated the better janitorial jobs.[25] Although both world wars stimulated migration from the South, most blacks who could find jobs in the North worked as menial laborers in factories, often at wages half that for whites doing comparable work.[26] In general, black employment opportunities, public education, and accessibility to unions were inferior to the economic and social resources available to other American subgroups.

Traditional black American churches and fraternal organizations, both of which had mutual aid benefits, never functioned as rotating credit associations. Rural southern churches organized sickness and burial societies, and fraternal orders mushroomed and vied for insurance benefits, but neither developed money pools earmarked for general business investment.[27] Voluntary organizations provided black Americans with opportunities for individuals to assume the leadership roles denied them elsewhere. But with a few notable exceptions, traditional black American voluntary organizations—while a source of political strength, social identity, and economic survival—have not served a specifically entrepreneurial purpose.

On the other hand, black American families share an investment in children, as demonstrated by the child-rearing networks described by Stack in her study of a black, low-income housing project in the late 1960s.[28] Families migrating to northern cities and towns have maintained strong connections with rural southern kin, and children frequently spend summers with relatives in both places. The care of children has constituted a moral obligation among black American extended families. A similar sense of moral purpose does not extend to credit and other business-related functions.

The Majestic Eagles, Inc.

The Majestic Eagles, a Washington, D.C.-based voluntary association of black Americans, provides a variety of support services to minority business

K

owners, aspiring entrepreneurs, and their families. United under the leadership of President John Raye, they propose to "redirect the black dollar by emphasizing black ownership of land, goods and services produced within the black community."[29] As a business development organization, they aim to bring together individuals with a variety of skills and experience to share information and expertise with each other. Members receive encouragement for developing their own concepts, talents, and ideas into viable businesses.

At present, the Majestic Eagles, Inc. administers a federally insured credit union for participating members; conducts weekly meetings, business, motivation, and entrepreneurship training seminars; and sponsors youth activity groups. Most activities take place at the organization's headquarters in a recently purchased building on Rhode Island Avenue, N.E. Plans are under way to purchase a group of homes in the northeast area of the District of Columbia, which Eagles members will then renovate and use for shared equity. In the near future, they intend to open a Majestic Eagles bank. They will also continue to encourage the formation of Eagles chapters in other cities in the United States.

John Raye and six friends founded the Majestic Eagles in 1983. They chose the eagle as a symbol to identify the shared purpose of the group, an image found in the Bible (Isaiah 40:31):

> But they that wait upon the Lord shall renew their strength; they shall mount up with wings as eagles; they shall run and not be weary; they shall walk and not faint.[30]

In addition to the image of the "majestic eagle" soaring to great heights, members identify with the Eagles motto, regularly stated at meetings: "God first, family second, and business third."

An introductory brochure for prospective members prescribes the economic empowerment of the minority community through the creation of small businesses and the encouragement of entrepreneurship:

> In this organization, you will find a number of serious and socially committed persons, who, like yourself, have a talent, skill or idea to share with others and who believe that the best and surest way for us to rise above our present status in life is to make maximum use of all the persons with various interests and avocations. Among them are: preserving our cultural heritage, traditions and institutions, fostering the economic development of the resources in our community, increasing our political awareness, and developing a solid business and financial base. To all of the above, we add the chief component, the development of our spirituality, the center of all our power.[31]

Clearly stated expectations accompany the membership application, from which members ascertain that they can count on the Majestic Eagles for the following:

1. Learning sound business principles.
2. Developing a solid economic foundation.
3. Self-enrichment seminars and workshops.
4. Investment opportunities.
5. Discounts on products and services from other Eagles.
6. Promoting business.

In return, the Eagles expect members to:

1. Provide quality products and services to customers and clients.
2. Give fair and competitive prices to customers and clients.
3. Uphold the highest standards of business practices.
4. Do business with other Eagles.
5. Discount products and services to other Eagles.
6. Be serious about the goals of the organization and work actively in the organization to achieve those goals.
7. Promote the Majestic Eagles organization.[32]

Members pay $250 cach year, $50 for family members and $75 for students. For individuals unable to pay the initial lump sum, a deferred payment schedule allows an initial down payment with the balance paid off in three subsequent monthly installments. Besides Washington, D.C., Majestic Eagles chapters exist in ten other cities of the Northeast, Midwest, and South: Norfolk and Richmond, Virginia; Baltimore and Cambridge, Maryland; Flint, Michigan; Newark, New Jersey; Hutchinson, Kansas; Charlotte, North Carolina; Atlanta, Georgia; and Brooklyn, New York. In order to extend the credit union to all chapters, the Majestic Eagles is in the process of legally establishing itself as a national organization—a predictably complicated process that involves filing, and then waiting for, the approval of myriad forms with various government agencies.

As of August 1987, the Washington, D.C. chapter had 800 fully paid, active members. About 80 percent are in business for themselves, either as sole proprietors or in partnership. Those who derive primary income from working for someone else usually have an entrepreneurial venture going on the side. Generally, they are above average in income and education. Five are millionaires. Overall occupational profiles of one hundred Eagle memberships break down as follows:

1. 38 in designated nonbusiness careers: 14 in education/administration (teachers, administrators, day care supervisors), 3 lawyers, 4 in medical services, 4 students, 6 pastors, 4 in food services, 8 in sales, and 2 secretaries.

2. 21 in intermediate business activities: 4 in financial planning and business consulting; 2 in investments; and 5 in insurance, public relations, advertising, accounting, and banking.
3. 41 in miscellaneous enterprises: computers, natural foods, real estate (6), facial and hair care, auto repair, telephone answering services, video productions, janitorial services, private delivery services, and flower shops.[33]

Information about members is currently stored in a computer. Office staff is paid by donation, and only recently has a full-time administrative assistant come on board. Florence King, an associate of John Raye, Inc., until recently administered the federal licensing of the Majestic Eagles Credit Union and worked full time in the Eagles office.

King worked for eighteen years in the federal government, fifteen as the branch chief of the Army Personnel Center, and three years in civilian personnal and management. She holds a B.A. in Sociology and a minor in Business Administration. In an interview with her in September 1987, we obtained the following information about the status of the federally insured credit union, thus far the largest and most successful joint business undertaking by the Majestic Eagles.[34]

Its holdings were approximately $540,000, extremely high for a credit union in existence for a mere ten months. The D.C. Credit Union League informed them that no other credit union in the District ever did as well in so short a period. Although the average depositor held only $1,000, the Majestic Eagles Credit Union had become the second largest black credit union in the country.

At this point in time, the union was limited in terms of its investments because of the relatively small gains made on loans. Most of the returns come from secured loans based on a twelve- to twenty-four month repayment schedule. From January to June of 1987, one hundred such loans totalling $150,000 were made, earning about $8,000 in interest. Other types of loans distributed by the union include signature, collateralized, automotive, and security loans in amounts based on the size of individual deposits.

Most of the union's organizational and managerial problems were due to a lack of financial resources. A full-time treasurer/manager, or at the very least an additional $25,000 to pay the part-time treasurer for full-time work, was required. The system of maintaining records in file cabinets would be obviated by a separate computer, an unaffordable luxury. King needed someone to manage—do the books, ledgers, and daily statements—while she attempted to generate additional funding. Thus far, only a small percentage of the assets could be spent, and salaries relied completely on earnings, a situation that translated into a paid full-time president and a half-time treasurer, two voluntary loan officers, and a sometime secretary whose scant remuneration derived from voluntary contributions by Eagles members.

By the end of October 1987, King anticipated the union would have reached the one-million dollar mark in deposits. The plan was to establish credit unions in all ten chapters around the country, and eventually to extend them into the international arena. Because of the number of blacks in Washington, King believed they had the potential to surpass other major credit unions in the area. In order to provide much needed space for the rapidly expanding venture, negotiations were under way to purchase the building next door to Eagles headquarters on Rhode Island Avenue.

Over the past year and a half, the credit union has had significant problems achieving its goals. As of February 1989, John Raye reports that poor management and a close to 50 percent default rate on member loans has created a crisis situation for the fledgling financial institution. Having completely reorganized the union's management, Raye and other Eagles are in the process of raising enough capital to cover the costs of restructuring and debts. In addition, national Eagles chapters have yet to receive the legal status necessary to establish affiliate credit unions. Strained finances have meant that while the Eagles rent and continue to hold an option to buy the office building that houses the credit union on Rhode Island Avenue, they have been unable to make a final purchase offer.

John Raye—an Inspirational Leader

A handsome, bright-eyed man in his late forties, John Raye began his journey out into the world when he left small-town, rural Louisiana to attend Southern University in Baton Rouge. John credits his maternal grandfather, a tenant sharecropper whose cotton fields John worked as a boy, with instilling in him the virtues of hard work and a need for self-improvement. In particular, said his grandfather, a man who wanted to get ahead needed a good education. John majored in horticulture, working on a hog farm and as a vending machine repairman to pay for tuition and board. On graduation in 1963, he married his hometown girl, Rosie, and they started life together as high-school teachers. When the U.S. Department of Agriculture offered John a position as an advisor to Oregon farmers, they moved to the Pacific Northwest. Eventually he went to work for the Job Corps, teaching Hispanic migrant workers in Washington state. A newspaper reporter visiting his classroom suggested to John that he apply for a job with a Spokane television station. He did, and to his surprise, got hired.

During the 1970s, John played the role of first black anchorman on a Seattle television station's weekend news program. When his advocacy activities in the black community became "too radical," he was demoted to the position of weatherman. During this time, he produced a controversial film, "Blacks in the Media," that criticized the media for portraying all black Americans as poor, criminal, or drug-addicted; that is to say, as the generally unsavory outcasts of American society. He wanted the media to accentuate the positive about black Americans in rural and urban areas, and dreamed of being a Charles Kurault among enterprising black American individuals and community groups. In the late 1970s Channel 5, an independent television station in Washington, D.C., offered John a job, and he moved his family to suburban Maryland. The station did not renew his contract, according to John, because of his ongoing criticism of the media's characterization of black Americans. Following a brief period of unemployment, John was hired by the U.S. Census Bureau to help solve the potential problem of a massive undercounting of black Americans during the 1980 census.

His campaign to engage black American community groups on a national level spread the word that the Big Count was of vital importance in getting blacks increased economic and political power. But John's presence in the federal bureaucracy, as in previous organizational settings, rapidly became problematic. From his point of view, he "spoke the truth and made people uncomfortable . . . I was considered difficult." During a late-night television talk show in 1983, John enumerated the ways in which black Americans were "worse off now than twenty years ago." His agency did not find this sentiment congenial with their policies. When he decided to resign from the census bureau to open his own public relations firm in 1984, his government superiors were reportedly greatly relieved.

John describes himself as a "loner, descended from a family of stubborn, hard-headed people—idealistic, generous, kind-hearted and a little weird." Ethel Payne, a reporter for the Washington, D.C. newspaper *Afro-American* and a friend of John Raye comments that John:

> is always going to be shaking the system. John has always been a maverick. He sees himself as a champion for little folks, who don't ordinarily have a voice and this is what he's good at doing.[35]

His firm, John Raye and Associates, Inc., provides motivational training, seminars, and workshops for interested businesses and community groups. He has produced a series of instructional cassettes on motivation, with titles such as "Selling Your Way to Success," "Don't Let Fear Keep You Down," "The Power of Positive Thought," and "Building Self-Confidence." He is a frequent radio talk show guest.

As an activist, Raye has a passionate commitment to the achievement of black economic and political power in America. To this end, he started the Majestic Eagles in 1983. John possesses charm, warmth, an infectious smile, and a booming laugh. At this point in his life, he engages the world with a message of hope and inspiration and appears to have succeeded in becoming a truly inspirational leader—a man among men.

John Raye's Message

The world view of John Raye, a personal synthesis of fundamental Christianity, Eastern spirituality, and Western entrepreneurial zest, stands as the philosophical underpinning of the Majestic Eagles. John's perspective circumscribes his vision of the past, present, and future of black Americans. It is his vision that generates the guiding principles and inspiration for Eagles members.

In that it focuses on worldly success in family and business, John's internal motivation has an explicit connection to the external world. He says:

> I'm very positive. I'm very sure of myself. I feel good about myself. I understand the power God has bestowed on me. I know I'm someone special . . . . I accept no limitations. The only limits on me are the ones I put on myself. I am in control of my thinking.

By personal example, he tries to teach others in workshops and entrepreneurial training sessions:

> Your first order of business is to clear up your own head. What do you really want to do? It's important to realize that whatever you can conceive in your uncluttered and cultivated mind, can be brought forth into reality if you persist. If you develop the right kind of thinking and maintain the right attitude, the money will come. Also, if you want prosperity, you have to be around people with a prosperity consciousness. If you want to be in business for yourself, then you have to be around people who are in business for themselves.

He considers the Majestic Eagles a nurturing ground for mutually supportive business interactions among its members:

> A young man came into the organization about five months ago who wanted to start a taxicab company, but had no real capital. He had been driving a cab for the past 12 years and his idea of a cab company was presented to us. As a result, about 30 of our members got together and raised enough money to get a cab company off and running. This is just one example of self-help and collective involvement.

John remembers long evenings spent with Richard Gregg during his Seattle period. An older white man married to a Japanese woman, Richard Gregg had a great influence on John in the formative years of his adult life. From John's perspective, Mr. Gregg "talked like Martin Luther King and Ghandi" and lived in a holistic manner, experiencing, as a direct result, positive effects in day-by-day reality. Richard Gregg's message consisted of knowing oneself in mind, body, and spirit—a message John conveys to the Eagles each day.

John recalls his stretch of unemployment after leaving the census bureau as a time of personal revelation, referring to it as his own "Great Depression." He grew a beard, went inside himself, and engaged in a battle strongly reminiscent of some Biblical prophet's struggle in the wilderness. He even describes himself in this period as "like a wild beast." John, since youth a religious man in the Baptist tradition, also prayed to God for guidance. Deeming it an "enlightenment that came along with age," his eventual "awakening" served as the source of his own motivation and grand vision. He came to the realization that "there was more to life than a GS-14 and I must do more." After his Great Depression, says John, his private raging demons "once so active became quiet." He had achieved a vision of personal strength and a possible future for black Americans:

> Life is a never-ending challenge. We are continually on the search. Once I figured this out, that being in pursuit is the meaning of life, I was healed.

At this point he believed himself in a position to heal and lead others to personal and economic salvation.

When John reflects about his role as leader of the Majestic Eagles, his first thoughts are about how this type of social movement happens so rarely, in his estimation about once every hundred years. He sees the impact he has on people and the growth of the Eagles. He knows he is making a big sacrifice of time with his children, one daughter and a son, but believes that all black people must be prepared to make big sacrifices, like others before them who have died (Dr. King). For John Raye, "Giving of time is life."

Jesse Jackson, keynote speaker at the first annual majestic Eagles Black Economic Summit Conference (held in July 1987 at the Mayflower Hotel), called John Raye "one of our visionary leaders."[36] A more inclusive description might refer to him as a "minister of black economic progress." Indeed, a deep spirtuality underlies his entrepreneurial spirit. Born and bred a southern Baptist, John has expanded his religious viewpoint to include a universal consciousness which connects human beings to the God inside all of us. For Raye, God is the single most powerful force in the universe. He experiences the consciousness of God within as the 'I AM Force." According to John, God Consciousness has the power to change the world. He provides an example from a recent master mind training session of the Eagles where collective meditation and prayer

> freed Menson and Winnie Mandella . . . . It happened right here and you can quote me. The system in South Africa is broken; it's just a matter of time. A new wind has started to blow. Last night we went over South Africa . . . the heat was burning

so to release them. By using the God Consciousness, the I AM Force, we can affect change inside the self and the world.

John views this time in human history as an Armegeddon. He continues:

> There have been so many violations of Divine Law. The forces to maim and destroy have been released and now the positive forces can return. God sends us messages and signals. When Reagan had to cancel the inaugural parade for the first time in history. When the Challenger blew up as a result of failures and lies. The AIDS epidemic, a plague . . . . The drug problem in America is God's wrath. Divine law says that energies you put out come back to you.

Raye says "the time is ripe for the Eagles" and black Americans have their time coming for social and economic parity:

> This is the golden age of opportunity for persons of color in the U.S. We are beginning to shake off the dry bones of ignorance, jealousy and envy. We are witnessing the beginning of a movement of unity among black people and this time it cannot be stopped.

His vision of the position of black Americans is hopeful, but also explicitly outlines problems internal to the black community. In his view, blacks suffer from a fundamental ignorance of the business enterprise. "Blacks," he says, "are financially illiterate." He would like to teach them "the principles of how wealth is acquired in America through real estate, equity securities, stocks and bonds." He observes that although blacks make up 75 percent of the population of Washington, D.C., "They own nothing." Why? "Blacks don't think of *owning* anything." John and fellow Eagles constantly remind one another of the success of recent immigrant groups, especially Asians, who have taken advantage of the dearth of businesses serving the needs of inner-city blacks. In an interview with Lee Green of *Financial Independence,* Raye insists:

> We have nothing against those who understand the free enterprise system. Our purpose is to encourage black people to understand it and use it to their advantage. Our dollars do not stay in our community for very long. Most other groups keep their dollars in their communities as long as possible by doing business with one another. Historically, blacks have not done that. Our money comes in and goes right out.[37]

Raye has committed himself to helping black Americans "change their thinking." He identifies fear as the central barrier to entrepreneurial ventures. "Blacks fear responsibility and obligation and are not confident they can fulfill obligations." Talking about his plan to apply for a Department of Defense contract that will sponsor information conferences for minority businesses,

Raye says bluntly, "If we make it complicated, black folks will mess it up every time."

He notes that when black Washingtonians shop they go to White Flint—a luxurious white-owned shopping mall—rather than to Sunboes—a high-fashion black-owned shop. Raye compares the average nouveau riche black American to "a kid in a candy store; he goes to White Flint and spends it all." He talks about the Koreans and the Jews, "who are close in business ventures, like peanut butter on a cracker." He exhorts black Americans to "pattern ourselves after them and do what they've done."

Raye summarizes the internal problem of the black community as the tendency to believe that black professionals are not dependable, don't work hard and have bad attitudes. Raye acknowledges, "There's some truth in that, too .... Many will choose to use the services of a white lawyer because . . . 'a white man's eyes are colder.' " He says black Americans traditionally "drift from day to day. . . without a concept of saving or planning for the future." His response to these problems incorporates the fundamental message of the Majestic Eagles: Number one, be positive; number two, have an idea; number three, make a goal; number four, develop a plan. Orientation toward the future constitutes a critical element in socializing Eagles for entrepreneurial success.

Raye perceives the strength of the black community as an enduring sense of righteousness and hope in the face of despair—the belief that if one holds on long enough, things will get better. Even though much of this strength derives from the beliefs and practices of traditional black Christianity, Raye believes black American churches have not stressed economic development enough. In particular, they have not invested the billions of dollars they collect each year into black-owned and operated enterprises. Raye wants to turn such institutionalized resistance around by inspiring a "movement of unity among black people; we're going to create businesses and buy from each other." In doing so, he believes he is calling for nothing less than the economic salvation of black America.

"Eagle Talk" and the Entrepreneurial Spirit

John Raye and the Eagles movement have created a language to help negate self-defeat among black Americans. As the metaphors start to fly at meetings, Eagle empowerment becomes almost tangible. John and others refer to the poetic imagery as "Eagle talk." Eagle talk represents a syncretic form of Baptist Christiantity, new age revelation, and the free enterprise spirit. John Raye tells his Eagles:

No other people have undergone such fragmentation. If you do wrong unto someone or a group of people, it will come back to you. Now the dominance is turning around.

He refers to fellow members as "brothers and sisters," a traditional form of address between black Baptist church members.

Jesse Jackson, in his appearance at the Economic Summit Conference, used Eagle talk to prime his audience. Asking for campaign funds he exclaimed, "Eagles don't like to be told how high they can fly, right? . . . Now give 'Guccily' . . . give like you dress."[38] Earlier, encouraging the Eagles to higher entrepreneurial heights, Mr. Jackson exhorted:

I argue, Brother Raye, anyone who needs an alarm clock to wake up is not an entrepreneur. We need to awaken by purpose, driven by cause. Let your bird take over, pass in your arms for wings. Remember you're not Chirping J. Bird, you're not buzzards, you're eagles who soar to the sky.[39]

John and the Eagles have chosen an Eagles theme song, a musical enactment of Eagle talk. Written and recorded on cassette by an Eagles member, the lyrics to "The Sky is the Limit" were written with the Eagles in mind. They express a "possibility thinking" type of conversation with oneself. "When you feel down, down, down, remember the sky is the limit, you can reach the stars, only the sky is the limit."[40] Michael Tait, the college gospel singer who made the recording, expects to put himself through his remaining years in college with the proceeds.

The basic John Raye formula for entrepreneurial success, "possibility thinking," forms a central feature of Eagle talk. The prescription for starting one's own business, as stated earlier, is think positive, have an idea, make a goal, develop a plan. A formula repeated often during meetings, for many members the concept is revolutionary. The step-by-step progression of planning and orienting one's present life toward future goals is frequently not a part of the life experience of many working-class black Americans. Raye maintains, however, that once blacks "know the unspeakable joy of going up against the odds, to press on . . . the joy is indescribable." The local Afro-American newspaper characterizes Raye's movement as "finding converts to economic salvation."[41] For John Raye, the Eagles movement is "divine . . . a movement for the masses . . . right now, the Eagles are a rocket and I have to control the throttle."

At the summit conference, John introduced two young male leaders-in-training, a law student and a business student. Both exuded excitement about the potential of the Eagles movement and maintained a solid stage presence. Said John, "The hallmark of a good leader is being able to replace himself; here are two young men, now being groomed."

A joking conversation between a man and a woman in their early thirties at an Eagles meeting represents the process of conversion to Eagle patterns of thought. Money is the color of freedom:

> "Are you a Majestic Eagle?" asked the man. "Not yet," said the woman. "I'm working at it, though." "Then will you loan me some money?" responded the man, and they both laughed.[42]

For the business novice, the Eagles meetings can function as an open university. A librarian in her early forties explained how her understanding of herself has changed since she has begun to think about the importance of a well-defined business plan and short- and long-term goals. As an Eagles member learning about business, she found one lecture on "How to Start Your Own Business" particularly helpful. The presenter, also an Eagle, had provided what amounted to new information to many members. Some of his points, among others:

1. Starting a business is not a nine to five situation; you have to be willing to put in the time.
2. You need to save some money or borrow from an uncle, aunt, or friend.
3. A business is not a hobby; it's for profit.
4. You must live for less while you start a business. Cut expenses and reinvest profits to get a business off the ground. You need tangible fixed assets to borrow against.
5. You need an advisory board to air your decisions. The Eagles can help here.[43]

Interviews with several Eagles members yielded further insights into shared Eagle patterns of thought. A man in his mid forties who has started several business endeavors, none quite successful as yet, told us, "The purpose of the Eagles is to provide a forum for the collective recognition that jobs are not the way to empowerment."[44] He continued:

> Eagles function as a network. If you need advice or help in your business or plan, you can go to an Eagle. You don't have to pay for a consultation.[45]

In addition to supporting economic self-reliance:

> What makes the Eagles "move" is an unquantifiable item, not attached to anything tangible. It is a shared sense of what is real and what is important. It is a shared perspective. We admire and respect each other for being here at this point in time, in full recognition of the difficulties Afro-Americans have at being in business. We've all come to the same conclusion. Whites understand the difference between employee and employer; it's in their culture and not in black culture.[46]

An important distinction drawn in Eagle talk is the difference between an employee and an entrepreneur. An Eagle with experience in several businesses comments:

> The Eagles with business experience are people who make decisions. The Eagles allow people to share the experience of being in a business environment, being among people who take sharp, definitive action. Blacks who know the obstacles—such as hard-to-get loans—and still decide to have a business . . . may try many times before they succeed. They really want the independence and the ability to be in control of something rather than being controlled by it. For a black person to act on this, whether in desperation or out of a challenge or a the result of a vision [like John, he adds]—to step out of the employee role, one steps into a new dimension, leaving the bonds of alienation. It is one way to lift the anchors of alienation for black Americans . . . . One of the main anchors is job security. Starting your own business is not a practical decision. Once you experience trying to make your business grow, to prove the institutions that support alienation wrong, it's hard to go back to being an employee once again.[47]

Inequality and devaluation, obviously deeply experienced by this man in his mid forties, is muted, and equality demonstrated by entrepreneurial activity:

> The true entrepreneur is "hooked" and is not happy any other way. Having your own makes you realize you're as good as anyone else, no better, but as good.[48]

The Eagles Meet

The Eagles building on Rhode Island Avenue, in Northeast Washington, provides a welcoming place for members and prospective members to meet, eat, conduct business, network, and find spiritual nourishment. The owners of the first Eagle product, Skybright Laundry Detergent and Dishwashing Soap, peddle their wares, as do the distributors of vitamins and other products. A member likened the interaction that goes on before and after Eagles meetings as "no different than what happens on the golf course between white business people . . . . We're here to talk about business, not exclusively, of course."[49] During meetings, John Raye often refers to fellow Eagles as "Brother X or Sister Y." He also emphasizes that members don't drink or "boogie" at meetings, following that with, "Can you imagine that!"

The weekly Saturday morning Expo (10:30 to 1:00) and Thursday evening Expo (7:30 to 9:00) include opening prayers, songs, and live music, a speech by John Raye or Florence King, a lecture on business or health, or a spiritual topic by an invited guest, a career history or business advice talk by an Eagles member, the pinning of new members, and a meal. Meals are an important part of the fellowship and practice of Eagle living; at $5, they are nutritional, low-fat, and catered by an Eagles member. At one Saturday morning breakfast meeting, a local chiropractor spoke about, "What is health?" She began with, "It's not just looking good or feeling good and being out for a good time."[50] Her talk focused on life-style modification, diet, and exercise as ways to combat high blood pressure and some cancers. She also spoke about her own business, a medical practice, and handed out business cards.

Another Saturday morning meeting drew visitors from the Atlanta and New York City chapters, who were welcomed with great fanfare. John Raye opened the meeting with a booming, "Good morning, how is everyone?" The audience replied in unison, "Fantastic!" He was enthusiastic about the Manhood Training Program, consisting then of five youths and five adults, which had met for one-and-a-half hours earlier that morning. He invited one youth to the microphone to share his experience in Manhood Training where "we talk some man talk." The twelve- or thirteen-year-old boy spoke about how his grades were high but slipped when be began to hang around some "bad kids." Since attending Manhood Training sessions, he has started doing his homework again and now wants to be president of his class. John asked him, "Why didn't you want to be president of your class before?" He replied, "Because I didn't want the responsibility." John beamed with pride, hugged the boy close, and said to the audience, "We must take responsibility for our own." This led into Michael Tait performing his Eagles theme song, "The Sky is the Limit." Later John spoke about the economic summit, the need to lease office space in the Eagles building, and the pending loan application for $900,000 to renovate the building. "This cash will be kept in our community, Eagles businesses will be hired to do the contract work," assured John.

Each Tuesday evening, John Raye teaches a Master Mind session to a class of approximately thirty students. Students in the current group had worked together for six months. As participants, they are asked to study the book *Three Magic Words* by U.S. Anderson and to write essays incorporating his wisdom into their thinking. John lectures and discusses the material and the group ends with a closing collective meditation. Possibility thinking is the general theme of the class.

In his lecture at one session, John reviewed the six areas of life that need to be balanced: physical, social, mental, spiritual, family, and financial. He talked about setting goals in each of the areas, beginning with good nutrition and putting less salt in our biscuits. He spoke about "the art of visualization" in getting what you want out of life:

> Get a clear picture in your mind of what you want. It's not enough to say, "I want a dream house." Go to a model home and see it! Write down your goals and put the list on your refrigerator. Record them on a cassette tape and listen to them in the car while your drive. Don't say, "I will become a person who is on time," say, "I am a person who comes to meetings on time." The difference between a goal and a wish is: a wish, you never do anything about it; a goal, you do something about it!

He moved on with the discussion of possibility thinking by stating the "law of attraction." Anderson discusses how, "You attract what you think," so John advised his students not to think negative thoughts. "Poor little ol' me is an example of contaminated thinking." John admonished his class to, "Write it down and claim it as yours." After reading positive thoughts from homework assignments, he acknowledged that, "Unlearning requires a lot of energy." He used the story of his wife's success in overcoming her public speaking shyness and an example from the group of one man's headway in combating his stammer. Although the man still stammered, he said, "I believe now that I can get up and say what I want to say." He was no longer embarrassed about his shortcoming, but proud of his progress. The devil was identified as self-doubt. Said one student, "The devil is on duty twenty-five hours a day." John wrapped up the session by discussing the possibilities for economic development, the Eagles chapter in Atlanta, and the power of Eagles thinking.

The "Tuesday Lunch Bunch" is an ad hoc group of Eagles in business who got together in June 1987 to help Eagles members apply for Department of Defense set-aside contracts. At the first meeting, a program analyst from DOD spoke about the set-aside program and efforts to attract minority businesses. He mentioned a request for proposal (RFP) for an organization or consulting firm to manage and sponsor meetings that were to be held all over the country to inform minority businesses about the set-aside program. John energetically endorsed the Eagles' applying for the RFP and helping members obtain set-aside contracts for their individual businesses.

As is pro forma at all Eagles meetings, the Tuesday Lunch Bunch began their meeting with a blessing by one of the Eagles founders, the Reverend Ewell, a Baptist minister and retired lawyer. Introduced by John as the "Chief Legal Eagle," he entreated God's help with the agenda:

> Bless our president and his family and help us bring up our skills to compete with others. Oh Lord, help us support our young people.[51]

The chair of the Tuesday Lunch Bunch, Ms. Ross, a woman in her late thirties, emphasized the difficulty of working as a group when a different group of people showed up every Tuesday. In addition, many people failed to arrive on time.

John wanted the Eagles to put together a "packet of Eagles skills"; that is, a group of services that could be provided by Eagles members. For him, the Eagles were a solution to the government's complaint of not being able to find qualified minority firms. Ms. Ross informed him that the Department of Defense does not do business with packets. She saw the role of the Eagles as doing workshops and familiarizing members with how to do business with the government, primarily learning the procedures to qualify for set-aside contracts. "The average black business person deals with a void of information," complained Ms. Ross. John wanted to direct the committee's attention to the July 10th deadline for the conference RFP. He reminded members that the Department of Defense "buys everything, from toothpicks to paper. . . . We all need to bid." Further, he admonished the group:

> You're moving too slow. It will be 1998 before you put together officers. Don't come back here talking no more. Don't waste the president's time rehashing something. Why has no one showed the RFP to me?

Ms. Ross stated calmly, "We can criticize and throw bricks and tear ourselves apart or get organized." At which point, officers were elected and Jim McBride was given the task of pursuing the RFP. John ended the meeting with an upbeat presentation of his trip to Atlanta over the previous weekend:

> They don't own nothing. It's pitiful. I told them, see what you don't own . . . and now the Eagles chapter there is organizing to buy a building!"

At the following Tuesday meeting, Ms. Ross did not come to the meeting, apparently offended at John's outburst against her leadership. Mr. McBride could not find a copy of the RFP. John arrived late and apologized to everyone. He had picked up the RFP and given it to an Eagles proposal writer. Having sidestepped the committee, he offered an apology to Mr. McBride, "You'll have to excuse me; I didn't know how to reach you." John has committed the Eagles to applying for the RFP and has asked that everyone's resume be included in the packet: "By yourself, maybe your package won't fly, but if you get together with others, maybe it will." This advice, in a nutshell, expresses John Raye's outlook on life.

Summary

The Majestic Eagles is a striking example of a grass-roots voluntary association where working and middle-class black Americans mingle and network. Its activities and purpose center around the inspirational leadership of its founder, John Raye. Members share an interest in acquiring entrepreneurial attitudes and in developing and implementing their own entrepreneurial ideas. The explicit goal of the organization is to assist its members in practicing entrepreneurship, a procedure defined by John Raye as having an idea, making a goal, developing a plan, and implementing it.

The Majestic Eagles organization provides its members with a range of *social resources* that foster entrepreneurship:

1. An active social support network for positive black American group identity and individual self-esteem, spiritual renewal, and the collective reinforcement of the entrepreneurial ethic.
2. Information and planning seminars for personal and business financial success.
3. Empowerment based on their voluntary membership in a social collectivity predicated on the recognition of one fundamental value—the necessity of achieving economic self-reliance.
4. The opportunity to participate in a federally insured credit union, as contributors and in leadership roles.
5. A weekly social arena in which to network with other Eagles members for business opportunities, advice, or information.
6. The formation of Youth Training Clubs to encourage self-improvement, financial planning, and entrepreneurship among the next generation.

"Eagle talk" is a supportive language that helps mitigate against internalized inferiority and promote risk-taking. The acquisition of Eagle talk as a way of speaking and thinking provides the keystone to empowerment and participation in the voluntary association. Although many of the individuals who regularly attend meetings have been socialized to speak Eagle talk, they generally view themselves as novices—vis-à-vis John Raye—in a spiritual and economic journey involving entrepreneurial success, personal growth and development, and spiritual salvation.

As a voluntary association, the Majestic Eagles has several internal, organizational constraints. Any voluntary group that centers on the leadership, vision, personality, and inspirational message of one individual is subject to problems of sustainability and replication. Even though two young men in their mid to late twenties have been identified as the next generation of leaders by John Raye, inspirational power and authority are difficult to pass on or delegate. With power and authority resting in the figure of John Raye, the future stability of the ten Eagles chapters is uncertain. Within the D.C. chapter, authority for solving internal conflict rests solely with Raye's efforts at conciliation; a more formal process for conflict resolution is simply not in place.

A Washington-based journalist who grew up in a Baptist-centered home suggests that inspirational movements that focus on the leader's vision and personality are part of a broad black American cultural pattern.[52] She argues that as a deeply rooted feature of black American culture, the preconditioned search for a Messiah to fulfill a tenacious longing for freedom and salvation causes problems in movements for social change. The leader of a black church or social movement often embodies ideals of liberation and deliverance. As a symbol, he is revered and supported by his followers. When the movement is political, fruition of objectives depends more on the personality of the leader than on the momentum and advocacy of members. As a result, inspirational movements are risky in terms of their ability to promote long-term social change. Thus, although John Raye's dream encompasses economic as well as spiritual salvation, the inherent dangers of black charismatic leadership could become an impediment to the sustainability of the Majestic Eagles.

As a four-year-old indigenous urban black self-help group, the Majestic Eagles relies largely on informal organizational principles. Kinship is not a membership criterion, nor officially is race. Compared with the social and economic functions of voluntary associations found among other groups seeking entrepreneurial success—immigrants to the United States or migrants from rural areas to central cities in the Third World—the Majestic Eagles has greater difficulty tying together a lasting moral basis for its communal activities. In contrast to other mutual aid associations, few members are involved in collective economic enterprises, although the possibility for such economic cooperation exists and may increase over time.

Finally, one suspects that the Majestic Eagles still lacks the critical mass of professional expertise needed to make a significant, nationwide impact on expanding entrepreneurship among black Americans. To meet its goals, it will have to attract a larger number of highly successful entrepreneurs interested in investing significant amounts of time in teaching members sound business practices. Competence among the current membership is far from uniform, as evidenced by efforts to gain access to Department of Defense contracts. The more successful members are involved in starting a Majestic Eagles bank and a shared equity program. The latter entails raising venture capital to purchase substandard housing for renovation by Eagles members. In the long run, the spiritual component necessary to bring the group together in the first place may also serve as its most limiting constraint; the new class of black urban professionals appears less likely to join groups that combine spiritual salvation with business success.

The Pittsburghers

During a 1963 summer weekend, Mr. Henry Wade of Pittsburgh visited the District of Columbia to spend time with six friends, all then residents of the Washington, D.C. area and former Pittsburghers. He suggested that they form a club to enjoy their common bond, and, over the next six months, the Pittsburghers was founded. The first members had moved to the Washington area during the 1940s and 1950s to compete for federal jobs, a number of which had become newly available as a result of changes in hiring policies under the Truman administration. A few had been stationed in Washington during their stint in the armed services and opted to stay. Washington was viewed as more open and less blue collar than Pittsburgh. The segregated schools were reportedly good and a growing Washington black middle class attracted migrants from up and down the eastern seaboard, including many from northern cities like Pittsburgh.

By the time the Pittsburghers came into existence, the civil rights movement had blossomed. In their own fashion, they committed their new social club to advocacy on behalf of the black community. They adopted the motto "Pittsburghers Promote Progress" and defined their purpose as developing "a social and civic program among the membership of former residents of the Pittsburgh Metropolitan Area in order to have friendly contact with each other."[53] Col. Henry Morgan offered his home as a permanent meeting place and was elected the first president in 1964. As its major goal, the club established a scholarship fund for Pittsburgh students attending college in Washington. Donations to Washington community organizations came next, along with contributions to a few charitable efforts in Pittsburgh. The current president of the Pittsburghers, Dr. Floyd Keene, summarizes the objectives of the organization as threefold:

1. To raise funds for a competitive scholarship program for needy students who were born in Pittsburgh and want to go to college in the Washington area.
2. To raise funds to donate to community service organizations in Pittsburgh and the Washington area.
3. To promote social contacts between Pittsburgh migrants to Washington.[54]

Between 1965 and 1981, $36,000 was awarded to students and $20,000 to community charities and organizations. In 1986, scholarships totaled $6,000. Club members use their personal contacts to interview eligible students in Pittsburgh and Washington, in addition to mounting a search for worthy candidates through high-school recruitment programs and radio advertising. Washington charities that have received funds include Friends of the Juvenile Court, the YMCA Summer Campership Fund, the Hospital for Sick Children, The D.C. Association for Retarded Children, No Drugs for Us, and the Metropolitan Police Boys Club. By contrast, contributions to Pittsburgh groups have tended to go to more exclusively black and less socially activist groups—Junior Mothers of Pittsburgh, Danette Civic Club of Pittsburgh, and the Pittsburgh Continental Society.

The main fund-raising effort is an annual autumn ball, initially held at the Presidential Arms, a segregated facility, but nowadays at the Shoreham Hotel. Each of the sixty members is asked to fill two tables of twenty people, but in general, about a third of the members carry most of the tables. Friends and relatives of the Pittsburghers have established a custom of visiting for the autumn ball each year and receive special recognition at ball ceremonies. The ball has expanded to include a weekend of festivities; a Friday formal ball and breakfast, a Saturday night disco, and a Sunday farewell brunch.

Recently, the charter was amended to include the children of persons born in Pittsburgh as members. Average age of current members is near retirement. The greatest source of new membership appears to be new professionals in the Washington area who originally hailed from Pittsburgh. New members must be sponsored by a current club member.

According to President Keene, the children of Pittsburghers have different social needs than their parents. They did not attend segregated schools, have generally followed upward mobility patterns, and do not currently reside in Washington. The president adds:

> Younger people now have so many greater opportunities to own their own businesses, earn MBAs and work for corporations. In my time, we couldn't get a loan without a personal contact.[55]

In addition, the once-steady stream of students from Pittsburgh to Washington colleges has lessened since Carnegie University began accepting large numbers of black students in the early 1970s.

Pittsburghers meet once a month, with approximately thirty members in attendance at an average meeting. The executive board also meets on a monthly basis. The club sponsors holiday parties and sends flowers to funerals and gifts for weddings. The president said he joined the club because he liked the values of scholarship and community service, wanted fellowship with others, and enjoyed the good name of the club in the community. Some members of the club, their families and friends, have become his patients. He has been most impressed by the fact that the Pittsburghers have stayed together for over twenty years.

Summary

As with the Majestic Eagles, but for very different reasons, the Pittsburghers face a sustainability problem. Most members are in their fifties and sixties and recruits have not been easy to find. The children of Pittsburghers are not as active and interested in the kind of club their parents founded at a similar age.

Pittsburghers support education and benevolent community service as a means to improve the quality of life in the black community. They emphasize deserving black youth from both lower-income and working classes. Scholarships are based on academic and social achievement, and selected individuals are honored at meetings and the annual ball. Recipients have used Pittsburgher Club members as valuable resources for advice, information, and in some cases, job contacts.

The Coalition of Black Professional Organizations

The Coalition of Black Professional Organizations (CBPO) was founded in 1981 by the New York City chapter of the National Urban Affairs Council. The current president, Darryl Gay, is a labor relations expert and attorney. According to him, similar organizations exist in Atlanta (the Atlanta Exchange), Miami (Black Professionals Coalition), and Washington, D.C. (D.C. Coalition of Black Professionals). The organization advocates sharing information and building a support network among black professionals. The stated goals are:

1. Sharing information.
2. Opening doors of communication between corporations and the black community.
3. Helping students enter the professional workforce.
4. Supporting black professionals in upward mobility.[56]

CPBO is literally a coalition of member groups created for a variety of reasons to serve the needs of the black community. It includes:

- One Hundred Back Men—founded in 1963, now 500 male members in industry, business, government, public affairs, and the professions who want to improve the quality of life for blacks and other minorities.
- Black MBA Association—gives seminars for professional development and has a scholarship program for minority MBA students.
- New York Association of Black Psychologists—founded in 1967 to promote a responsible application of psychological intervention strategies in the black community.
- National Urban Affairs Council—a professional placement service promoting black community visibility and a black legislative voice.
- One Hundred Black Women—founded in 1970, has 500 members promoting leadership among black women.
- Council of Concerned Black Executives—founded in 1968 the day after Martin Luther King's assassination to support members in corporate careers, assist corporations in minority executive recruitment, and teach black students about corporate life.
- Urban Bankers Coalition—founded in 1971 to help members achieve high job performance, promote economic development by financial counseling, support organizations raising the standard of life in black communities, and assist high-school and college students in career planning.[57]

Darryl Gay describes CBPO as "a round table" rather than a hierarchical, parent organization. He explains, "The purpose of the Coalition is to encourage black professionals from various specialities to meet each other, to expose ourselves to important local and national issues, and to cooperate in a mentor program for junior and senior high school and college students."[58] Speaking about the state of black professionals, he says:

> In the 1960s there were possibilities for black professionals in law and the government, not in Fortune 500 companies. Since the early 1970s the number of black graduates of professional schools has been explosive. We are missing, both personally and in our organizations, an older generation of black professionals. We have no one to look up to . . . . We are the pioneers.[59]

Gay mentions a broad concern among black professionals about limited minority promotions and states that the Coalition's networking function has alleviated this problem. It helps to identify shared difficulties as "part of the problems of *my* community." Gay considers the mentorship program very successful. As president, he contacts individual members to speak at a junior high school assembly or sponsor a summer intern. He finds the voluntary spirit refreshing and has rarely been turned down by prospective mentors.

Summary

The Coalition of Black Professional Organizations is composed of a diverse group of organizations based in New York City. Its members are fifty-five years old and younger; the group misses the presence of a generation of elders in the black American professional scene. An occupational type of mutual aid voluntary association, the CBPO has focused on the upward mobility and career advancement of black professionals. Most member groups have a community outreach function for exposing younger black Americans to professional opportunities and successful role models.

Comparison of Three Contemporary Black American Voluntary Associations

Similarities among the black American voluntary associations we have covered are worth noting. Although member needs are at the forefront of most activities, all three groups have an explicit orientation toward the next generation of black Americans. The Coalition extends itself to the young by conducting effective outreach programs for students at secondary and college levels. Pittsburgers contribute to the lives of individual college students in the form of cash outlays. Over the past twenty years they have invested in the future of hundreds of young blacks. The Eagles conduct Saturday morning classes for its youth, boys and girls in separate classes, and have plans for involving them in entrepreneurial sales and neighborhood clean-up campaigns.

All three voluntary associations advocate self-help, group solidarity, and mutual support. The Eagles view entrepreneurship as the hope of the future, while the Pittsburghers support educational endeavors and community benevolent activities. The Coalition attempts to increase networking among black professionals, another step in upward mobility.

Besides function, differences among the three voluntary groups rest on the fact that they represent different segments of the large black American community. The Coalition has defined its interests along occupational lines and primarily represents the interests of the new generation of "Buppies"—black Yuppies. The Pittsburghers have defined themselves by geographical roots and concern themselves with both social solidarity and an investment in the education of the younger generation. The Majestic Eagles serves as a multifunction voluntary group attempting to resocialize black Americans to save, take entrepreneurial risks, and thereby improve the economic and spiritual life of the black community.

As we have shown, different segments of the black American community have successfully represented themselves in voluntary associations. Although they provide new opportunities for leadership development among successive generations, none is free from internal limitations. John Raye and the Majestic Eagles confront the difficulties inherent in an excessive reliance on charismatic leadership. The Coalition of Black Professional Organizations lacks sufficient role models from the generation that preceded it. The Pittsburghers, who are the preceding generation, suffer the reverse dilemma of passing on organizational resources developed in a different time for different reasons. Nevertheless, each group serves important social and economic functions within the black community. Above all, they foster the in-group identity and positive self-image that appear essential keys for unlocking the full economic and social potential of black Americans.

Notes

1. Marcus Garvey, Daddy Divine, The Black Muslims, and more recently the Reverend Leon Sullivan are well known examples of blacks who have developed voluntary associations for entrepreneurial ends in black American communities. Brotz has observed, "An ideology together with an organization can do things which individual entrepreneurship among Negroes cannot achieve." Cited in Light, Ivan H., "Church, Sect and Father Divine" in Light, Ivan H., *Ethnic Enterprise in America: Business and Welfare Among Chinese, Japanese and Blacks* (Berkeley: University of California Press, 1972, p. 150).
2. Cummings, Scott, *Self-Help in Urban America: Patterns of Minority Business Enterprise* (Port Washington, New York: Kennikat Press, 1980). See also Han-

nerz, Ulf, "Ethnicity and Opportunity in Urban America" in Cohen, Abner (ed.), *Urban Ethnicity* (London: Tavistock, 1974).

3. Little, Kenneth, *West African Urbanization: A Study of Voluntary Associations in Social Change* (New York: Cambridge University Press, 1965). Also Mangin, William, *Peasants in Cities: Readings in the Anthropology of Urbanization* (New York: Houghton Mifflin, 1970). As well as Meillassoux, Claude, *Urbanization of an African Community: Voluntary Associations in Bamako* (Seattle: University of Washington Press, 1968).

4. Vincent, Joan, "The Structuring of Ethnicity" (*Human Organization,* vol. 33, no. 4, 1974).

5. Light, op.cit.

6. Mangin, op. cit.

7. Ibid.

8. Mangin, op. cit.; Little, op. cit; Meillassoux, op. cit.

9. Mitchell, William, *Mishpokhe: A Study of New York City Jewish Family Circles* (New York: Mouton, 1978).

10. Light, op. cit.

11. Ibid.

12. Ibid.

13. Ibid., p. 14.

14. Interview with Dr. Keene, current president of the Pittsburgh Club (Washington, D.C., July 3, 1987).

15. Light, op. cit.

16. Ibid.

17. Interview with Collin King and Allan Brathwite of the Washington, D.C. Government Minority Business Opportunity Commission (Washington, D.C., June 24, 1987).

18. Ibid.

19. Davidson, Joe, "Melting Pot Boils as Influx of Asian Merchants Into Black Neighborhoods Is Greeted Grimly" (*Wall Street Journal,* July 31, 1987).

20. Ibid.

21. Ibid.

22. Light, op. cit.

23. Mullings, Leith, "Ethnicity and Social Stratification in the Urban United States." (*Annals of the New York Academy of Sciences,* no. 318, 1978).

24. Young, Harding B. and Hund, James M., "Negro Entrpreneurship in Southern Economic Development" in Young, Harding B. and Hund, James M., "Negro Entrepreneurship in Southern Economic Development," in M.L. Grunhart and W. T. Whitman (eds.), *Black Americans and White Business* (Chapel Hill: University of North Carolina Press, 1964, pp. 112–157).

25. Mullings, op. cit.

26. Ibid.

27. Light, op. cit.

28. Stack, Carol, *All Our Kin* (New York: Harper and Row, 1974).

29. Green, Lee, "Interview with John Raye" (*Financial Independence,* September/October 1986, pp. 34–35).

30. Ibid., p. 33.

31. Membership and Orientation Committee, *The Majestic Eagles, Inc: Membership Manual* (Washington, D.C., September 1986).

32. Ibid., p. 10.

33. Interviews with Florence King, May 30 and September 6, 1987.
34. Ibid.
35. Payne, Ethel, "Faith and Detergent: The Raye Formula for Success" (*Afro-American,* December 1986).
36. Jackson, Jesse, Keynote speech at first annual Black Economic Summit Conference (Mayflower Hotel, Washington, D.C., July 24, 1986).
37. Green, op. cit., p. 36.
38. Jackson, Jesse, op. cit.
39. Ibid.
40. Tait, Michael, "The Sky is the Limit," Majestic Eagles theme song (cassette tape recorded in 1987).
41. Payne, Ethel, op. cit.
42. Majestic Eagles Meeting (Washington, D.C., May 30, 1987).
43. Ibid.
44. Majestic Eagles Lunch Bunch Meeting (Washington, D.C., July 16, 1987).
45. Ibid.
46. Ibid.
47. Ibid.
48. Ibid.
49. Majestic Eagles Meeting (Washington, D.C., July 1, 1987).
50. Ibid.
51. Ibid.
52. Interview with Washington-based correspondant for a nationally syndicated black magazine (Washington, D.C., June 24, 1987).
53. *The Pittsburghers: Tenth Anniversary Souvenir Journal. Autumn Ball* (Washington, D.C., October 19,1973).
54. Ibid.
55. Dr. Keene, op. cit.
56. Interview with Darrell Gay, current president of the Coalition of Black Professional Organizations (New York City, July 13, 1987).
57. Ibid.
58. Ibid.
59. Ibid.

6

Building a New Agenda:
Entrepreneurial Perspectives

Building a New Agenda

The five preceding chapters present a preliminary sketch, based on existing evidence, of black entrepreneurship in America. We have attempted to ground our efforts in the social institutions closest to the daily lives of black Americans—families, schools, and voluntary associations. Looked at from an entrepreneurial perspective, they suggest a variety of practical solutions to overcoming the economic and social barriers to black entrepreneurship.

Many pieces of the puzzle are missing. Cultural and sociological studies of black entrepreneurship have been rare and incomplete. Most anthropological research on economic development, including entrepreneurship, has been limited to Third World countries or small, exotic segments of American culture. Sociological analyses have tended toward sweeping generalizations based on little or outdated evidence.

Starting from the bottom rather than from the top seems to us the commonsense way to find culturally relevant entrepreneurial solutions to black economic problems. Adopting this method of entrepreneurial research may incur "political" problems analagous to those faced by small, entrepreneurial companies:

> It is not easy to abandon policies that worked so well in the past in favor of an unknown, widely scattered, fine-grained collection of small enterprises, none of which contributes much, but the collection of which is keeping the older cities alive.[1]

Birch's observation of the relatively low political favor enjoyed by small entrepreneurial companies provides a neat metaphor for the types of research applied in the past to economic development and those that remain to be done.

As a research construct, black economic culture is in its own pioneer stages of development. Like entrepreneurial businesses, it needs to be approached

169

from a large number and variety of discrete, seemingly disconnected perspectives. The totality of these efforts, we suggest, may indeed provide the insights necessary to keep American cities alive.

In our study of black entrepreneurship, we have emphasized the importance of an entrepreneurial culture in the economic development process. We have stressed the need for understanding how the individual economic choices of black Americans relate to surrounding economic and social conditions. In particular, we have tried to show how the mediating institutions of family, school, and voluntary association—in conjunction with external conditions in the marketplace—have enhanced or restricted entrepreneurial opportunities among black Americans.

We believe black Americans have the resources to propagate their own economic development. As realists, we know the task will not be easy. Changing the anti-entrepreneurial attitudes and behavior patterns ingrained in black economic culture will take, in addition to changes in the objective circumstances of many blacks, a change in black perceptions of entrepreneurial possibilities. Our first recommendation is that solutions begin with a clearer understanding of the problems involved.

The Problem of Culture

Cultures encompass the socially transmitted beliefs and behavior patterns of particular human communities. By extension, economic cultures reflect shared beliefs and behavior patterns governing the production and distribution of wealth.

Within both the dominant American culture and the black American subculture, black economic culture has been subsumed by the belief that, as victims of white racism, blacks must be insulated from the depredations of the marketplace. Accordingly, blacks progress only to the extent government protections or spending on black economic programs expand. We believe this view is antithetical to the economic progress of black Americans. With many experts, we agree that economic development depends first and foremost on innovative, risk-prone activities that governments, rigid and ponderous by nature, cannot manage effectively. The entrepreneurial activities that stimulate development are best carried out through efficient and properly regulated markets. At base, economic development is a private activity organized around the talents and resources of a particular community. It can be frustrated or facilitated by government; it cannot be done by government.

We do not advocate the wholesale elimination of protections that have allowed blacks and other minorities a fair opportunity to compete for jobs, housing, and business opportunities. As long as protective or compensatory statutes reinforce productive economic behavior, they enhance economic development. When, however, they undermine entrepreneurial creativity by encouraging dependence, they block development progress. In the end, blacks must rely on their own entrepreneurial ability in a rapidly changing, multifarious marketplace.

Breaking the bonds of black entrepreneurship will require changes in the economic culture of the black community. Not only must blacks turn less to government for economic resources, they must also focus less on racism as the primary cause of their economic problems. Few would deny that the current plight of the black poor originated, in large measure, from the abusive power of white racists. But continued attacks on racism will not wipe out black unemployment or welfare dependency. If more laws were passed tomorrow mandating better treatment of blacks by whites, they would not have one iota of impact on the economic problems facing black Americans today.

Finally, the black community must change its dominant perceptions of economic risk and reward. One of the most crippling effects of racial discrimination was to sever effort from accomplishment, investment from reward. First as slaves and then as poorly paid sharecroppers and laborers, many blacks learned that for any given level of effort, the reward was identical, little or none. Prohibited by law from competing with whites for economic resources, sharecroppers and wage laborers who worked very hard could not reasonably expect to be better off than those who worked very little. When, regardless of the amount of invested effort, economic reward remains constant or absent, few people expend more than is necessary to survive from day to day. In this kind of world, the world in which many blacks lived most of their lives, economic culture was not organized around hard work, investment, and risk.

Sustained economic progress throughout the black community will require blacks to overcome negative beliefs based on lessons of the past. Whether and how much they achieve will depend to a large degree on what they believe achievable. Consider the case of two men, one entrepreneurial, the other risk-averse, looking at a vacant factory in the middle of an urban ghetto. The entrepreneurial man sees the potential for a successful assembly plant and pursues his belief with effort and money. If smart and lucky, he will be rewarded with a successful entrepreneurial venture creating new jobs and wealth. If his project fails, a few people will lose money, but the community will be no worse off than before. The risk-averse man may see the same possibility, but believe his effort and money would be lost by making the investment. Turning away, he will avoid failure but he will also foreclose success. His decision will have left the community at best no better off and at worst, worse off.

The Problem of Structure

New economic activity tends to spring up where resources, especially money, are available to support it. The black community, though not nearly as rich as white America, is not nearly so poor as its cultural mythology would have it believe. In terms of percapita income, American blacks are among the richest people on earth. Yet blacks know their savings—in the form of life insurance, pension plans, or bank deposits—finance office buildings in downtown New York, shopping centers in Orange County, and retirement homes in Florida. Little goes toward financing new economic activity undertaken by blacks in black neighborhoods. Have blacks purposely directed their hard-earned savings toward financing business deals outside the black community? Hardly. Rules governing financial markets make investments inside the black community illegal or unattractive, even when their potential rates of return are extraordinarily high.

In the theoretical world of perfectly efficient capital markets, capital always flows to where it can earn the highest returns. Real-world markets are not perfectly efficient. Scarce information about certain types of investment, high transaction costs, and the absence of intermediaries to pool and spread risk prevents capital from flowing to many people and projects. For example, banks may refuse to lend money to a neighborhood based on incorrect or biased information about its property values. Investors may hold back from a deal because of the high cost of documenting and monitoring its progress. Blacks themselves may not invest in their own communities because black banks, insurance companies, and other financial institutions either cannot or will not pool risk and spread functions to reduce investor risk.

Governments also shape markets in the real world through tax, spending, and regulatory policies. Governments can encourage investments they deem to have a high social value, even when private investors are not willing to make them. Conversely, governments can discourage investments in which, left to their own devices, private investors would invest heavily. Low-income housing is an example of the first type of government intervention, South African kruggerands of the second.

Reasonable people do not always agree on what will enhance social utility or market efficiency. One person's market correction is liable to be another's distortion. As a result, legislators are constantly pressured to implement tax and regulatory policies altering the relative advantage of various investments. Frequently the results reflect the triumph of cupidity over utility. During consideration of a recent tax bill, the securities industry successfully lobbied to change a rule fixing the length of time certain stocks must be held for their sales to be treated as taxable capital gains. Security industry economists argued that the change would increase the efficiency of capital markets, but the real effect was to increase the income of brokers by allowing people to trade stocks more frequently without incurring tax penalties.

A few economic ideologues may insist that God created markets, like human beings, to be free. Hard evidence tells us that markets are constantly reshaped to accommodate shifting, and not always sound, ideas about how capital should be allocated. Unfortunately, blacks are rarely involved in debates about markets, savings and investment taxes, insurance regulations, and bank charters. Largely due to their historic dependence on the public sector as well as to their historic mistreatment in the marketplace, blacks tend to view financial markets as entities other people use to generate income. As a result, market structures rarely advance black economic interests and, indeed, are frequently inimical to them.

Entrepreneurial Perspectives

Herb Wilkins

> Our worst option is to do away with the notion we are a community. The black middle class can't go home and enjoy the fruits of the labor they have supposedly earned by their own initiative while leaving that kid in the ghetto unable to compete.[2]

A handsome, robust man in his mid forties, Herb Wilkins fits the profile of the well-educated, high-powered black in an "emerging" field of minority enterprise. He is married, the father of three children. He holds a Harvard MBA in finance and control. In 1977, after a series of job stints in mainstream corporate America, he broke away to form his own company, Syndicated Communications Incorporated. Headquartered in Washington, D.C., SYNCOM is the only minority-owned venture capital firm created to finance minority entrepreneurs in the communications industry. To date SYNCOM has a portfolio of thirty-two minority-owned communications companies representing over $13 million of invested capital.

Although $13 million seems a considerable sum, Herb emphasizes that in the broadcasting business it represents a mere drop in the bucket. The price of one good FM station in a large metropolitan market ranges between $25 and $70 million. When we talked, Herb was negotiating a deal for a small consortium of minority bidders to buy a Chicago FM radio station. To be taken seriously, they would have to submit a minimum bid of $25 million. Ten years ago, says Herb, he could have bought the same station for $3 million. The rapid escalation of broadcasting property values, up 800 percent in a single decade, reflects tremendous growth in the advertising bases of individual stations. Explains Herb, "There's a fixed relationship in this country between advertising revenue and consumer spending. As disposable income has gone up, the number of dollars spent on advertising has risen accordingly."

When Herb started SYNCOM in 1977 there were fifty minority-owned broadcasting operations in the United States. Today, out of 10,000, there are 175. To further illustrate the competition minorities face, Wilkins parallels the situation of two operations, one minority-owned and the other not, in a single metropolitan market. WKYS and WHUR are both powerful FM radio stations in the high end of the Washington, D.C. market. WKYS, the non-minority station, earns between $14 and $15 million a year. WHUR, owned by Howard University, brings in between $6 and $7 million. A few years ago, WKYS lured away WHUR's top programmer. In addition to being minority-owned, WHUR operates as a public broadcaster, while WKYS is both privately owned and operated. As a result, even if WHUR could afford the $1 million in salaries WKYS pays for top people, the potential hue and cry from an outraged public would make it impossible. Because most minority-owned firms' broadcasting operations receive some kind of government or public support, different standards are commonly applied to minority and non-minority owners. Laments Herb:

> Typically, minority owners never have a clear shot at the unencumbered business environment nonminority firms operate in to develop a business. They're always tied in somehow to the community or somebody's federal program. They can't even try to pay somebody $1 million a year.

WKYS reflects another commonplace reality in broadcasting. WKYS serves a predominately black clientele. All of its top programmers and disc jockeys are black. It is the single most powerful and popular "black" radio station in Washington, D.C. WKYS is owned by NBC, which in turn is owned by General Electric. Over 80 percent of Washington, D.C. residents are black, but only four out of its forty AM and FM stations are owned and operated by minorities. In Philadelphia, New York, and other large American cities, most of the people benefiting from black audiences are white. Herb notes the same situation obtains for Spanish-language stations around the country. Hallmark, which he describes as the prototypical middle-American company, headquartered in Kansas City, owns and manages the largest group of Spanish-speaking broadcast operations. Herb shrugs as he details the daunting environment of minority broadcasting:

> That's just the nature of broadcasting and the way it's always been. Except today we have a few minorities who are attempting to get into these markets. It's tough because it takes a tremendous amount of capital to buy a station.

As in other competitive industries, the answer for blacks has been to find an appropriate niche in the market. Since 1980, SYNCOM has focused on cable acquisitions. "Since no one else was doing it, we saw it as an interesting opportunity." Cable systems offer several important advantages to minority broadcasters. For one, it's easier to get into the business. Most of the big, powerful radio and T.V. stations were created twenty years ago. The dearth of significant new frequencies combined with tremendous growth in the profitability of existing stations has placed noncable broadcasting beyond the reach of most minorities. Cable networks, on the other hand, are still in their infancy. Blacks can come in on the ground floor with everybody else and take advantage of a range of opportunities at affordable prices. As a consequence, Wilkins believes black and other minorities can potentially build stronger bases in cable than in traditional broadcasting.

Cable networks also attract minorities because of their relative freedom from control. Cable systems have multiple channels, allowing their operators to input as much and whatever type of information they choose. Recent legal changes have practically eliminated outside influences from the cable industry. In reality, says Herb Wilkins, because cable operators can directly control the number and type of channels going into a house, they have more First Amendment control than newspapers or individual radio and T.V. stations.

Throughout the country, an average cable system controls thirty-six channels. In the larger markets, sixty channels or more are typical. For the next few years cable operators are legally bound to include network programs, but beyond that, competition between traditional broadcasters and cable stations becomes an open field. The major networks have already positioned themselves to compete directly with cable companies. Even though broadcasters operating a single frequency will have the advantage of covering much larger geographical areas, Herb believes cable systems will eventually surpass them by using interlocking systems. It's a possibility on which he's willing to stake his own future and that of his company.

As with most minority group members in the communications business, Herb has received support from the government. The federal government provides no direct financing, per se, for broadcasters. However, the FCC has developed a series of policies to facilitate minority ownership in separate areas and at different levels of the broadcasting industry. Women or minorities who meet basic qualifications may receive preference in obtaining new broadcasting licenses. A "stress scale" policy also gives a leg up by permitting already licensed but financially troubled broadcasters to sell their licenses to women or minorities at less than fair market values.

Herb's own company, SYNCOM, is 50 percent owned by OFC, Inc., a holding company with controlling interest in Fulcrum Venture Capital Corporation. Fulcrum Venture Capital is a government-sponsored MESBIC. Herb

Wilkins is president of SYNCOM and OFC, Inc. and the managing director of Fulcrum Venture Capital. As a MESBIC, for every dollar of private capital it raises, Fulcrum can borrow four more from the government to lend to minority firms.

Wilkins finds partnership with government onerous, but necessary. Rising costs have made minority entry into the broadcasting industry extremely difficult. And even if they can come up with the money, big lenders prefer nonminorities. For a simple reason, says Herb:

> They believe nonminorities will make even more money from a $25 million investment. It goes back to the age-old bottom line: maximization of effort and minimization of risk.

Even as he defends the necessity, Herb Wilkins chafes under the impositions of government. "We are as regulated as you possibly can be. . . . At every turn we're hamstrung on what we can do." He outlines some examples. For the past three years, the company has been extremely profitable. In order to hold onto those profits and successfully reinvest them, Herb has incurred heavy legal fees. Government officials in charge of his MESBIC have restricted the amount he can spend for legal fees—about an eighth of what he has actually paid to maintain the firm's earning power. "It's the most ludicrous thing in the world," he declares, "but that's what the minority entrepreneur has to endure." In turn, Herb's company must impose rigid rules and reams of bureaucratic paperwork on the minority firms it capitalizes. Even if some of the rules simply reinforce standard business practices, too many others are "arbitrary and unnecessary."

The federal government is not the only offender; local regulations also cramp the ability of minority firms to compete. In return for receiving preferences on a contract, a city or county government may also require a company to hire a set percentage of labor or services from the locale. In reality, the particular locale frequently does not have the required number of skilled workers and services to do the job. Wilkins sums up the problem:

> Too often we are asked to do what is socially significant instead of what is economically important for the success of our companies. To the extent minority firms are forced to choose social commitment over economic requirements, they will not be as competitive as they should be.

Herb looks down the road five or ten years and sees a world market in which American companies will not be able to entertain "anywhere near the social commitments they entertain today, unless the commitments can generate positive economic effects on company performance." Although he be-

lieves there are often economic benefits to be derived from social commitments, "the connection is more often coincidental than intended."

In an increasingly competitive global marketplace, the issues of productivity and competitiveness pose big questions about the future of minority entrepreneurship. Herb views the American economy as part of a larger global
economy whose overcapacity and efficiency are cutting more and more people out of the system. In the United States, black workers, who have served as
the country's reserve labor supply for the past hundred years, are no longer
needed. Wilkins points to the labor demands of his own company. While
output and profits have grown rapidly, his workforce has remained stable.
"When I have new functions, I simply add computers instead of people."

Herb believes black Americans can choose one of two ways to further their
own economic development. Either they can opt for development by exclusion, restricting market access to their own communities, or they can choose
full integration, as individuals, into the larger American economy. He favors
the exclusion method: "If they want to develop from within, blacks have to
learn to control their markets as almost all other ethnic groups have . . . without breaking any laws."

Herb calls the full integration choice "laissez-faire Republican bullshit":

> I tell people I was a Democrat from birth and still am today, even though I've
> become somewhat successful. A lot of my friends have become Republicans.

Wilson thinks Democrats and Republicans have fundamentally different
views of minority problems:

> The person who says he is a Democrat is a person saying there's still a problem that
> has to be solved and we've got to find a way to solve it. A Republican says the
> problem is solved, the solution is in place. The problem is one of people, not
> resources.

Herb concedes a balance might be struck between the extremes of economic development, suggested by his interpretation of Democratic and Republican viewpoints. Furthermore, he acknowledges that some people are not
going to develop no matter how many resources you give them.

Our discussion turned to the underclass and black culture. Herb deems
culture in general "a function of the governance of institutions within the
community." He thinks of economic culture as "the governance of that part of
the institutional framework directing resources to different parts of the community." To elaborate, he spoke of his youth in Roxbury, Boston's mostly
black, inner-city neighborhood.

Herb Wilkins grew up in a housing project next door to St. John's Episcopal
Church. When he wasn't going to school, studying, or playing basketball at

the local YMCA, he was at St. John's. He spent all day Sunday in church, attending services until four and meetings of the Young People's Fellowship between four and seven. He rarely saw his friends on Sunday because "every kid was tied up in his church on Sunday. . . Baptist, Catholic or whatever." Two additional afternoons of the week were taken up by choir practice.

Against the advice of his teachers, who encouraged him to enroll in a trade-oriented public high school, Herb decided to compete for entry into prestigious Boston Tech. Herb passed the entry exam and, four years later, was one of six blacks in his class to graduate. "Tech was tough," recalls Herb. All of Herb's brothers and sisters performed similarly. His older brother graduated from high school at fifteen and entered Boston University at sixteen. His sister went to Boston Latin and his two younger brothers to Boston Tech.

Herb attributes his family's success to his parents and a strong, supportive community. "Everywhere you went there was institutional support." Life wasn't perfect. There were people who used drugs, people who hustled on street corners, people who drifted jobless. But they were not the norm. When kids dallied with temptation, as most invariably did, the system worked to keep them in line:

> Every cop in Boston who patrolled Roxbury—back then they were all white—knew my father. If I ever did anything wrong, a cop would grab me, drag me home by the collar and hand me over to my father.

When he goes back to visit, Herb no longer sees the kind of community interaction he remembers from his youth. "It doesn't exist today." Ozzie Jordan, the lawyer who "took care of things" for his family and many others, still lives in the same house he did twenty years ago. But his functions have dissolved:

> Before, if anybody had a problem at city hall, the state house, or some other agency, they would go see Ozzie. He'd tell us where to go, phone somebody, make the connection. Now, instead of Ozzie, people go directly themselves and stand in line with everybody else.

As Herb's mother puts it, "The lines are integrated now, so you are treated just as badly as the person in front or in back of you."

Herb ascribes the institutional breakdown he has witnessed in Roxbury to two phenomena: economic changes outside the black community and social changes within. Lack of demand for unskilled or semiskilled black labor has resulted in widespread joblessness and social disintegration in inner cities. At the same time, many middle-class blacks, freed by civil rights reforms, have advanced and moved away. "The traditional caste system," as Herb calls it, dissolved and with it the institutional glue that once held inner-city neighborhoods together.

Like Herb, many others of his generation have left inner-city ghettos for "comfortable, drug-free" lives in predominately black urban suburbs. Admits Herb, "I don't know if I'd be middle class if I'd stayed." Their exodus has left the younger generation in inner cities essentially leaderless at a time when economic competition in the United States and the world has reached an all-time peak:

> Even as America is moving away from unsophisticated labor it is importing overseas talent—Chinese, Indians, South Americans, Europeans. We take the best-educated persons from abroad. It's a world meritocracy. Now every black kid left in the ghetto has to compete not just with 250 million Americans but 5 billion people worldwide.

Herb emphatically places the responsibility for solving the problems of the black underclass on middle-class blacks. Most, like himself, still have relatives in the inner city. They have worked hard and competed successfully to have a decent life in America. They are also, Herb Wilkins maintains, "going through the worst psychological and emotional crisis of their lives." He believes middle-class blacks must either choose to develop the whole black community "by ourselves, for ourselves" or maintain a limited participation at the periphery of mainstream America.

Wilkins knows the challenges are formidable. He's not sure how institutions lost to economic change and middle-class black advances can be reestablished in inner-city territories. If the black underclass has lost the undergirding of a traditional caste system, they have also rejected the middle-class values of a larger society. "In the ghetto today there is no regard for your money or your poverty; there is no structure."

The first task for black Americans is to stand together politically and economically as a community. Herb knows blacks have enormous wealth that has not been pooled to their own advantage. Again the problem is both cultural and structural. Black teachers who put billions into pension funds managed by Prudential and Allstate "never sit down together and say 'you know, we've got a lot of money. . . we ought to pressure these groups to fund some housing projects or finance a mortgage for a black housing development.' " Simultaneously, "The system protects these companies from letting pension holders demand that they do certain things with their money." Even if black teachers decided to put their joint savings toward black development they would quickly run into "tortuous rules for registering mutual funds which prevent investment in minority groups by keeping money within long-established channels."

Despite the awesome challenges, Herb Wilkins believes black Americans can pull their resources together for the benefit of the entire community. At one point he distilled the issues down to a single factor, attitude.

> We're probably our own worst negative. We could be doing better; we say we're doing worse than we really are. Sometimes it turns out to be in the interest of both groups [black and white] to say we're doing worse than we really are . . . an interesting phenomenon that needs to be looked at.

Marcus Griffith

> The development of a community revolves around economics; everything else depends on the business community. Unlike entertainers, technicians, and record-keepers, who are on the periphery of the economic mainstream, businessmen create wealth.

Marcus Griffith founded and presides over the Hairlox Company, one of the largest, minority-owned U.S. manufacturers and distributors of black hair-care products. He objects to using the word "traditional" to describe his type of minority enterprise:

> Blacks have succeeded at hair-care products more than at any other type of manufacturing, but I wouldn't classify the manufacture of hair-care products as "traditional."

Griffith rates manufacturing first in importance among American business activities. "More than most businessmen," he asserts, "manufacturers create wealth and value by transforming raw materials into finished products." He points out that black Americans have rarely attempted to manufacture products of any kind. Even in the formerly segregated, "protected" markets of the black beauty industry, the vast majority of black businesses confined themselves to small retail and service establishments selling or applying nonminority products to minority customers.

Marcus Griffith is a soft-spoken patrician man in his early sixties. The son of an Episcopalian minister, he was born and raised in the South American nation of Guyana. While still a young boy, he decided that the greatest need for the black population, after education, was economic development. To him, economic development meant success in business:

> I had no desire at all to follow in my father's footsteps. I had white and Asian classmates whose fathers were businessmen and I could see the power and security—the economic independence—they were able to provide for their families. When they died their sons would walk in and take over; when my father died his accomplishments and wealth would die with him.

Marcus set out on his uncommon path by moving to New York City in 1948. After a year as a cosmetics salesman for a black-owned firm, he joined Fuller Products Company in Chicago. S.B. Fuller, the founder of Fuller Products, was a pioneer in the manufacture of black cosmetics. He also made a concerted attempt to attract promising young blacks into the industry. According to Griffith, most of today's prominent black cosmetics producers went through the Fuller Products "school of manufacturing."

By 1955 Griffith had moved to Washington, D.C. and started his own business, manufacturing cosmetics and operating beauty salons. Beauty Queen Company expanded rapidly into a nationwide chain of black-owned beauty operations. At its peak in the 1950s it was the largest black business in Washington, D.C., operating over 150 salons and employing 400 people.

Under pressure from stockholders, the company dissolved in 1960. Griffith revamped his resources, scaled down, and continued to operate seven of his salons as an individual proprietor. In 1970 he returned to manufacturing with the Hairlox Company. This time, he narrowed his business to the manufacture and distribution of hair-care products.

Over the past thirty years, the business environment for black businesses catering to an exclusively black clientele has changed dramatically. When Griffith started in the beauty business in the 1950s, most of the large, non-minority cosmetic firms ignored the needs of the black consumer. Several declared publicly that they would never make products for blacks. Today, a plethora of black and white companies in the cosmetics industry vie for black consumer dollars. The market has grown both numerically and "aesthetically." As black tastes have become more sophisticated and their range of product choices has widened, demand for black-produced products has fallen. Hairlox has nevertheless maintained its profitability and has even taken advantage of new opportunities. Hairlox products are distributed by wholesalers and chain stores in forty U.S. states and twenty foreign countries. Annual sales are in the millions of dollars. "Luck," emphasizes Griffith, "is being in the right place at the right time with the right qualifications."

> In the '50s I told my salespeople, "One day black will be beautiful. We have to become qualified and ready to seize the opportunity when it comes."

Over the years Griffith has seen repeated cycles of black business advances and retreats. Taken together they have added up to significant overall gains for black entrepreneurs. According to Griffith, black business growth, and by the same token, black economic development, entails:

> a slow gradual process, an amalgam of education, inspiration, role models, the inculcation of better habits, outlook, and mindset, and the removal of artificial barriers.

In particular, a steadily improving racial climate has opened many more business opportunities for younger blacks. Inevitably, says Griffith, as blacks have made more money, white companies have needed more qualified blacks as middle managers and executives. They have had to seek blacks to operate franchises and participate in joint ventures. Although many young black MBAs have opted for secure jobs, a number of others, bottlenecked in white corporations, have begun to set out on their own.

On the other hand, Griffith is concerned about the widening gap between black haves and have-nots. He believes the problem of the underclass requires a mixture of government spending "to prime the pump" along with development within the black community itself. Griffith stresses that government spending is not the sole or even the primary answer for black economic problems. "You obviously can't spend or finance someone into prosperity."

He outlines the role he thinks government should play in helping to move blacks forward. In his view, the Reagan administration did little to encourage black economic development. Many of the programs put into place during the "Black Capitalism" phase of the Nixon era have been scaled back or discarded. Some, especially MESBICS and set-asides, Griffith rates as having been highly effective. Whereas Nixon reallocated resources from other government programs to stimulate black business growth, the recent trend has been to remove resources altogether.

Welfare reform is another area the government has neglected to the detriment of blacks. Griffith notes that his own business has suffered as a result:

> Welfare is necessary in any human and humane society. But I am one of the victims of welfare. My company operates in the ghetto, where people constantly walk off the job to get welfare.

He advocates jobs rather than welfare for able-bodied young mothers. He believes black mothers who can should work, both to learn the value of independence and to become less often victims of abuse by the fathers of their children. He categorically objects to paying unemployment compensation for people who walk off the job:

> I have seen too many irresponsible young men who need to work but who, for some sociological reason, have not developed the work ethic. Absenteeism is rife in my work force.

Griffith assigns government a third area of responsibility, providing moral leaders and responsible leadership. Rapid social and economic change, together with a lax moral climate, has led to a serious breakdown in the fabric of American society. Part of the lack of motivation among the black poor, says Griffith, can be attributed to immoral conduct at the top:

All the wrongdoing in high places over the past fifteen years hasn't helped. We have seen government, business, and religious leaders getting rich through devious means. The young underclass dude watching all this feels he should become rich, too, without having to work very hard.

Griffith thinks blacks themselves, especially the black middle class, have the primary responsibility for raising the moral standards of the black community. Middle-class blacks must also fuel entrepreneurial growth within black neighborhoods. Despite the millions of dollars they now have, blacks still do not control their own purchasing power. The ideal, Griffith maintains, is for blacks to pool their funds in black banks, savings and loans, and credit unions. The few black financial institutions that exist endure what he calls "the Catch 22 of black banks":

> Black banks are at higher risk because they suffer great losses by lending to blacks. Blacks must be encouraged to repay their debts, to go to every extreme to maintain their credit.

Griffith also harbors a strong bias in favor of developing the manufacturing base of the black community:

> Getting trademarks for products is the key to the emancipation of black distributors. Black control of brand names offers security and independence for black dealers who otherwise may receive the thirty-day notice at any moment.

Black Americans must see to it that their children receive the encouragement and resources to succeed in business. They should apply their combined economic and political strength to open more business opportunities for young blacks. Griffith, who is president of the Washington, D.C. Chamber of Commerce, ran for the office on a platform of stimulating more black business opportunities, including management education for black entrepreneurs. He has subsequently obtained contracts from major nonminority corporations to enter joint ventures with, subcontract to, and find executive placement for qualified blacks.

Marcus Griffith observes ruefully that "not nearly enough" of his black classmates chose the same route he has to economic success. Over and above racism, most blacks have simply not made the conscious choice to go into business:

> All careers, including sports, entertainment, medicine, politics, which blacks my age have entered in large numbers, present obstacles and difficulties. All people, blacks included, make choices about careers. They choose to obtain a particular set of qualifications.

At the same time, Griffith sees American society moving in a slow but positive direction toward a "color-blind" future:

> All is not lost. The system is developing slowly in favor of black progress. But it's a gradual process, evolution not revolution.

He observes that capitalist forms of economic development were initiated thousands of years ago within the context of particular societies:

> This form of free enterprise we enjoy in our times took 2,000 years to develop. Blacks have been exposed to it now for just a few hundred years. Given the barriers they have faced, it's not logical to expect the black community to behave with the same entreprenurial zeal or to exhibit the same ingrained, instinctive, business acumen as the Jewish community, for example.

Marcus Griffith is married, the father of two teenage children. He is grooming his son to take over the business. Under his son's leadership, he expects the company will diversify its manufacturing base, perhaps move into some state-of-the-art high-technology area. He hopes he will have provided the inspiration and financial underpinnings to secure the company for generations of family to come:

> Mine is the first generation of blacks who will bequeath their offspring multimillion dollar ongoing businesses. There are several around the country. The next generation will be more educated, more sophisticated, better prepared. They will have been exposed to the intricacies of management by schooling and practical experience. As they amalgamate their resources, they will be able to capitalize many new black businesses.

Unlike their pioneering fathers and grandfathers, Griffith's son and his colleagues may have the opportunity to participate in an entirely new stage of black economic development. If successful, they may pass onto their own children a less tangible but equally important gift bequeathed by their fathers: an entrepreneurial attitude toward life. In the words of Marcus Griffith:

> Black business development is not a question of opportunity only; it's not a question of training. It's a question of mindset . . . the entrepreneurial spirit.

T.M. Alexander

> I don't think there are any shortcuts to achievements. I go slowly, if necessary, and pay a lot of attention to the community around me. That's part of what I mean when I talk about building fellowships.[3]

Widely known as "the dean of the black American insurance industry," T.M. Alexander is a sprightly, charming man in his late seventies. In 1931, during the nation's worst recorded economic disaster, he founded Alexander and Company in Atlanta. Today Alexander and Company, which does about $9 million worth of business a year, stands as one of the nation's oldest and most successful minority-owned insurance companies.

T.M. Alexander embodies the kind of Renaissance man his alma mater, Morehouse College, aspires to produce. In addition to starting his own highly successful business, he has enjoyed two long, fulfilling marriages, fathered three accomplished grown children, and has six grandchildren. He has written and recorded a respected history of the black man in America and is a published poet. He continues to hold numerous positions on city boards and committees and maintains an active interest in organizations for children and the elderly. In 1957, he was the first black man in ninety years to run for alderman in Atlanta. He lost but ran again for public office in 1961, this time for the U.S. Senate. Again he was defeated, by a black Democrat named Leroy Johnson. Both campaigns opened new doors for black politicians.

T.M. retains a lifetime membership in the Republican Party. He chuckles when he thinks of the consternation his party affiliation has sometimes caused fellow citizens, white and black. American presidents, including Ronald Reagan, have sought his advice and received his criticisms. Observes T.M.:

> If the President can get this nation back on solid economic footing, I'm for him. I'll go along with cutting waste and bureaucracy, and bringing down interest rates so construction can take off again. That's what we—blacks and whites—need most.[4]

At the same time T.M. staunchly supports civil rights and pushes for new black business opportunities.

An anecdote illustrates just how vital the business savvy of T.M. Alexander has been to the black American community. In 1955, sparked by the protest of Rosa Parks, Dr. Martin Luther King, Jr. organized the famous bus boycott in Montgomery, Alabama. In order for the boycott to be effective, black workers had to find alternative transportation to their jobs. Black church station wagons enlisted for the purpose ran into a hastily constructed ruse from white opposition. Insurance companies throughout the South were prevailed upon not to provide liability or property damage to any of the vehicles involved in the boycott. King turned to T.M., a close friend of King, Sr. since Morehouse days, for help. Through a Chicago friend, T.M. obtained the required insurance from Lloyds of London. His own company assumed the enormous risk of providing physical damage coverage—a fact T.M. withheld from his board of directors. For both insurance companies, the risk paid off. Physical property damage during the year of boycott amounted to one small claim and Lloyds suffered not a single loss.

That kind of calculated risk boils down to what T.M. considers his basic philosophy of good business and life, "What goes around, comes around."

Alexander's own father was in the construction business, which he left under the direction of T.M.'s older brother. In the 1950s, the family decided his brother should take care of ailing parents while T.M. simultaneously ran the family business and his insurance company. Overextended, the brothers lost $40,000, and T.M. had to borrow heavily against his own business to pay off bad debts. In the end, T.M. managed to pay back the entire loan considerably ahead of schedule. The loan officer in charge, a white man Alexander never met personally, handled the case with unusual sensitivity and competence. A grateful T.M. wrote a letter to the loan officer's supervisor praising him for a job well done. Many years later, T.M. introduced himself to one of the major stockholders in the Altanta bus company. Alexander and Company was one of several major competitors vying to insure the newly formed transit operation. Much to T.M.'s surprise, the stockholder not only knew him but thanked him for having boosted his career at a pivotal point. It turned out T.M.'s letter to the banking supervisor had been a deciding factor in promoting the young loan officer into an important position at the bank. Not surprisingly, Alexander and Company won its bid to insure the bus company. What goes around, comes around.

Despite his own business and personal success, T.M. worries about the future of America. He has recently finished a book titled *The Demise of Service and the Birth of Greed*. He wonders whether blacks have "tried to turn the clock back" with an overemphasis on racism and an underemphasis on putting their own affairs in order. Is racism still the threat of twenty years ago or are blacks operating from a residual well of insecurity? Alexander holds the Reagan administration at least partly responsible for the current atmosphere of uneasiness between blacks and whites—"key advisors," he elaborates, "not the President." Still, T.M. concludes, blacks themselves have the primary responsiblity as well as the capacity to move themselves forward. "Too many see what they don't have and want it all at once . . . . They have become complacent and are preoccupied with image instead of substance."

T.M. offers several dos and don'ts for black business development. The first big don't is letting government get involved in the day-to-day operations of business. "Businessmen (unlike politicans) are practitioners not theoreticians." A second and equally important don't is a lesson T.M. learned early from one of his own business mentors, a white banker: "You can't start a business on borrowed money." Alexander believes blacks have enough money to invest in themselves, "but they can't beg with one hand and demand with the other." The first thing to do, then, is for black business aspirants to establish good credit, either by saving or raising their own start-up capital. Second, in the insurance industry as in others, they must diversify. Third, they have to start where they can now and gradually learn how to assume control over the larger tools of business and finance. T.M. recalls that he chose his own insurance niche, property and casualty, precisely because he wasn't allowed to do life insurance at the time. When he started out, all of his business had to be brokered, or "signed for," by a larger white company; his agency was too small to cover the financial risks involved. Today life insurance makes up one small department within Alexander and Company.

In addition to learning the technical rules of the game, blacks must strengthen themselves from within by improving their business networks. T.M. points to the huge recent success stories of black-leveraged buyouts in the food industry—Beatrice Foods and Godfather's Pizza—as examples of just how far blacks have come and where they can go.

In particular, Alexander likes to talk about the success of the black and white business coalition in Atlanta, his hometown city. In many ways Atlanta has become a model of what can happen when black and white economic interests converge. T.M. concedes that Atlanta started out with distinct geographic and demographic advantages. It is racially better balanced than many large American cities, 60 percent black and 40 percent white. It has a large, well educated labor force, a pleasant climate, and has long served as a major regional distribution center. According to Alexander, the Action Forum, a voluntary association of black and white businessmen, meets once or twice a week "to decide what's good for Atlanta." All the banks and big corporations send representatives to the Forum. Members meet for large social events several times a year, bringing along their families. As a result of their combined strength, the black and white business community of Atlanta "works on government, not vice-versa."

T.M. Alexander has groomed Horace Tory, a 1971 economics graduate of Morehouse College, as his successor. His own son, T.M., Jr. was, until his tragic death a few years ago, a senior vice president of public finance at E.F. Hutton. One of T.M.'s daughters is an educational researcher, the other a social worker. Following the death of his first wife of forty-one years, T.M. remarried to Dr. Lenora Cole, vice president of Howard University. Family and community play a preeminent role in his life. "They are our future," he says.

In 1983, T.M.'s children and grandchildren presented him with a book of essays and poems he had written for family and friends over the years. In "Reaching for Higher Plains" he compares an owl, who sits reflecting as he looks over "the darkness of his timberland," to an eagle who "soars over white mountains, gold brush and purple plains." Although the two sustain themselves on the same resources, they inhabit two different terrains of the same world and do not join in common endeavors.

> Yet never did the two form a pair
> Each go their separate ways
> Searching for that perfect day
>
> Wisdom's agelessness
> No room for new   maybe more
> Sometimes pride stood in the open door
> Strength
> Not force
> Withstands time
> Little fear enters between each flight   each climb.
>
> To the heavens the eagle has soared
> To mingle among the other stars
> Yet his strength remains
> To the owl
> Who still reaches for higher plains . . . .[5]

These words of T.M. Alexander, dedicated to his granddaughter, provide a fitting testimonial—and challenge—to the spirit of black American entrepreneurship.

Notes

1. From Pierce, Neil and Steinbach, Carol, "Reindustrialization on a Small-Scale— But Will the Small Business Survive?" in *Expanding the Opportunity to Produce* (Washington, D.C.: Corporation for Enterprise Development, 1981, p. 8).
2. Unless otherwise noted, the following material derives from a series of interviews conducted between February 1986 and October 1988 with Herb Wilkins, Marcus Griffith, and T.M. Alexander.
3. Rock, Maxine, "Profile: T.M. Alexander, Atlanta's Mr. Insurance" (*Business Atlanta*, August 1981).
4. Ibid.
5. Alexander, T.M., *The Things I Said to Me I Say to You* (Atlanta: Alexander McCown, 1983, pp. 25–26).

Index

189